SHADOWS OF ETERNITY

THE CHILDREN OF THE OWLS

REVISED EDITION

FROST AND FLAME TRILOGY BOOK 2

BY RICK KUEBER

STELLIUM BOOKS

Grant Park, Illinois

Shadows of Eternity: The Children of the Owls

is the second book of the Frost & Flame Trilogy

of fictional books by Rick Kueber.

These books are, however, based on true events.

www.stelliumbooks.com

Manufactured in the United States

ISBN: 978-0692482452

Second edition

<u>Dedication</u>

For my son Daniel, who has inspired me to
be the best person I can be, and has taught
me the true meaning of unconditional love. I
will always be with you and will always
watch over you. You are the greatest miracle
I have ever experienced. I love you, and I
thank you, for being you.

Dad

Special Thanks to:

Sanela Leila Kubiak — Cover Photography.

P.E. Kubiak — Cover Photo Effects

Special Thanks to our Cover Girl :

Ayane Rayne Kubiak

Shadows

of

Eternity

Shadows of Eternity is a novel based on actual events and investigations which includes some fictional elements. Though some of the locations and names have been changed, most remain accurate. The team members of Evansville Vanderburgh Paranormal Investigations, and Psychic/Mediums- Theo Kostaridis and Rick Hayes are portrayed as themselves, and a short bio on each has been included-

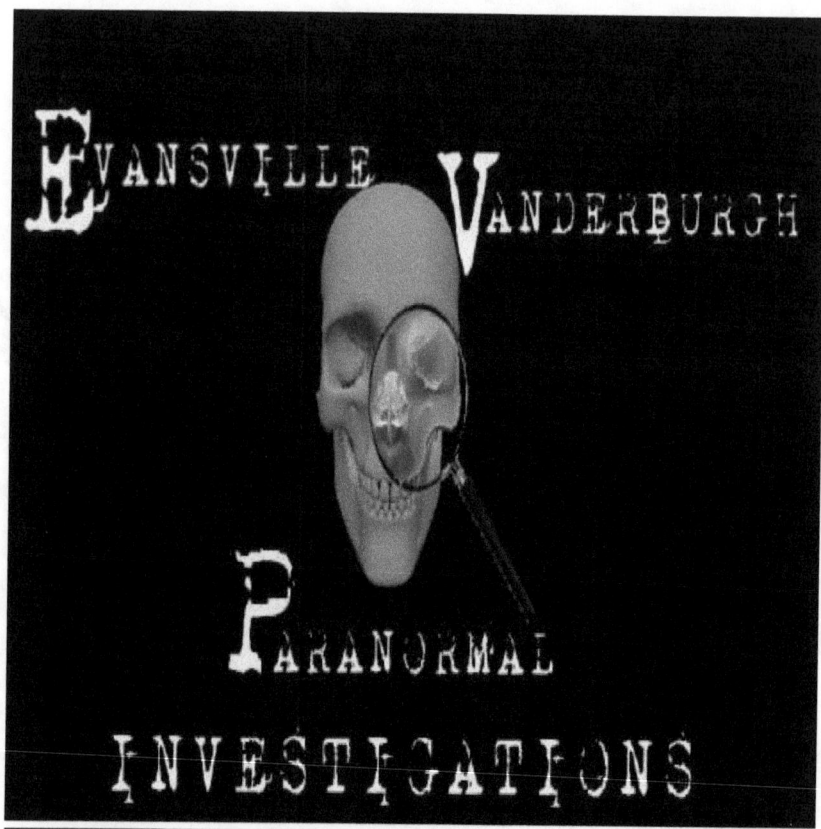

Special thanks to the following people involved in this project:

Barb Heerdink, Christian Russel, Del Heerdink, Sterling young, Fred Sammet, Linda Sammet, Karen Daugherty,   Tabitha Linton, Amanda Gish-Morris, Sterling Young, Jordan Beck and Robby Denton

Photography credits: Evansville Historical Society, Barb Heerdink, Jenn Kirsh, Katie Collins, T.J. Kueber, Sanela Kubiak

CHAPTER INDEX

FOREWORD

Parts of this foreword are repeated from book one of the series, but other parts contain previously untold information:

I've always been one of those people who never grew out of the "why" phase of childhood. If I didn't know the answer I would find it in books or the wisdom of those I trusted. Maybe that's why I have been fascinated with science as far back as I can remember, and still am to this day. If I could have been anything growing up, I would have chosen to be a scientific researcher. What could have possibly been more rewarding than answering a question for the first time in history? Life sciences were always my favorite, but now I find myself researching just the opposite, and as puzzling as it may be, it is exponentially more rewarding.

My life changed when I was in my late twenties while I was at work in a very rural setting. I was outside of a small furniture factory, working up on a ladder when I heard a sound that reminded me of an approaching helicopter. Suddenly it felt as if I had been hit in the ear by a flying baseball. What had actually happened was that I had been stung by a hornet and the venom was dangerously close to my brain. I came down off of the ladder and as I passed my coworker, he asked if everything was alright. I explained what happened and then went inside to splash some water on my face. On my way out of the factory, everything began to bleach out and become the brightest white I could imagine. I found my way along the wall until I made it back outside, and I heard my coworker saying I looked bad. I began to itch all over, and still could barely see anything.

He helped me into the work truck and sped off towards the emergency room nearly twenty minutes away. The entire way there, a voice in my head kept telling me to let go and just go to sleep. When we arrived, a team of nurses pushed a gurney next to the open truck door, and I climbed out of the truck and sat up on the gurney while they rushed me into the E.R. doors. I wasn't sure what the rush was, but I went along for the ride. Shortly after entering the E.R. my memory failed me.

I woke up in the hospital room, and my buddy from work smiled rubbing his forehead. He said 'I thought we lost you' which confused me. According to him, he thought I stopped breathing for a period of time on the way to the hospital. I argued that I wasn't in that bad of shape, or I wouldn't have been able to get on the gurney and ride it into the E.R., to which he responded, 'four nurses picked you up and laid you on that cart.' I repressed that memory for years, but the more I thought about it, the more I began to realize that what I happened was most likely what is labeled an 'out of body experience'.

Then a few years later at the young age of thirty one, when my first child was born my life was changed again. A cotton topped little boy who reminded me of myself more and more every day. Fourteen months later, there was another life altering event. It was 2001 and I still didn't have a cell phone. It wasn't that unusual to not have one, but they were becoming more commonplace and I was behind the times.

Arriving back home after spending the afternoon of my birthday at the orchard, I found a distressing message on the answering machine. It was from my sister-in-law. The voice on the recording was shaky and obviously crying. My brother was in the hospital and he had a stroke. I was asked to come as soon as I got this message.

Part of me was in shock and another part of me was in disbelief. There was something in my gut that made me gather myself together and head to the hospital. Without going into too much detail, let me put it as simple as I can. My brother had a massive stroke on my birthday, and for the next two days, the whole family and many friends lived at the hospital in the intensive care unit until he died on October the first.

Over the course of a few years, I had nearly died, seen the birth of my son and the deaths of far too many family members and good friends. My faith was shaken and I found myself asking once again, "Why?"

It was at this same time that the home that we lived in had some unexplained things happening. The house never made me feel uncomfortable, but I must admit there were many times, at night especially, that it just seemed a bit 'creepy'.

Nothing phenomenal ever happened there to my knowledge. There would be the odd sounds from the attic or basement that I attributed to an animal getting inside, or old pipes...you know, the normal weird noises an older house makes at night, but occasionally there were things like a set of keys left on the coffee table would come up missing, only to be found on the same coffee table later that day, or a door being closed and a few minutes later being open again when no one had been in that part of the house. One example that is burned into my memory is the sound of a shrill scream as I lay in bed trying to go to sleep. I had always told myself that it came from outside, but if it truly did, the screaming woman must have been right outside my bedroom window.

It wasn't until years later after living in two other homes that I saw a show on paranormal activity, and how different electronic devices were used to capture what was labeled as 'evidence of a haunting', that I thought back on how I would have loved to have known about this when we lived at the troubled house. Why couldn't I do just what they were doing on TV? I began going to my public library and studying every book I could find that surrounded the supernatural and paranormal.

Eventually, I searched for the lead paranormal investigator on the web and soon became friends with him. We chatted online, sent emails back and forth, and even exchanged numbers. During our friendship, he encouraged me to begin investigating the paranormal if I had the desire to do so, and had even given me a few pointers.

It took a few months, but I purchased a few pieces of equipment that I had seen on the show, a Mel-meter, a digital recorder and a K-II meter. I already owned a couple of digital cameras and a video camera. While I excitedly waited for my new online order to arrive, I began to build a website and used social media to begin letting people know I was a paranormal researcher. My first real investigation came before the website was up, but after my order had arrived.

The location was teeming with paranormal activity on several different levels and it is where I met Jennifer Kirsch. The house she lived in was quite haunted, and Jenn had a prior knowledge of the paranormal as well. She became the first member of my team. I could go into details about that investigation as well as several nights when we captured some incredible audio and video evidence at her home, but that is another book in itself. We have been through an assortment of team members who never worked out for one reason or another, but Jenn was the first and remains the lead investigator to this day. A few years later we picked up a young woman named Katie Collins, and she is also still with the team. This unlikely trio became the team that is now commonly known as Evansville Vanderburgh Paranormal Investigations.

PROLOGUE:

The team of Evansville Vanderburgh Paranormal had just finished up an incredible case. We had been confronted by a mysterious haunting and through several investigations, and many personal experiences, we were eternally changed and enlightened. My team had impressed me with their historical researching skills as well as their relentless search for the truth.

What began as an investigation of either a very malevolent spirit or a demonic haunting, ended quite differently. Our investigation spanned several weeks and a couple of states. It was during this investigation that we discovered that the evil presence was actually a negative energy that had attached itself to the spirit of a child.

This poor child, a young girl by the name of Ashley Sue, was burned as a witch at the young age of nine. The negative energy had twisted her over a very lonely century. My team and those who were touched by her were 'shown' her story in bits and pieces. Those bits often included very real dreams and visions of being burned to death. These memories are something we live with every day and will remember for the rest of our lives. Though she eventually found her eternal peace, this young spirit often visited our team in both private settings and during other investigations. The burning girl befriended us, and Ash, as we called her, became a vital part of more than one of our cases.

Chapter 1

FINDING ME

The celebration of Katie's pregnancy announcement, and the gathering to celebrate the success of our last investigation, was slowly winding down. At nearly 11pm Theo, Katie, Jenn, and I were finally saying our good-byes to Dr. Em and her family. Our typical, late night chatter bounced back and forth between us as we headed to our cars. "Buzz". My phone vibrated again. Pulling it from my jeans pocket, I glanced at the screen to see what this latest notification was. The EVP website had forwarded another email and this time the subject line simply stated, 'please respond'.

"Now what?" Jenn asked as she unlocked her car door.

1

"Another request from the website... Looks like we may have our choice of investigations coming up." I smiled.

Katie stopped short of her car, almost as if the news caused her heart to sink. "Hey guys, if this is another one like Ash, I'm gonna have to sit this one out."

"Of course." I said trying to hide my disappointment. "Is everything alright?"

"Yeah, it's just now that I know I'm pregnant, I don't think it's a good idea to expose myself to that kind of evil... not to mention the mental trauma we all went through." Her own disappointment was apparent in the solemn tone of her voice. "I just don't want to do anything to put my baby in any danger."

"You're right." Jenn said regretfully.

Theo broke into the conversation. "If it isn't malicious and you want to take part in the upcoming investigations, I can do a blessing and help you with protection on several different levels. I think that's a good idea for any future investigations... probably for everyone."

"Yep." I had to agree, "We should have asked for your help with the last one earlier than we did, and yeah... we should make it a habit of doing some form of protection before we begin any investigations, or even interviewing anyone."

After our last investigation, and our experiences with Ashley, and the shadow demon that plagued her, I was rethinking the seriousness of what we did as a team. It wasn't anything to take lightly, and we had all seen and experienced things we would never forget, though I am sure we all desperately wished we could.

"Hey..." Katie blurted out from the other end of the driveway, standing beside her car. "It's kinda weird standing out here talking about this stuff... I mean... maybe we should meet up someplace more private, but not tonight."

"You're right, as usual." I felt awkward thinking that Dr. Em's neighbors might overhear us, if any of them were still awake. "Let's call it a night. I'll take a look at the emails

2

tomorrow and I'll let you all know if they're anything that needs our attention." I opened the door to my car and before getting in, I waved to my team mates and friends, "Good night guys. Great job..." I hesitated, because I knew how cheesy it was going to sound, but I continued, "I'm proud of each of you and I'm proud of the team." the darkness hid the blushing, but I could feel the heat rising in my cheeks.

"Thanks for making this group a real team." Katie said as she slid into her truck and started the motor with a growl.

"Yeah, and thanks for having me help you with that investigation. It was incredible!" Theo added with his typical smile that made his eyes all but disappear.

"You're welcome pal, but really... you may not be with us for every part of every investigation, but you are just as much a part of this team as any of us." And with that, I believe, his eyes disappeared completely as his smile grew even wider.

"Thanks, that means a lot." He waved, and climbed into his silver blue Subaru. Then, sticking his head out of the open window as he drove away, shouted over the hum of the motor, "Let me know about the emails too. I'd be glad to help out with anything you need."

"Will do." I shouted back. "See ya later."

After passing out her inevitable hugs to all, Jenn had slipped out with Katie, so once again I was the last to leave. I stood in the driveway contemplating the investigation we had just finished and the horrors of the burning girl, Ashley Sue, which we all had been subjected to. I could not help but wonder if we would ever experience an entity with powers that extreme again. I wondered if I even ever wanted to... probably not, on both counts.

I pulled out of Dr. Em's driveway and headed out into the night. It was a short drive from the doc's suburban house to the more rural setting of my apartment a few miles away. Though the radio played loudly on one of my favorite 80's stations, I hardly noticed the music. My head was still filled with countless memories of our adventures at the doc's old family farm, mixed with curiosities

3

about what our next investigation might entail.

As the surrounding darkness of the countryside whizzed by, giving way to only the road ahead, I daydreamed. This was my typical nature. I loved to fantasize about everything from the possibilities of future investigations to winning the lottery.

Not a car on the road, I gazed ahead and focused only enough to keep my car from drifting off and into the ditch. In the blurred focus of my vision, I could see the white flashes of the lines on the road, and dots of bugs and moths that flew too close to my headlights, and on occasion, a mailbox, shrub or tree. The sound of my little convertible sports car grew louder, echoing, as I passed by the same cornfield I had passed a thousand times on my way home.

The flashing green of the wide leaves on the seemingly never ending rows of corn stalks gave me something else to be distracted by. The warm, wet spring we had experienced here in the Ohio Valley had given the crops a great head start. The old saying 'knee high by the fourth of July' was now more like knee high by mid-May. This field had always done well, but this year, it was already nearly four feet high. As I neared the end of the field something caught my eye. Stepping to the edge of the corn row was a small girl, dressed in white. Her long blonde hair fluttered in the breeze as I drove by, and her stare caught my attention... the burning stare of her fiery eyes.

In the split second that I saw her eyes, and spun my head as I passed, I also jerked the steering wheel. The front tires screeched as the rear end of the car slid across the lane to the left. My car spun wildly out of control and as I tried to correct it, I over corrected. The car bounced off of the road, and my head hit the driver's side window. With a thwap-thwap-thwap of corn stalks against the front and side of the car my foot pressed hard against the brake pedal. In a cloud of dust and flying shards of green stalks, my car came to rest nearly fifteen feet into the field. I tried to gather my senses, but it was no use. I only had one thought on my mind... there was only one possibility that I could believe. AHSLEY! Dear God! It was Ash! I was sure of it.

I threw the car into park, shut off the motor, and covered my face with my shaking hands. I rubbed my face and pulled my hands down across my cheeks and lips hard, stretching my face slightly as I did. My hands slid into a prayer position and my lower lip was caught

4

and pulled between my index finger-tips. I exhaled heavily and tried to regroup myself.

Climbing out of the car, I wandered to the road, leaving the door open and the door alarm dinging. I whirled around, frantic and bewildered, calling out, "Ashley! ...ASHLEY!" But, there was no response. "Ashley Sue!!! Are you here?" Again, there was nothing. I stood there silently in the middle of the road and wondered how long these visions and glimpses of the past would continue.

Meandering towards my dinging car, I surveyed the situation. Other than a few rows of irreparably damaged corn and some scratches to the already somewhat dulled paint on my little car, things seemed mostly unharmed. My car started up with a whir and I counted my blessings that there had not been a ditch between the field and this stretch of road. I placed the gear shift into drive. Slowly and cautiously, I pulled back onto the road and was clearly alert and focused for the remainder of the drive home.

I opened the door to my apartment and stepped inside. Locking the door behind me, I dropped my keys on the end table and stumbled through the darkness to my room. I tried to lie down and sleep, but it was no use. I had to tell someone what had happened... I had to tell everyone. I pulled my phone out of my pocket and sent a group text message to Jenn, Katie and Theo.

***

Theo walked through his front door and was greeted by his tiny companions, Cleopatra and Precious, his Chihuahuas, starving for attention and scolding him in their own way for leaving them alone again. The three curled up in bed to finish watching the movie he had started earlier that day, but it was to no avail. Theo quickly fell asleep as the movie played and Cleo and Precious nuzzled up next to him. For such little dogs, they certainly knew how to hog the bed.

Barely minutes into sleep, a vivid dream came to him. Some twisted mix of memories and imagination had invaded his peaceful slumber, or perhaps it had nothing to do with memories *or* imagination. He found himself being chased through a huge old house. It was empty and dark and he had no idea who or what he was running from. All he could sense was that he was running for his life and fear was all he could feel. He found himself fleeing down a set of wooden stairs, and halfway down his footing failed him. Theo felt himself banging against the stair nosing and landing hard on the oak floor at the bottom. The fear remained all too real and over whelming. Turning, he took off with a shot down the hallway next to the open spindles of the banister. Midway down the wall was a glowing, brass doorknob. He feverishly grabbed the knob and with a turn opened the door, rushed into the empty storage space under the stairs, and quickly shut it tight behind him.

His eyes began to adjust to the faint light that came in through the crack at the bottom of the door, and between he and the door stood someone. A young girl was there facing him. As she spoke, the space between them began to lighten somewhat. He could clearly see the sadness in her bright blue eyes, and hear it in a voice that seemed to come from her, though her lips never opened.

"Help them. Help the children, before it's too late."

"Ash, Is that you?" Theo thought out loud.

"Help the children, before it's too late!" Her only response was now pleading, desperately, with his heart.

The light between them grew brighter and brighter, until it was nearly as gleaming as the light of day, and the floor and walls surrounding them began to growl and grumble.

"Ash! What am I supposed to do? What Children?" He begged for an answer.

The growling had grown to the point of rattling and rumbling, and the dust grew thick in the air between them. The walls began to shake as he watched them crumble around him. Ashley began to crumble along with everything, and her voice echoed one last time, "Help the children, before it's too late."

When the dust began to settle, the rubble simply disintegrated as if it had been absorbed into the floor that Theo was kneeling on... the floor of his own bed room. Hearing the familiar 'gwuff' he looked to his left to see the two Chihuahuas still sleeping soundly in his bed.

Before he could stand, there was another familiar sound.

"Beep-Beep...Beep-beep" The text alert on his phone was going off, announcing a new message. He pulled the charging cord from his phone and opened the message. All it said was, EVP RICK: "I saw Ash tonight. I'm not crazy."

***

The rest of the night, which didn't include much sleep, and a good piece of the next day, I sat in my room and wondered when she would visit again. When lunchtime had come and gone, I realized I couldn't just hide in my room forever, besides, I already knew she would find me wherever I was. I finally grabbed up my laptop and logged into my email account. There they were, like two foreboding omens, the unopened emails awaited my attention. Scanning over them in the inbox list, I noticed quickly that they were from the same sender, which eased my mind slightly. I opened the first, which had the subject line: 'Numerous spirits frightening our patrons. Please help!' and the sender was barb-owls@xxxxx.com.

The email read:

Dear EVP Investigations,

I am writing on behalf of our private club, the

Order of the Owls #30. We have been in the same

location for many years, and there have been

several patrons die here over the decades.

Our members have always had experiences,

and now they have become more frequent

and some of our membership is becoming more

and more uncomfortable. We would like you to

come and either validate or disprove our ghosts.

Please respond as soon as possible.

Thank you,

Barb and Del Heerdink

I breathed a sigh of relief. This sounded like just the kind of investigation we needed, not menacing, no one fearing for their lives. Even the fact that these experiences have been happening for years made this more of a 'ghost hunt' than an investigation. I smiled, returning to the inbox to read the second email.

Email #2:

Dear EVP Investigations,

I just wanted to let you know that as soon as

I sent that email from the office here at the Owl's Nest,

there was a chill in the room. The door was closed and

the A.C. was not running. I saw someone's shadow out-

side the door, so I went out to see who it was, but no one

was there. We hope to hear from you soon.

Thanks,

Barb and Del

I was actually looking forward to telling the team about this one, and even felt pretty positive about the case itself. Not to make light of paranormal research on any level, but this investigation almost sounded like it could be fun. I had begun to reclaim my desire and drive to be a part of the paranormal research community once again. It was time to make a few phone calls and get the interview scheduled.

It was Sunday at 3p.m. when I sent the text message to Katie and Jenn, telling them about the emails and asking when they might be available to meet to do some initial interviews. They were both quite eager to get this new investigation started. Something told me that they were most likely feeling the same as I was, ready to put some distance between us and the burning girl, Ashley Sue. We had all decided that Tuesday, Wednesday, or Thursday evening after seven would be options. So, I responded to Barb and Del with my typically professional sounding email.

Barb, Del, and the Order of the Owls,

The team of Evansville Paranormal would be

pleased to meet with you to discuss your

experiences and the situation you believe you

have. We would like to conduct our interviews

with you one evening this week. We can be available

at, or after, 7p.m. on either Tues., Weds., or Thurs.

Please respond as soon as possible so I may add

this to our schedule.

Sincerely,

Rick Kueber- Founder, EVP Investigations

'Keep your eyes and mind wide open'

With the click of the mouse, the email was sent. I ventured out of my bedroom, popped a breakfast bowl in the microwave and opened an ice-cold Mountain Dew. I turned on the television, and heard the sound of 'Tears for Fears' playing on one of my favorite 80's movies. All was right with the world. I was feeling much more like myself, and less like someone who had just returned home from a true life horror movie. I put the fiery terror of the past month out of my mind, and lost myself in Mt. Dew, bacon, eggs and cheese, and Molly playing another charming high school teen looking for love and acceptance.

***

When the movie was over, and I was feeling very couch-potato-ish, I decided it would be best to get up and at least wander around the apartment for a bit. I eventually found myself in the office, clicking the mouse to clear the screen saver. Much to my surprise and pleasure, there was a reply from the Order of the Owls.

EVP Team,

Thank you for responding to us and agreeing to meet with us. Wednesday evening after 7pm would work best for us. I will gather up all of the information we have and see you then. We will meet you by the front door. Just call the number below when you arrive.

Thanks, Barb and Del – 812-454-xxxx

Quickly, as if it really mattered, I sent a text message to Jenn and Katie, confirming the time and date of our interview. Within minutes I had their enthusiastic responses. Once again, it was time to play that dreaded waiting game. Wednesday was only a few days away, but this new potential investigation was all I could think about. Three different times that week I had to stop myself from casually 'popping by' the Owl's Nest just to peek around, but I managed to control myself, though it wasn't easy. I just kept telling myself, 'it wouldn't be fair to do that without the rest of the team.'

With each passing workday, and evening, I found myself thinking less about the last investigation, though it still crossed my mind several times a day. Every day, I was feeling more like me, and less like someone who might never get past those recent life changing experiences.

12

Chapter 2

AT FIRST GLANCE

Wednesday evening had finally arrived, and so had I. I had scrubbed down, and dressed up...in my favorite EVP shirt and hooded team jacket. I stood in the parking lot of the huge building, and was awestruck by its sheer size and the interesting mixture of architecture that encompassed several periods. It was quite obvious that there had been a few additions and changes to the structure over the years. Though the original brick building was still quite intact, it had an eerie appearance. Several of the upstairs windows had been boarded up, tastefully done and painted, but boarded up just the same, which gave the place that 'abandoned, haunted house' look. I had a good feeling about this place... haunted or not, I knew it would be interesting to investigate, and the history alone would be an adventure to uncover.

I hadn't stood there long, in the cool of the evening, when Jenn showed up, eager to move on to another 'ghost hunt' and, much like myself, put the past behind her.

"Welcome, welcome! Glad you could make it." I called out across the rows of cars to where Jenn had emerged from her black

Camry, with its silver scorpion emblem, shining in the bluish glow of the parking lot lights.

"Wouldn't miss it!" she said and chuckled as she crossed the parking lot to give me a hug, as always. I was surprised to see her carrying a notepad. Jenn had always been a digital recorder kind of girl.

"Notebook, huh?" I teased lightheartedly. "Your digi broke?"

"Nope." She replied smugly. "Got that too... Just brought this in case there was anything I needed to actually write down, or draw out... or you know, if somebody else needed to write something down..." She trailed off, leaving the statement open ended, but I knew what she was getting at.

"I know, I know... I'm notorious for leaving the note taking to you and Katie when we're all meeting for interviews. I don't do it intentionally, I swear!" I defended myself as best as I could.

"Yeah, yeah... sure you don't." Jenn teased as Katie's truck pulled into the lot slightly too fast and almost screeched into its parking spot.

It was five minutes until seven when Katie rushed over to us. "I'm sorry I'm late." She said out of breath with that one of a kind, puppy-dog-eyed, bottom-lip-stuck-out, chin-crinkled, pouty face look, that only Katie has.

"You're not late chica. We're just early." Jenn said reassuring Katie with a smile. "You aren't gonna believe what E.V.Prick here just tried to B.S. me with... He actually said that when we all come for interviews, and he doesn't bring anything, no note pad, no pen, no recorder... that it's totally unintentional."

Katie rolled her eyes up and to the left, in my general direction, and said, "Really? And we're supposed to believe that?" She stuck out her bottom lip and crinkled her chin again. She was mostly kidding around like Jenn, but I knew deep down, there was a little part of them that believed I did it on purpose.

"Think of it as a compliment... I know you two will be well prepared and my brain just automatically blocks that I'm supposed to bring that stuff." A poor defense at best, I knew. "It's all I got..."

14

"Well, we'll forgive you this time, but don't let it happen again." Jenn truly enjoyed ribbing me at every opportunity.

"I may not have been late when I got here... but we're all late now! We better get inside." Katie said, looking at the pink dial on her watch.

I snatched my phone from my pocket and called Barb as we strolled up to the door. It was still ringing when I reached for the pull bar and opened the door to see a very happy and very smiley couple, around my age, or a few years older, standing in the doorway. The woman had her ringing phone in her hand, so I pressed the end button on my phone and spoke.

"Barb, Del?" I queried.

"Yep, right on both counts." Del said cheerily and shook my hand. "You must be Mr. Queber." Almost everyone mispronounced my name, and it was something I had grown all too comfortable with.

"Oh, no... That's my dad. I'm Rick, and it's a German spelling, so it's actually pronounced- KEEBER." I jokingly said. "And this is Jennifer Kirsch, with a 'c', and that's Katie Collins... also with a 'c'." I said, actually remembering to introduce them for a change, (I had always been horrible about that) and most likely confusing the heck out of our new acquaintances with my 'c' comments. The truth was that for some reason, when I was writing or typing her name, I often spelled it 'Kirsh', when it was actually 'Kirsch'... yet another thing that Jennifer scolded me about, which, I think, she enjoyed just a little too much.

"Come in, come in." Barb smiled, ushering us in and directing us down the hall way. "We knew who you were from your website."

The interior was very dated, but not in a bad way. The walls were plaster in this area, and covered in rows of photographs of Order of the Owls presidents, past and present, along with numerous photos and paintings of various owl portraits. That in itself gave us a foreboding first impression. We walked down the short hallway and it seemed that the owl's eyes followed us (and even a few of the presidents) until it opened up into a bar room, which was actually fairly quiet.

"Is this alright?" Del asked pointing to a long rectangular table with eight chairs.

"Seems fine to me." I answered looking back and forth at the girls, raising my eyebrows and shoulders, asking for their approval.

They both looked back, wide eyed and awkwardly nodded, saying nothing. So... we sat down, Jenn, Katie and I on one side, and Del and Barb on the other.

"So..." I began awkwardly, "tell us about what kind of activity you have here, and where it happens, who it might be... if you have any ideas, that is... just the basics for now." I started off, and prepared myself for some incredibly hokey story about flying apparitions, and screaming banshees, and of course the gruesome and ghastly, chain-rattling victims. Don't get me wrong, I didn't think they were trying to fool us, or have any reason to distrust them, but we had learned through some past experiences, that often times a business would have an investigation as a publicity stunt. So, as always, I hoped for the best, but prepared for the worst.

The tales of their encounters as well as the experiences of patrons, (some of which were actually there and were called over to recant their stories) were all quite legitimate. Most were similar stories of unexplainable cold spots, the shadow of someone passing by when no one was actually there, the same man in a yellow shirt seen in the same place, the strange feeling of being touched on the shoulder, or on the ear as Barb had experienced numerous times, and the sound of someone walking upstairs, even though that area was closed to the patrons, and was only used to store holiday decorations and things such as that.

We took a brief tour of the main level which included the bar-room, a large dance hall, a card room (for those Texas hold 'em fans), an enormous kitchen filled with stainless steel appliances, work areas, and bustling people prepping orders for the customers. We were then shown the offices, and miscellaneous hallways and restrooms. As we explored the areas, Del and Barb explained to us which areas were parts of the original house, and which were additions.

The music played in the background, along with the smoky conversations of longtime friends and new acquaintances. As we crossed the bar room, Del pointed to a door with a push/pull bar, telling us that it would lead us to the lower level. We followed the two of them through the door and down to the lower area. Going through the door at the bottom, we found a large room filled with cafeteria style tables and folding chairs. At the far end was another bar, complete with a bartender. Only a few people were in this room, and they were gathered in huddled groups of three or four at the end nearest the bar.

The cheerful couple offered us a seat at one of the tables and followed up by offering us a drink. We accepted graciously, and though it was not our policy, we all enjoyed one adult beverage of our choice... Crown and Coke for me, as always. There were several closed doors down the left side of the room, but Del suggested that it would be better to leave that for the night when we have the building to ourselves. I believe he was afraid that we might have some of the customers and members follow us if we opened those doors.

Barb laid a crisp, manila file folder on the table in front of her and proceeded to open it up revealing several pages of research she had done. She had a half dozen or so photographs of the original home, the current structure, and different phases of its existence through the past century. The documents included newspaper articles about a prominent area family, the Bettigers, who lived in the home originally until it was purchased by the Owl's in 1922. Barb even had some records from the old Willard Library that was just up the street from the Owl's club, which gave the original owner's (Charles Bettiger) birth and death dates, some of his wife Amelia's information, as well as the names, and birth and death dates of all of his children.

We passed each documents around and briefly scanned over them. Katie paused when she held the records page, and spoke out to all of us in general, and none of us specifically, "Did you notice the dates on the children?" Del and Barb nodded, as did Jenn.

"No, I didn't look that closely at them yet, why?" I asked curiously.

"Seems that all of Charles and Amelia's children died by the age of...ummmm...about eight, or younger in most cases... and most of them died in the same year. Now that's just spooky!" Katie elaborated.

"Yes it is!" I responded and then turned to the Heerdinks, "Barb, can we get copies of these documents for our files, and so we can study up on the history and maybe do some digging ourselves?"

"These are actually copies that we had printed off for you to have. So, I guess the answer is yes." Barb said, and she and Del smiled, knowing they were at least one step ahead of us on this request.

After a brief review of the documents and photos, we left the lower level, following Barb and Del up the steps, through the bar room, and discretely down the hall, being sure we hadn't been followed. We stopped at an area near the front entrance where the hallway suddenly doubled in width.

"These two walls and this door were added in the 1940's to restrict access to the upstairs. It was never really used at all by the Owl's, except for storage." Del enlightened us about the wall to our right where the hall was notably narrower, as he dug deep into his front pocket for his keys. He fumbled through the numerous keys on the ring, and locating an older looking, yet unworn key, unlocked the door, and pulled it open to reveal an old hard wood set of steps and a spindled, dark oak bannister that ran up the right side, and curved at the top where it was open on three sides at the upper landing.

The darkened stairs creaked and groaned as if they we were pained by our treading on them, or detested our presence. Reaching the precipice, it seemed as if we had almost stepped into another time. The dismal second floor was dank and dust covered, except for a pathway of many past footprints that had ventured into this unchanged space to store, or retrieve items from storage. The paint was chipped and peeling. It was an odd, greenish-blue color, and was dated to a time long before any of us had existed. We entered the room to the right at the top of the stairwell, and slowly browsed the areas. There was a defunct restroom and kitchen, both small, and out of use for decades. The main room was a multifaceted rectangle, with outcroppings near the windows on the left side and two doors on the right.

The first door was halfway down the wall to the right, and oddly enough, also entered into the stairway landing. Past that, the room widened by a few feet and the second door was near the far end of the wall. The ceiling was nearly 12 foot high, and much like the walls, had random spots where the paint was bubbling and peeling away, giving the space the appearance of an old abandoned house one might expect to find in a Hollywood horror film.

Turning the corner, we made our way, single file, through the second door. It was opened with a pop and a high pitched squeal of the hinges. This room was a conundrum. It was a six foot by four foot space, wider than it was deep, and had a door to our right, which, once again, led to the stairs. It felt too large to be a closet, too small and confining for any other obvious purpose. We filed into the room, and other than opening the other door to peek out into the hallway, we circled through and exited swiftly.

We reversed our path through the large room until we found ourselves back in the stairway. Barb took the lead and opened the doorway opposite of where we had been. We curiously followed her into the final upstairs room. With one exception, this was also a rectangular room. Nearly two-thirds of the way through the room, there were one foot thick and deep turnouts on either side of the room that met a bulkhead at the ceiling of the same dimension. The area was very open, but due to the turnouts and bulkhead, felt divided into two distinct and separate spaces.

Unlike the other two levels, the second floor was devoid of life and had a certain sinister air about it. The emptiness called to us stay, but we fought against the desires to wander the desolate abode any longer and ended our tour feeling an irrefutable need to return soon. When we eventually exited the stairway, we found ourselves near the entrance, and it was then and there that we chose to say our good-byes. As we shook hands, or exchanged hugs (as the case may be), Del and Barb let us know they would soon meet with the trustees and officers of the club and choose a Friday or Saturday night when they could close the doors to the public early, and grant us unlimited access to the entire building from midnight until 8am.

It was nearly unbearable, having to wait to find out when we would be given our date to discover what mysteries this captivating treasure might hold. We had no choice but to go on with the humdrum of our daily lives and await the phone call, or email, that would give us a definite point we could prepare for.

The week passed as many do, with work, family, and friends. There were still the random emails from fans, and curious band-waggoners, and even one or two haters, who were mostly jealous that their limelight was being taken by our tiny paranormal team who was not seeking fame or fortune, but only to help those in need and to attempt to answer the questions that have been asked since the beginning of mankind itself. It was incredibly upsetting to find that people we used to consider our 'paranormal family' were turning their backs on us and letting envy and jealousy feed a growing negativity. If only they could see how obvious it was to those outside of their own close circle of friends, perhaps they would come to their senses, and realize they were creating and growing their own negative shadowy energy from the lies and treachery they had initiated.

Day by day, our lives went on despite the hate and the love we received. Monday, Tuesday, Wednesday... ahhhh... Wednesday, and at the end of the work day, I found various ways to keep myself busy, thinking if I could get through 'hump day', I could get through the rest of the week.

***

The trustees of the Owl's Nest #30 met on Wednesday evening, and I received an email late that same night. They offered us either of the next two weekends to do our investigation (Saturday, June 12th or 19th). I sent a text message to Jenn and Katie as soon as I read the email. It wasn't until the following evening that I received their responses, and the date of June the 12th was chosen, which only gave us two days to test and recalibrate our equipment, and double check out ever dwindling battery inventory. (I could always count on Jenn and Katie to have the spare batteries I was lacking.)

The day arrived, and passed quickly with the enthusiasm and expectations of exploring a new, potentially haunted location. We met at a local steakhouse for dinner and to discuss a possible 'plan of attack' for the evening, and because we couldn't wait until midnight to get started. It was a productive meeting, and I always felt better going into a new place knowing we were all on the same page, to some degree.

We finally decided to leave the restaurant at just after 9, and drove the short distance to the Starbucks, inside the east side Barnes & Noble Bookstore, to kill a bit more time. As we sat and filled ourselves with a dose of much needed caffeine, we rambled on about everything from past investigations, to personal anecdotes, and the future of the team.

"I almost hate to bring this up..." I wasn't sure how to start.

"Then, by all means, don't bring it up." Jenn cut me off with her humorous sarcasm.

"Well, I really think it's something you may want to know, even if you really don't want to know." I confounded them, and had almost confused myself.

"I don't know what the heck you are trying to say, so, just spit it out." Katie laughed as she spoke.

"Okay, here's the thing... When we left the Doc's house, what was it...a few weeks ago, on my way home I drove my car off of the road and into a cornfield." I gathered my thoughts trying to decide how to finish the story.

"Oh my gosh! Were you alright?" Jenn asked.

"Why didn't you call one of us... we were obviously still awake. We would have come to get you." Katie responded.

"I didn't want to bother you, and my car was okay, mostly. I just drove it back onto the road and then home." I continued.

"Did you fall asleep or something?" Jenn asked.

"Yeah, what happened?" Katie slid her question in.

"I was getting to that... you see, just as I was passing this corn field I saw a little girl step out to the edge of the field." They gave me looks of bewilderment, wondering why a girl would be in a corn field in the middle of the night. "That little girl was Ashley. I'm sure of it. But when my car came to a stop, and I got out, she was gone. I don't know why she was there, or if it was some sort of a hallucination, but I don't think it was. I just thought you might want to know... she may be at peace, but she isn't necessarily gone."

"So that's what that text message you sent was about." Jenn said, putting the pieces together. "I was waiting for another text from you explaining it, but when it didn't come, I thought I'd just leave it alone."

Katie nodded in agreement with Jenn's deduction and staring down at her coffee cup, not making eye contact, said, "Alright, now I'm officially freaked out." We could feel the fear in her quiet voice that cracked in the middle of her statement.

"Sorry, that was not my intent, but I thought it was only fair to tell you." I said to them both. "I don't want you to be scared, but I just wanted to let you know, we haven't seen the last of her... I don't think." I falsely half smiled and shrugged my shoulders.

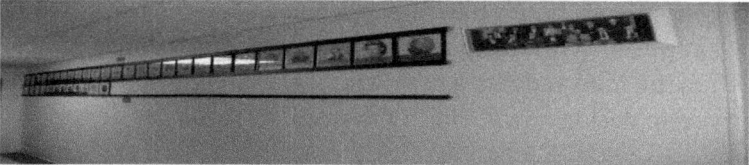

Hall of Presidents

Barb gets a chill.

Chapter 3

SHADOWS OF THE PAST

The conversation ran on for almost an hour when we decided we should head to the north side of town. I pulled into the parking lot of The Owl's Nest on First Avenue at twenty minutes before midnight and found both Jenn and Katie had beaten me there. Walking up to the door alone, I met Del and Barb who were waiting, anticipating our arrival. After a brief discussion, I returned to the girls, who were eagerly awaiting my return in the parking lot. The sky was starless and the wind was warm, growing stronger from the southwest when we began the tiresome task of unloading and carrying in all of our equipment.

"Rain's coming." I said, as I carried a couple of the cases through the dimly lit, empty sea of striped asphalt.

"I can smell it in the air." replied Katie.

"Yep. We had better get a move on if we don't want to be packing this stuff in wet." Jenn added, and we all instinctively quickened our pace.

It was just before midnight when we gathered in the bar on the main floor of the Owl's Nest. A storm had been brewing to the west when we arrived, and occasionally we heard the distant rolling thunder. Del and Barb were the only ones in the entire building besides Jenn, Katie and myself, which gave the typically lively atmosphere a dark and desolate tone.

"If you can give us a few minutes, we have to get everything turned off here and downstairs." Del said.

"Is it okay if we take a look around upstairs and you two can join us when you finish up down here?" I asked.

"Sure, just be careful. There's a lot of boxes and things upstairs, so you might want to keep your flashlights on." Barb answered me.

"Thanks." I said to her, and then I turned to the girls, "Grab a few things and let's get this investigation started!"

One by one, the rooms went dark, and the hush of the enchanted blackness before us brought goose bumps and chills as we prepared ourselves for what may lie ahead. There was a spellbinding and magical allure to the utter darkness, silence and emptiness that we had not anticipated. With flashlights, meters and cameras in hand, we found the stairway and headed up to the second level. At the top of the stairs there were three options. There was a door to our left, an open doorway to the right, and the short corridor that ran to the right of the stairway, next to the banister that held two doors at its end. We chose the open doorway to the right.

24

We entered the room with caution. Lacking the incandescent lighting, the second story of the home had a worrisome overtone, spine-tingling and ominous. Looking around with our flashlights, we located the stockpile of decorations and business supplies like toilet paper, paper towels, and other miscellaneous boxed sundries and took note, so as not to stumble over them in the pitch black when our lights went out.

We hadn't brought our DVR and infra-red camera system, but Jennifer did have her hand held night vision Sony camcorder. Once we had all of our meters on and recorders running, our flashlights were extinguished. We had taken a semi-circled seat on the floor near the doorway we had entered, and began to casually whisper to each other as our eyes adjusted to the near pitch-blackness of the room.

"Do you think this place is really haunted?" Katie asked.

"I don't know, but I really hope so." I answered back. "It sure has that weird feeling in the air, ya' know? I'm already on edge."

"I have a really strong feeling about this place, and with the history of the children and the patrons that have died here, I think we may have some activity." Jenn added.

Thunder rumbled again, now closer than before.

"And then there's that..." I joked, referring to the brewing storm outside, and its connection to our last investigation and Ashley Sue.

The oppressive darkness was suddenly overwhelming and the air in the room grew heavy. Our conversations had come to an abrupt end and we sat in silence staring into the darkness at the other end of the room. There was a building energy in the air that none of us could deny.

"What is that?" Jenn asked. "There's something over there by that boarded up window."

"Yeah, I swear I thought I saw something move." whispered Katie. I could feel the fear trembling in her voice.

I strained my eyes to see through the dark, attempting to focus on something that I had yet to see, and then there it was, a shadow moved at the other end of the room, no wait, there were several shadows. I studied and thought, and tried not to speculate, but the longer I looked, the more positive I became that there were several shadows, three to four feet in height moving independent of any possible light source.

I depressed the on button of my flashlight, and it flickered for only a fraction of a second, and in a brief moment of pale, electric light we all saw them. There were four shadowy child figures holding hands, two on either side of a taller female child who was less shadowy, with more definite features. They all stood there hand in hand, staring back in our direction. And a split second later, the lightning flashed through the cracks in the boarded up windows, and they were gone.

I didn't do it mean to, but intentional or not, I blurted out, "Ashley!"

Katie sucked in her breath hard and reflexively scooted her butt backwards across the floor, away from the now empty space.

"What the hell is she doing here?" Jenn reacted and didn't bother to whisper.

"Oh crap, oh crap, oh crap..." Katie muttered over and over. I moved back to where she was and placed my arm around her shoulder.

"It's alright. If you aren't comfortable, you just say the word. Del will let you out." I squeezed her shoulder.

She drew a couple of deep breaths and with a shaky voice, said, "No, I'm okay for now. If it gets too bad, I'll go, but not yet." She paused for only a moment to catch her breath and continued with, "I'm sure that was her, wasn't it?"

"Yeah, I'm pretty damn sure it was. I just hope she's here to help. We don't need another case like the last one." Jenn said and drew back memories to us all about the terrible experiences of being burned to death that we had experienced when we were trying to help the spirit of young Ashley Sue.

Now that Katie was pregnant, neither she, nor the team wanted her to be in any kind of situation that could have a negative effect of any kind on her or her unborn child. The mere possibilities caused me to physically shudder. Jennifer and I were stunned when Katie jumped to her feet.

"Well come on, guys!" She said with a rekindled spark in her tone. "Let's go... they're still here somewhere, and I bet we can find them!"

Clumsily standing up, I turned to Jenn. "You heard her, let's go see if we can drum up some activity. I don't think we need to question if the place is really haunted."

"Well, duh!" Jenn regurgitated her sarcasm. "Maybe we should keep it quiet about Ash being here."

"Agreed." I said.

"Come on!" Katie pleaded.

We took our meters to the other end of the room, checking high and low, slowly moving from side to side. There were random e.m.f. fluctuations that we couldn't explain. Random bursts of free moving energy were caught by our meters and quickly vanished until we would catch up with them again. Though the apparitions were now invisible to us, we felt their presence. An uneasy feeling had overtaken the three of us, and while the apparitions may have appeared as children, a foul and ghoulish fog had filled the space we occupied. I had the distinct feeling we were not the only ones occupying this place, not tonight.

We stood frozen in our tracks for a moment, and the hair on the back of my neck stood on end. A cold breeze came from nowhere and crossed my neck and face, chilling me to the point of a physical shiver. I had been monitoring my MEL-Meter and while the e.m.f. range was at a 0.0, I watched as the temperature reading quickly dropped from 74 degrees Fahrenheit to 69. Then as if on cue, the e.m.f. spiked to a 2.1 and immediately declined.

I called out, "2.1! Did you see that?"

"No but I felt a cold spot." Jenn said.

"My K-II meter spiked for a second too." Katie responded to my question.

Then, as if being directed by some unknown force, our trio turned simultaneously toward the odd shaped, 'non-closet', mystery room. We darted into the room, elbow to elbow, with meters in hand. The energy in the space was obvious to us all, in fact at times it was off of the charts and beyond what our meters could reliably measure. Lightning flashed brightly through the cracks once again and a thunderous growl shook the very building itself. Without warning, the meters went calm, and the energy seemed to leave the air. We immediately (but not literally) turned into ravenous 'monkeys', with arms and meters flailing around searching for the lost energy of the shadow children and Ashley. Our efforts slowed as we all found ourselves with our devices pressing against the wall opposite of the door we had entered. The e.m.f.s were coming from the opposite side of the wall, but were now weaker and slowly dissipated until they were completely gone.

"That was incredible!" I whispered loudly to the pair of brunettes who were crammed into this small space with me.

"I know right!" returned a whisper from Katie.

So far, this investigation *was* incredible, but not terrifying... yet. Our now energetic trio exited the non-closet space. Only a half dozen paces into the larger room, and Jennifer stopped dead in her tracks, and Katie and I both nearly ran into her. A painful silence immediately filled the air, and then... 'Tap-squeak....tap-squeak....tap....tap-squeak...tap'

"Someone's on the stairs." Jenn whispered in a barely audible voice.

"Barb and Del, maybe?" Katie whispered back, paradoxically answering the statement with a question.

We had frozen to listen to the ascending footsteps within arm's reach of the second door to the stairwell landing. My left hand stabbed out into the darkness and grasped the doorknob. With a swift turn, a pull, and two purposeful steps, I was on the landing. I stepped into the open stairs and clicked on my LED flashlight, as it lit up the steps, the thunder cracked loudly outside, and it's after rumbling trailed off slowly. I stared in disbelief as my flashlight scanned the empty wooden steps.

"Nobody." I said over my shoulder to the girls in my full voice. The two quickly joined me.

"I swear I heard someone on the steps." Jenn said, as if she were trying to convince us that she hadn't made it up.

"I know, Jenn. We heard it too. No doubts." I reassured her, and Katie nodded in the dim LED lighting.

We stood there, for what seemed like an eternity, looking over the stair railing onto the dimly lit stair treads, waiting for some mystical-supernatural revelation that never came... well, it didn't come that night. When we had come to the realization that the occurrence was not returning, we ventured into the last room, at the top left of the stairs.

The room was feverishly scoured by the three of us using the hand-held devices to check for energy fields and cold spots, unexplainable noises and irrefutable shadow movement. With the exception of a few random e.m.f.s the room was oddly inactive. The searching for anything paranormal had led us to the opposite end of the room, which was actually the front of the house. Standing side by side, we peered through the dust and dirt covered windows and out into the darkest night sky. Watching the distant electrical storm, and hearing the low rumble of the lightning's aftermath, we each had a moment filled with wonder, excitement and memories of past events that we shared and yet were somehow our own.

I turned away from the window just as a stabbing shard of lightning flashed much closer and lit the room for a millisecond. I had turned to my left and in that flashing moment of revelation, I stood facing a door that we hadn't even realized existed yet.

"Check it out." I said to Katie and Jenn as I turned on my flashlight with a click and lit up the ornate wood carved door, and multifaceted, red glass doorknob.

"Sweeeet!" whispered Katie grinning through the darkness.

Jenn became immediately obsessed with the intricate lock and reaching forward, clutched the glass knob in her hand. With a gravelly twist and a pull, nothing happened. From that moment forward, Jenn had an insatiable desire to find out what was behind that door. Her fascination with old locks and keys was simply part of her character, but this was a consuming curiosity.

"Can you get it open?" She directed her question to me. The door was secured with a skeleton key styled keyhole-deadbolt lock. I knelt down and shined my flashlight into the keyhole but could see nothing. I then placed my light on the floor, and pressing it against the door, shone its light underneath and into the hidden space. Jennifer giggled out loud as I pressed my cheek to the door and peered into the key hole. Nothing. Not even a hint of light was seen. Holding my light in hand, I stood up.

"I can't see anything, not even the light." I said to the girls.

"Maybe there's a key." Jenn responded to my statement.

"Shhhhhhh!" Katie hushed us quickly.

"Tap...tap-squeak...tap-squeak...tap...tap...tap-squeak..." The noise continued, even louder and more pronounced than before. The three of us walked as quietly and cautiously as we could, while still trying to reach door at the other end of the room before the sound disappeared once again. When we reached the door, Katie grabbed the knob, and pulling it open with a rush of wind, we burst onto the upstairs landing.

"AAAHHHHHHHH!" Came a shrill scream and heavy fast breaths from the steps below, followed by "Oh, crap! You guys scared the 'you know what' outta me!" The voice came from an exasperated Barb, and boisterous laughter came from Del who was right behind her. For the next few moments we all enjoyed

30

a good laugh, as Barb and Del finished their climb up to the second floor.

Once we had regained our composure, Jenn had a question for the pair of long time members and officer of the club.

"So, do you know where the key is to the door in this room? You know... the one with the red doorknob?"

"There's a funny story about that...Del, why don't you tell it." Barb said.

"Okay..." Del answered her and rubbed his goatee with his hand, pulling down, as if to straighten it, though with its shortness, it was never mussed up. He began, "I guess it was about three or four years ago." The two exchanged looks, and since there was no discrepancy, Del continued. "Two of our trustees were up here getting a list together to order some sundries, and taking inventory of the stock. One of them, I think it was Kenny," The two exchanged looks again.

"Yep, it was Kenny." Barb confirmed.

"...so anyway, Kenny came downstairs and asked our president, at the time, if he had the key to that room. He wanted to see if there was anything stored in there, or room to store anything. Our president, Fred, said 'Nope, we've never had a key, and never been in there... since the Owl's bought the building, as far as I know.' I think it's always been one of those hushed mysteries."

"It's one of those things that everybody used to know about years ago, and it's something that a few of us still know, and it's sort of an 'Owl's Nest curiosity'...something that comes up in conversations around Halloween as part of somebody's spooky story." Barb added.

"Yeah, it's talked about in 'ghost stories' but most of our members don't even know if the *'door with the red knob'* even exists. I think that the 'so called' legends and stories about *'the room we've never been in'* is why we've never just had the lock picked or replaced."

31

"Very curious story, I'm intrigued." I said, and I honestly was, but Jennifer was beyond intrigued, she was literally captivated by it.

"Do you mind if we join you while you investigate?" Del asked.

"We promise to be quiet as mice." Barb said with sincerity in her voice and a smile on her face.

I looked at my team mates for their agreement, and then turned back to the polite and smiling couple. "Sure, just follow our lead, and try to just be observers unless we ask you to step up."

"Thank you! We can definitely do that!" Barb said grinning like a youngster on Christmas morning.

We went through the motions of the investigation with Barb and Del alongside us. We spent most of our time in the room where we had seen the shadow children with the ghost of Ashley Sue, sitting or standing, and patiently waiting. The sound of rain on the flat roof of the building, and the occasional tremor of thunder, broke the silence and though the room still had a mysterious and chilling feel about it. There were no spectral visits for quite some time, so we decided to show Barb and Del how our different e.m.f. detector worked, and how we used them to disprove paranormal activity, or to find it. We let them hold the meters and sweep the room for rogue energies.

"1.2 … 1.4 … 1.9" Barb whispered loudly, "2.1!" calling them out in the manner we had explained- '2.1' was said as 'two point one' Her voice and excitement escalated, and then declined, "1.6 … 0.8 … 0.2 … and it's gone."

I approached her as she called out the readings, and when the numbers went flat, I took the meter from her and began to sweeping the floor and wall in the area where the random energy was caught.

"I am looking for the rational man-made source of the high reading you just caught. Usually there is a simple explanation for these occurrences. I always try to find the logical explanation to things, and when I can't find one, that's when things get interesting." I explained to Barb how my logical, scientific brain worked these situations, and just as I finished my explanation, a chill ran up my spine, causing the hair on my neck top stand on end.

We continued our re-investigation of the upstairs, but the remainder of our time there was quiet except for the continuing storm outside. We were growing anxious for more activity, and hopefully more answers to the haunting of the Owl's Nest, so I suggested we venture to a different level of the building and carry on with our investigation.

"Is everyone ready to investigate some more of the building?" I asked everyone.

"It *is* almost 2 o'clock already... I'm ready if y'all are." Jenn informed us, sounding a bit countrified...and so we headed towards to stairs.

The rest of the group wandered down the stairs, holding onto the beautiful, but antiquated, dark walnut stained handrail, in an effort to not stumble to our deaths in the dimly colored glow of our equipment's l.e.d. lights. Remaining behind, Katie motioned us on, as if we could make out anything she was doing in the blackness at the top of the stairs.

"Go ahead. I want to hang out up here by myself for a few minutes and see if any paranormal activity occurs when we aren't all up here together." She half whispered, leaning over the top rail.

It had always been our agreement that no one investigate alone, but against my better judgment, I whispered back, "Okay, just don't stay too long." and then fumbled through the darkness to catch up to Jennifer and our hosts.

Taking a seat on the dusty hardwood floor of the upper landing of the staircase, Katie quickly began to feel uncomfortably 'not alone'. She had her K-II meter and digital recorder turned on and placed neatly in front of her, but said nothing, asked no questions, and remained utterly still. The eerie feeling of an unknown presence grew around her, causing her to shiver and the hairs on the back of her neck stand on end. She peered into the darkness, hoping to see something, anything, that would explain the unexpected coldness she felt.

A sudden feeling of dread came over her as she instinctively recalled her experiences with Ashley Sue, the burning girl, and how horrific and frightening those encounters had been. She had been called a witch child, and considering her short life had occurred in the late 1800's, I can imagine that some people may have believed that she was. We knew better, but that didn't make many of our meetings with her any less dreadful.

Gathering up her courage, Katie whispered softly into the musty night air, "Hello?" Then as if in response, she felt a presence, almost a pressure from behind her, causing her heart to race and her skin to crawl. The slightest movement of icy air was felt on the side of her neck, and as she leaned away from it, a disembodied voice chuckled a low and devious laugh in her ear. Katie snatched up her K-II and recorder in one fell swoop and flew down the stairs, catching only every other stair, at best. Bursting through the door at the bottom, her feet planted on the main floor landing with a thud that echoed in the empty darkness.

From the bar room, we all heard the 'Thump...thump...thump ...thump...Bang-thud!' followed by the scuffling sound of footsteps down the hall. Jennifer and I dropped our attention to investigating in the bar area, and we quickly rushed into the hallway to meet Katie halfway. I turned on my flashlight with a click, and lit up the area enough to see the startled look, mixed with a half-smile, on Katie's face.

"Everything okay?" Jenn blurted out quickly.

"Yeah, I think so... I was just a bit freaked out... guess I'm just a little jumpy after the last investigation."

"Understandable... I shouldn't have left you up there alone. I'm sorry. So what happened up there?" I asked.

Katie went on to tell her story with precise detail and we took note of it and decided from this point on, it would be

best to continue our initial investigation on the first floor
together and then finish up in the lower level.

Chapter 4

A RUSH OF SOULS

I excused myself to use the restroom, and the girls rejoined Barb and Del in the bar room.

Barb continued recanting the tales of a man in a yellow shirt who has been seen in the area of the bar and always walked the same path, disappearing into the Coke machine. "He would usually be seen somewhere around here," she pointed with her light, "and walks in this direction until he disappears into the Coke machine, and a couple of times it's been said that he walks into the dance hall right there."

"Hey Rick...." Jenn called out. "What's he doing heading down *that* hall?" She said in quieter tone to the other three standing with her.

"I thought he was in the restroom?" Del replied. "It's down the other hallway, but they all connect in a sort of loop." and as he finished speaking, I emerged around the opposite corner, out of the hall.

"I **was** in the restroom, why?" I asked, having been able to hear the whispered conversation from across the otherwise silent room.

"How did you get back there so fast? I swear I just saw you go down that hallway over there." Jenn said with a tone of surprise as she pointed to the hall leading out of the opposite side of the room.

"Awesome!" I answered. "I was never in that part of the hallway. We are the only ones here, right?"

"Yep, just us." smiled Barb.

"Let's get a camera set up here and aim it where you thought you saw me. If it's a residual haunting we might catch it again." I turned toward Barb and Del and explained. "A residual haunting is one that is like a recording. It plays the same thing over and over, usually at the same time and same place. It doesn't interact, it doesn't want anything. It is not an actual spirit. Usually it's a trapped energy, but not quite the same as the energy of a 'ghost'."

"We've done some research ourselves, but thanks for the explanation. That could explain the man in the yellow jacket." Barb said, being somewhat proud of their knowledge of the paranormal.

We continued on through the main level of the club and after we had finished our typical routine investigating, we made our way down the wide, 1950's, school-like stairs into the basement. The stairway opened up into a huge room that we were told was often used for bingo, crafting and other member activities. There was an antique bar, for serving liquor, at the far end of the room, and down the wall on the left side a few doors could be seen in the glow of the flashlights we carried.

"Let's go in this room first." whispered Katie.

Del pushed the door open to reveal a long rectangular room with a low ceiling. There were two pool tables to the left as we walked in and a few small round table and chair sets scattered about to our right and on the back half of the room.

Once we were all in the room, Jenn said, "Yeah, good call Katie. Can you feel it?"

"Brrr." Barb shuddered and rubbed her arm. "Is it just me or is it cold in here? I though the heat was supposed to still be on in here."

"It is." Answered Del, with a flat tone that gave us the feeling he was confused by the obvious chill in the air.

"Whoa!" Katie let slip out, and then continued with, "Did you just feel that breeze?"

"I think so." I answered, though I couldn't be sure.

"I felt it." was Jenn's comment. "It blew behind me and the around my right side...kinda low, like it was only around my legs."

"Precisely! That's how it felt to me." Katie agreed.

"Okay, let's get set up in here." I directed everyone as to where I would like to set the equipment. Once it was set up, I began with all of the generic, typical e.v.p. questions, with a 30 to 40 second pause between each one.

"Is there anyone with us tonight? ... Can you tell us your name? ... Do you feel trapped here? ... Is there anything we can do to help you? ..." and so on. Although there was an energy in the room that we could all feel, it was unnervingly quiet, and there was no apparent activity.

Jennifer decided to try a different approach. Opening up the bag she carried on her shoulder like an oversized purse, she withdrew a stuffed toy duck, an old wooden toy train, and

39

placed them on the floor. Looking around she noticed the pool tables she was between and chose the red pool ball from the table top and also placed it on the floor in front of her. She knelt down on the floor and began to speak. "Hi... my name is Jennifer. What's yours?" she paused for a few moments, and rolled the red ball forward. It came to rest a few feet from her, but nothing seemed to happen. The rest of us watched silently as Jenn reached out and pulled the ball back to her and rolled it forward a few times in a row with the same results. Jenn pretended to play with the toy train and the duck and then rolled the ball forward once again. The ball came to rest a few feet away, but only for a moment. It unexpectedly rolled nearly a foot to the right and then just as it was coming to a halt, rolled directly back to Jenn as if it had purpose. Though obviously shaken, Jenn rolled the ball one more time, but it stopped abruptly and returned to her at an even faster pace than it had been sent. She caught the ball in her hand and continued in her lighthearted, yet slightly quivering voice. "I want to talk to the children that are here."

"CRACK" A sound, as Del so accurately put it, 'like two large hammers smacking together', very metallic and heavy, seemed to echo from some distant place, yet somehow, still within the same room. Everyone in the room flinched, especially Barb and Del.

Though I knew the answer, I had to ask, "Did you hear that, it sounded heavy, maybe metallic?"

"Yeah, that was pretty interesting, huh?" Katie said.

Jenn looked up at us over her shoulder and smiled. "Sometimes you just have to know how to talk to them." She turned back around. "Can you do that again?" She asked politely, but there was no other sound or reply. In fact that was all of the activity we experienced in that room during this particular visit, and eventually we moved on to the next door.

"On through here is the room we call the 'rat room'." Del said as we entered the next room.

"Oh gawd!" Barb grumbled, and then laughed as she pointed up to a spot where the water damaged ceiling was coming down slightly... and there it was... a dead rat, hanging out of the edge of the open crevice in the ceiling. We had seen worse, but it **was** awkwardly morbid.

"Ewww, that's just creepy." Jenn said jokingly.

"I know, and apparently it's mummified. It's been up there for years, and now it's just a part of this old building, and no one can bring themselves to get rid of it." Del explained.

We left the rat room after a short round of investigating and headed up a couple of steps and into an oddly shaped sort of a hall. The rafters were dusty and cobweb filled. We now found ourselves in another part of the original basement of the home. Old jars, bits of wood and an assortment of boxes were scattered about in disarray. There were doorways to our left, and up ahead there was an opening to the right and one straight ahead. I was beginning to feel one of those uncomfortable, eerie sensations again. This area truly had the look and feel of a haunted house you might see in a Hollywood thriller. To our right was one of the most curious things I had seen yet. Just before the opening on that side of the strange corridor, there was an old rickety, uneven, and un-level set of open wooden stairs that led up to the rafters above, and then simply ended.

We all took our turns peering into the doorway to the left, which was a storage room that held shelves full of regularly used items such as bingo cards, markers and the ball cage, but for some reason we did not enter. Instead we stealthily made our way through the doorway that stood directly in front of us and found ourselves in a puzzling room that had numerous round air ducts that cut across the room at various angles and caused the entire space to feel 'off-kilter'. While the others took their turns looking around, and taking readings, Jennifer and I ventured into the room at the foot of the stairway to nowhere.

The walls in this area were original to the home, and built of old red clay bricks. Now they were brittle and crumbling, and hidden behind decades of dusty cobwebs. We had to duck as we entered the creepy space. The floor was concrete and had a deep 'cut out' in the center. We would later learn that this 'pit' was where the old steam boiler, that was used to heat the home, had once been located. The brickwork was not particularly remarkable, it was average at best, and like the other areas, had a dirty, musty, web covered surface.

Our attention was immediately drawn to an antique wooden wheel chair that must have been from the same era as the original home. It too was dust and web covered and had the appearance as if it were growing into, and becoming a part of, the house. The wall directly behind it was the same as the others with one exception, just up and to the left of the wheel chair was a cut out opening that lead to a crawlspace.

Katie popped her head in the doorway to the boiler room and said what the two of us were already thinking.

"Wow, it's totally creepy in here. This is what paranormal investigators dream of...and that wheel chair. That's amazing!"

We had decided, without a word, that this place was worth spending some time investigating. Jennifer and I both turned on our digital recorders to capture any electronic voice phenomenon that may occur. She set hers on the far side of the room, and I placed mine in the seat of the wheelchair. The hair on the back of my neck stood up, and I had the unmistakable feeling that I was being watched....that we were not alone.

Katie depressed the on switch of her K-II meter and sat it near the open hole in the concrete floor. We stepped back and began our typical, routine questions. Once we were all in the room, we turned off our flashlights and slipped into the dank, darkness of the moment. When our eyes began to adjust, the faint glow of the red recording lights, and the single green light telling us the K-II was on, gave the small room beneath the ground level a sinister glow and a cavern like feeling.

"This is one of the spookiest places I think I have ever been." Barb whispered to everyone.

"It definitely has an unnerving presence about it...but it's not the creepiest place we've ever been." Katie whispered back.

"Helmach farm?" I responded with a question.

"That one has to be the most haunted and creepy place *I've* ever been." Jenn popped in with a comment that none of us could deny.

It was just then that the room went silent. We all stood frozen in place as if Medusa herself had appeared and turned us to stone, when there was a sound, a low murmuring whisper that trailed off into the night.

"What was that?" Del whispered loudly.

"I heard it to." I answered back. "I can't say for sure, but it sounded like voices."

"Shhh..." Jenn hushed us all, and pointed to the K-II meter on the floor.

It was beginning to slightly flicker and I stared at it like a kid watching his first fireworks display, afraid to look away and miss something phenomenal. In a matter of seconds, it had stopped. There was a collective exhale, which made me realize that I was not the only one holding my breath.

I began to speak to the nothingness around us. "If you are here with us, we'd like to communicate with you. I think we may have heard you trying to talk a few minutes ago ... if that is too difficult, you can talk to us by answering our questions using this little box on the floor with the green light on it. If you touch this box, it should light up when your energy comes in contact with it. The more energy you exert, the more lights you will light up." No matter how haunted a place seemed to be, or how many times I had done this, it always felt awkward to speak to someone who simply wasn't there.

"Would you like to try that? If so, touch the little gray box." Jennifer said politely. In mere seconds the light flickered.

"Do you feel trapped here?" I asked and waited, and once again the flicker of green drew us in like a magnet.

"Did you used to live in this house?" Katie took her turn and immediately there was a flickering light, which quickly went out.

I leaned toward Del and Barb and whispered "You can ask a question if you want." It was too dark to really see, but I was pretty sure they were smiling through their uncomfortableness.

"Are there many of you here?" Del spoke up. At first there was nothing but darkness and silence. Just when I was about to give up and ask another question, the light flickered one more time, a long slow intermittent flashing and then went still.

"Whoa!" Katie said. "I guess we aren't alone at all. I wonder how many there are here? ... Can you make the light flash once for each of you that are here?" Nothing happened. So, we waited for what seemed like an eternity. Nothing. We shuffled around the room a bit trading places and trying to stir things up. Still... nothing.

"If you use a little more energy, maybe try to squeeze or hit this box, more lights will light up. There are green lights, and yellow and red..." As soon as I said the word red, the K-II meter lit up fully, every light and remained lit for a few seconds. Everyone in the room felt a chill and goose bumps were raised. We stayed in that room for another half an hour or more, but we experienced no more notable activity.

On our way out we were all abuzz whispering about the impressive K-II interactions in the eerie 'wheel chair' room. When we stepped out of the older area and into the newest part of the basement where the bar and bingo tables were set up, it was like the entire feel of the space had become oppressive, and suddenly uncomfortable to be in. A few steps in and Barb and Del stopped without warning, staring ahead and into the far left corner of the odd rectangular room. I can't say if we all noticed it at the same time, but when I looked in the same direction I clearly saw something moving...something low, and large. I held my breath, watching as some vacuum of blackness sucked every bit of light out of the already darkened corner, and moved slowly, awkwardly, yet purposefully to our right.

Jenn carefully raised her video cam and pointed it in the direction of the shadowy motion. Depressing the record button, the infra-red lights came on and the electronic hum of the camera filled the otherwise silent room. Perhaps it was the red lighting that was pointed in the corner, or the sound of the running video camera, but something provoked the shadow. In a rush of sound that seemed to grow inside my head, like the shrieking of a dying animal, multiple shadowy figures flew directly across the room, straight towards us! The entire group was terrified and stumbled backwards a few steps. I managed to accidentally find the step that led into the older area, and catching my heel on it, fell backwards and onto my butt with a painful smack. I watched as the shadows passed through my new friends and team mates, and then brushed by me as well, with what almost felt like the cold movement of air, like a nearby air-conditioning vent had suddenly turned on and then back off.

I jumped up immediately, before the experience even had time to sink in, and turned my flashlight on, chasing the shadows into the old boiler room. I was followed within inches by the rest of my companions. Jenn and Katie burst into the room with me and stood shocked as we watched three shadowy, full bodied apparitions standing in the pit where the old boiler used to be. In the second following our visual discovery, as Barb and Del peeked into the room over our shoulders, the shadow people sank into the brick covered pit and disappeared from our sight.

"That was intense!" said Del. "We've had plenty of experiences here, but nothing that up-close and personal!" The excitement shook his voice.

"Yep!" Katie answered back. "It was kind of an 'in your face' moment, huh?"

"Ya think?" Jenn chimed in with her sarcastic comment, almost chuckling.

"And did you feel how cold it was?" Barb said raising her right arm and rubbing it with her left hand. "I still have goose bumps!"

"I hope that didn't freak you out too much, but it's kinda what we're used to." I said to Barb and Del. "We totally understand if you want to sit the investigation out and just hang out in the bar room, or something." I tried to offer them an 'out' because most people are not interested in face to face spirit activity, and after our last investigation, I didn't want to put anyone in that situation with us.

"Oh no... That was great!" Del answered back, and even in the dim light, I could see the grin on his face. He and Barb had true paranormal investigator blood running through their veins.

"Yeah, I hope everyone at the club believes us when we tell them about it!" Barb added excitedly.

The air was thick in the room as we all found our way into the former boiler room. Thick lint-like dust covered the pipes and Romex wiring that hung across the floor joists. An uncomfortable feeling overwhelmed us all. It was that sickening feeling when you are asked to identify a loved one after a tragic accident, mixed with the repulsive nature of a high school visit to the county morgue to deter teens from drinking and driving. None of us could say, at the time, why we felt these things, but we all agreed that it took everything we had to remain in that room awaiting another visit from the shadowy presences.

Chapter 5

OUT
OF THE
ASHES

My mind drifted back to only a month prior when we came in contact with the shadow demon at the Helmach farm and how its attachment to little Ashley Sue had caused her to become the most evil of creatures at times, and how it had even turned my team into angry and sometimes bitter people. My stomach turned, as thought about the possibility of three of these 'demons' in one location...

"Oh... fuck..." The whisper escaped my head and slipped out of my mouth. "Oops...so sorry! I really don't usually talk like that." I apologized to everyone in the room.

I think Barb and Del were a bit shocked, but chuckled under their breath. I could see Jenn's smile in the dim LED light of the meters.

"What?" Katie asked. "Something must have made you say that, right?"

I didn't want to answer, not right then, but I suppose it was only fair not to keep something like this from them. "Do you remember the shadow we 'ran into' at the Helmach farm?" Katie and Jenn's faces went blank, and I could almost see the blood draining from them as they went pale, remembering the shadow demon that brought us all such terror and other worldly horrors.

"Don't get me wrong. I'm not saying this is the same at all... we have encountered lots of shadow people in the past who were not out to do anyone any harm, but the feeling I was getting in here..." I trailed of never ending my sentence.

"I can feel it too... kinda sickening feeling in the pit of my stomach." Jenn spoke quietly and gravely.

I stood up and was visibly shaken by my thoughts. I squeezed between Jenn and Katie to where Barb and Del stood, near the door. I whispered to them, "Come out here with me for a minute, if you don't mind."

"Sure." Whispered Del and they followed me out to the large room where we had first seen the shadow people. We stopped and before I could speak, the lightning stuck just outside, and the thunder sounded a deafening boom. I took a moment to regain my composure before I addressed my concerns.

"I'm not trying to frighten you, but I think maybe we should call it a night here. We have a lot of audio and video to review already, and our last encounter with a shadow haunting was not so good. I would like to possibly come back with our friend Theo and do some more investigating here. Theo is a psychic medium, and he is very good with using holistic means to purify and protect people and places." I spilled my guts to

48

them and waited for their reply. The two looked at each other in the dim lighting, and then Barb spoke up.

"That sounds great!" She began, and the two smiled at me. "We were honestly afraid you might come here and not have any activity and then leave us with no answers, so coming back and bringing more help is a wonderful idea!"

"I have a feeling that there is more to this haunting than we know, but I will do everything in my power to get you the answers you need, and proving this place is legitimately haunted, well... I'm pretty sure we're beyond that already." I reassured them.

***

While I ushered the two out to the newer area, Jenn and Katie remained behind, seated on the floor near the open pit.

"I don't like this place. It feels...wrong" Katie said with a mousey voice.

"Me either." replied Jenn. "Leave it to E-V-Prick out there to walk off and leave his team in this..."

'BOOOOM!!!" the lightning and thunder announced their arrival together so dramatically, that the girls wondered if the building had been directly hit.

"You think that struck the building?" Jenn asked, but Katie was distracted.

"Yeah...I know it did." was her only response.

Jenn turned to see what it was that had Katie's attention. She followed Katie's stare down to the pit in front of them, where they both saw the glowing embers and tiny flames of a phantasm. They watched as the miniature fire and its fuel began to grow and flourish. What began as the size of a few pebbles and match flames grew and grew becoming a mound of red-hot coal embers that would more than fill a wheel barrow, and flames that now licked the dusty cobweb covered rafters, but did not seem to radiate any heat.

49

The pile of burning embers began to move. The uppermost coals tumbled down followed by the next and so on, until it appeared to be a landslide of embers revealing what appeared to be bones.

"You seeing this?" Katie whispered so quietly that Jenn barely heard her. She did not budge, and her lips moved less when she spoke than those of a seasoned ventriloquist.

"Mmm-hmmm" Jenn made the noise without even parting her lips, and the two gazed at the burning embers as they continually revealed more and more.

The mound of red glowing coals soon exposed the chalky, white, ash covered skeletal remains of three adults. One of the skulls rolled to the side and seemed to be looking towards the two girls, and its boney hand and arm reached out to the girls, but fell lifeless as the fire was rekindled. The girls sat horrified and speechless as they watched the flames once again grow. The fire, though it seemed to now have no coals on which to feed, became a powerful inferno, hissing and blowing like an acetylene torch, or flamethrower, billowing out flames with intent. Just as the flames reached their fullest potential, Ashley appeared within them, arms spread wide, palms upturned, and her hair a float on the waves of rising 'heat'.

"These monsters are not the end of the story, but the beginning." Ashley called to the girls in an otherworldly voice that gave them chills and retrieved a fear they had been trying to forget... the fear given to them by Ashley Sue, the burning girl.

Jenn found her courage while Katie sat dumbfounded by the spectral girl. "There are no real monster's Katie..." she whispered trying to comfort her friend.

The spectral voice began softly, and then filled the room with a frightful power and caused the room to brighten and glow with the orangey, dancing light of the fire, "I never believed in monsters either... until I became one!" The fiery glow dimmed and Ashley seemed to shrink somewhat in stature.

She whispered loudly to the girls as she and the embers crumbled into ashes and dust and disappeared into the cracks between the brick-laid floor of the pit.

"Monsters do exist...Save the children, before it's too late." Her voice echoed in the nearly empty room, and her words haunted the girls' thoughts.

"You two ready to get outta here?" I said, poking my head around the corner. The two jumped as if I had thrown a bucket of ice water on them and I couldn't help but laugh, which earned me a pair of 'brow-beating' scowls and spluffs.

"Cheese and crackers!" Jennifer yelled out. "You scared the crap outta me!"

"Ya think?" Katie mocked Jennifer's sarcastic comment from earlier in the night.

"Let me gather myself together... and yeah, I think we are ready to go." Jenn's voice trembled.

"Yeah, but we aren't finished here. We have to come back." Katie added with conviction. "There are children here, and monsters... we have to see this through."

"I will talk to the Heerdinks, but I am pretty confident that we will be welcomed back." I didn't even question Katie's comment about monsters. Our brush with Ashley's shadow demon taught me that monsters may not be what we have been taught they are, but they are as real as you and I.

The next half hour or so was spent gathering up our equipment and packing it safely away. Our black and silver hard cases were stacked neatly near the entrance, and after taking a second run through the building to be sure we hadn't left anything behind, we headed back to the main level. The five of us gathered in the open bar room, under the dim green light of exit signs and erratic bouncing flashlight beams.

"Thank you both so much for having us out. It was a night to remember, most definitely." I said as I shook the hands of Barb and Del. "I hope we can schedule a follow-up

51

investigation very soon. There is a lot happening here, and we have only scratched the surface of this mystery."

"Of course! You are welcome back anytime... We are very impressed with your professionalism and we've seen some things tonight, we have never seen before." Barb said with excitement.

"Yes, we would love to have you back soon... I will just have to let the trustees know ahead of time, so they can plan for it... normally the bar doesn't close until 1, and we have a hard time getting everyone outta here before 2" Del added.

"Sure thing. Plus we hope to be back soon to let you know if we caught any evidence." Jenn explained.

"I'm really looking forward to that! I hope you guys caught something." said Barb.

"We want to have something to show the trustees and the officers, so they can see it was worth while having you out." Del finished her thought.

"I'd be surprised if we don't have any evidence. It was a very active night." Katie chimed in correctly. It was rare that we had been to an actively haunted location and not captured some form of evidence, in fact many times when we left a place certain it wasn't haunted, we would later find bone-chilling evidence proving that we were 'dead wrong'. (Pun intended)

We shook hands, said our good-byes and as always, Jenn passed out her hugs. The equipment was loaded in the cars and we were about to leave when Katie stopped and looked up at the old building. Her eyes grew wide, and her jaw dropped open as she covered her open mouth with her hand and gasped.

"You okay, chica?" Jenn asked, looking from Katie to the building and back again.

Katie's huge brown eyes filled with tears, but didn't spill down her cheeks. "I know it wasn't real, but I swear I just saw a woman in a dress falling from the second floor of the building."

"I didn't see or hear anything, but I wasn't looking the right direction." I said sheepishly.

"It was silent... but she was a ghostly white, and fell almost in slow motion, but not quite... either way, it was a terrible thing to see."

I remembered back to when I had seen a troubled young man jump from a parking garage in downtown Evansville, in such desperation that he felt he had no other option. The sound of his body smacking the pavement, like a raw steak dropped on a tile floor, still haunts me to this day.

"Just another question that needs answered, and another reason we need to get back here as ASAP!" I meant every word I said.

"And we need to get with Theo before we come back. There is something evil there." Jenn said looking to Katie with a look of knowing more than she was saying.

"Okay girls, what's going on?" I had to know everything. It was the only way to prepare for our return.

"Well... when you left us alone in the boiler room, Ash came back for a 'visit', I suppose you could say." Katie shrugged her shoulders looking down as her foot stirred the bits of loose gravely pavement. "She said there are 'monsters' here and to 'save the children' before it was too late.' Not sure what all that means, but I agree. We should get Theo's help."

I was disappointed and relieved that I hadn't been a part of Ashley's second visit that evening. I wanted to know every detail, but instead of asking for more, I simply continued on in a way that let them know I didn't doubt them, and trusted them 100%.

"Jenn, you want to try to dig up some research on this place, and maybe you can help too." I said turning to Katie. "After we review the audio, video and photos, and get that all put together for an evidence reveal, maybe you two can find some more history to share with Del and Barb. That way, if by some rare chance we don't have any evidence, we might still be able to offer them something."

53

"Sure, that could be pretty interesting, trying to dig up some dirt on dead people." She said jokingly. I knew it was only in an attempt to be humorous, and avoid the obvious fear-factor that this haunting already had instilled in us.

"Great. Then, when I get finished going over my footage and audio, I'll contact Theo and see if he can make himself available. You want to come over tomorrow afternoon or evening and use the computers in the office to review everything, as a team?" I blurted it all out at once.

"That'd be good. Then we can get each other's opinions on what we think is legit." said Katie.

"Sounds good to me too... I'll give you two a text when I am awake and back among the land of the living." Jenn said in her typically sarcastic and somewhat morbid way.

We parted ways for the remainder of the morning. It was already going on 5am, and I didn't expect to hear from either of them until, at the soonest, tomorrow evening.

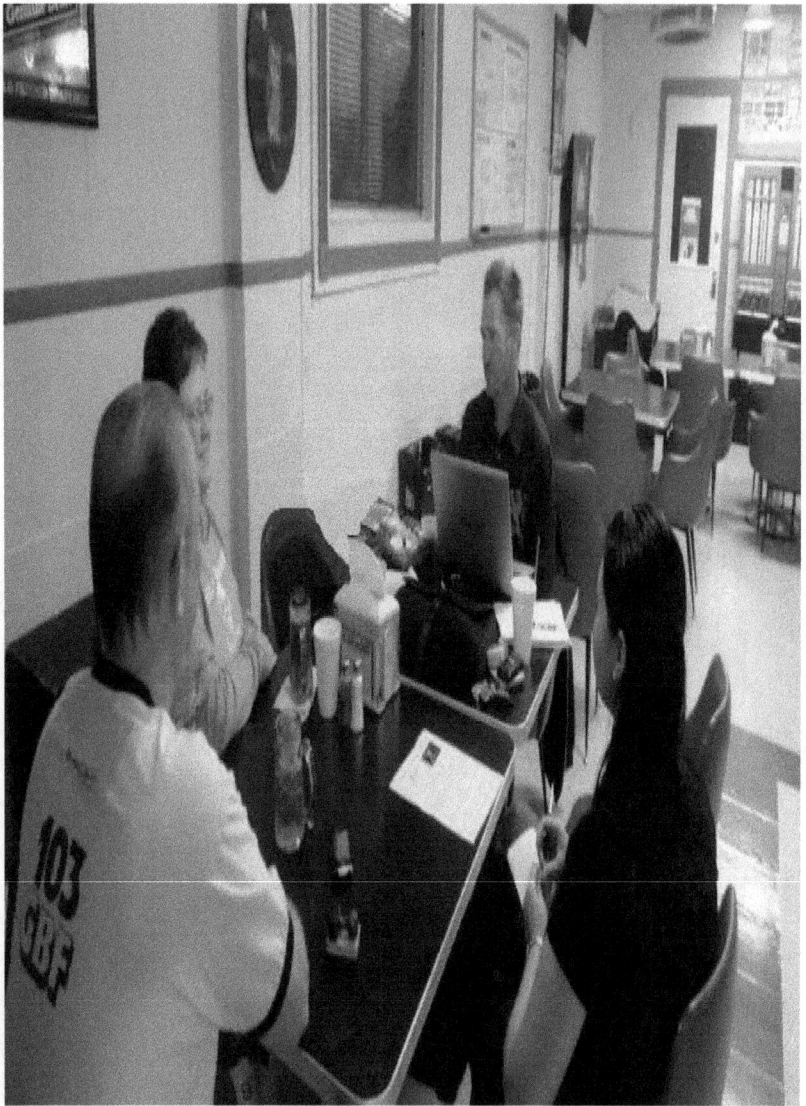

Chapter 6

VOICES

OF THE

DEAD

I had fallen asleep as quickly as I had turned the nightstand lamp off. A deep and restful sleep was what I needed, and it is exactly what I had, until my phone rang at 2pm on Sunday. I rolled over and pulled it off of the charger.

"Hello?" My raspy and groggy voice struggled its way out.

"Hey Rick! I didn't wake you did I?" The overly cheerful voice on the other end belonged to Barb Heerdink.

"Um, no... I've been awake for a little while already. What's up?" I tried to sound more awake than I was, though I don't think I played it off as well as I had hoped.

"Well, I just wanted to say thanks for coming out last night, and I had to call you because I have a couple of pictures from last night for you to look at *and* because of a conversation I had with my friend Linda. She and her husband Fred, who is the local President, actually live next door." Barb spoke, and I could hear something inside her bubbling over. I wasn't ready for a real conversation, but I felt the need to find out what had caused her to be so energetic and peppy this ....ugh... afternoon. I couldn't believe it was already 2pm.

"You're welcome, and thank you for having us. It was a great investigation and the team is getting together later to start reviewing our evidence. So, send me the pictures and we would love to have a look at them. Now... tell me about this conversation you had." I was now up and moving around. As I walked into the kitchen to put on a pot of overly strong Colombian coffee, Barb began to tell me about her discovery.

"Okay, I usually help out during the lunch shift here at the Owl's on Sundays, and even if I'm not, I'm always here. So I wasn't working today, but I couldn't wait to get there and tell all of my friends about the crazy shadows and everything last night. So, I was waiting for any of my friends to show up, and Linda was the first. She came in for lunch and I was getting her a refill on her coffee, I just do that kinda thing even when I'm not working, and out of the blue she actually asked about our 'ghost hunt'..." Barb's tale had been broken and a bit scattered, but I knew she was getting to a point, and I was following her. I could also tell that the more she spoke, the more excited she was getting.

"Go on..." I tossed in politely, to show her that I was listening and interested.

"Well, I was shocked that she showed an interest that we had you guys out last night. She isn't a fan of spooky things. But, when she asked about it, I was so surprised, that I sat the coffee pot down, and I sat down too, right there at her table." While she spoke, I poured the first of many cups of my own coffee, and added a few cups of sugar and French vanilla creamer. Okay, that was a bit of an exaggeration about the sugar, but not too far off. "So I sat there for a few minutes and told her about the investigation last night, but left out the scary details, and I told her about the history that Del and I had found about the Owl's Nest, and the building, and the family that lived here before. That's when she said something that shocked me."

"You have my complete attention." I was on the edge, waiting to hear what the woman had told Barb that was not only shocking, but could possibly relate to our paranormal investigation.

"Alright, here is the jist of it... She said she used to know a woman named Allison **Bettiger**! And she was supposed to be directly related to the Bettiger's that owned this place. Not only that, She said she was pretty sure that she was still alive, in her 90's, but alive... well, that's what I wanted to tell you. I just thought you might want to know." Barb finished up and I could feel her waiting to hear my response.

"That *is* pretty incredible. I have to admit. I'm going to share that with the girls, when they get here, and maybe they can do some research on her too." I was actually quite intrigued by the thought of a living relative to the family that had so many tragedies. "Thanks Barb. I'm going to have to get off of here and get the office opened up and ready for our review." Although what that mostly meant was opening the door to the spare room, turning on the computers, and hooking up the video monitor. We said our good-byes and hung up the phones.

The girls arrived together just after 4pm, packing in their cameras and digital recording devices. We crowded into the ten foot by thirteen foot room. Office style work stations lined one wall and two desktop computers and one laptop filled the space. There were two large, high backed, black leather office chairs, and one smaller one. I snatched up the smaller one positioned in front of the laptop, calling it as mine, and left the two more comfortable ones for the girls.

"Can I get you something to drink?" I asked them both in one question.

"Dr. Pepper?" Jenn asked.

"Bottled water?" was Katie's choice.

"Yep." I said pointing to each of them. I quickly returned from the kitchen with their drinks, and a Mt. Dew for myself in only a couple of minutes, but by then, the two had selected their computers and were already hooking up headphones and digital audio recorders. Once we were all situated, I'm sure it would have been a sight to see from an outside point of view, the three of us lined up wearing headphones and holding them tight to our ears as we listened, every minute or two stopping our recordings to back them up and give a second or third listen to a clip in question. About thirty minutes into the audio analyzation, I was listening to the file that was recorded in the 'pool room'. After replaying the clip nearly half a dozen times, I paused it and slowly removed my headset. Turning towards Jenn and Katie, who sat to my left, I watched them for a few minutes until they felt my stare and stopped what they were doing.

Katie smiled at me and said, "What?"

"You get something?" Jenn asked.

"Oh, I just want you to hear something... just to see if you hear the same thing I do?" I said, as I handed Jenn my headphones. "This is down in the basement. Remember when we heard that loud metallic bang?"

"Oh yeah!" Jenn said enthusiastically. "I have been dying to hear that playing through the program, and I thought if we analyzed it we could, maybe, figure out what made the sound."

"I don't think we need to analyze anything here... it seems pretty obvious to me, but I want you two to hear it to get your impression." I was quite impressed with the clarity of this particular clip.

Jenn slid the headphones in place and cupped her hands over them. I pressed the play button, and watched as she closed her eyes tightly. Her lips moved with our voices as they

60

played out on the recording. When the interesting part played, her eyes and mouth opened wide.

Jenn pulled the headphones back and rested them around her neck, "Shut up! ... Are you freakin' kidding me?" I grinned back at her.

"What? Don't keep me in suspense!" Katie said, reaching her hand out to Jenn, coaxing her to pass the headset to her.

"Wait, I wanna hear it again!" Jenn said in a whiny, pouty voice that did not accomplish what she had hoped.

"Tough cookies, girl! Hand 'em over, and nobody gets hurt." Katie chuckled as she poorly attempted to be the 'tough girl'.

Jenn reluctantly passed the headphones to her while I reset the audio clip. Katie put them on, closed her eyes and concentrated on the loud, static filled recording. She listened through the noise and tried to concentrate on the background sounds and our voices as we talked.

She clearly heard Jenn say, 'I want to talk to the children that are here." and she awaited the metallic hammer smacking sound that never came... in its place was a completely different sound, a voice. Amidst the painfully loud static, a voice, that of a child came across coldly and clearly, "You can't find us."

"No flippin' way!" Katie said in an overly boisterous voice, still having the head set on. "That was so clear!" She said as she removed the headphones and handed them back to me. "What do you think it means?"

"I don't know, but it seems to me that the ghost children feel the need to hide, and not be found, for some reason. Now we just have to figure out why."

"Yeah, that's probably going to be hard to figure out, unless we find some ancient book of local stories... again." Jenn said raising her eyebrows and rolling her head towards Katie.

"Yeah, I doubt that's happening. You know, we could maybe ask Ash." The room fell abruptly silent. "Sorry.... but Jenn and I had a message, or warning from her. She said we needed to 'help the children before it was too late.' I'm not sure what that meant, but maybe we could ask her?" Katie was braver than she realized. Just offering to try to contact Ashley on purpose took an immense amount of courage.

Katie and Jenn shared the task of recanting the tale of Ash's visit with them in the boiler room, leaving out no detail, no matter how gruesome it may have been.

"So, Ash is saying there are monsters in the old house, and the children need saved... geez! This is getting weird." I was beginning to question our experience and our level of understanding, but I knew we had been brought to this case for a reason, not just by chance. "Can we handle this?"

"All I can say is... we have to try." Jennifer's statement was honest and sobering. She was right. How could we make the decision to turn our back on these shadow children, when they obviously, and so desperately, needed our help?

"I don't know if this will help, but we might be able to get some more information about what happened to the kids... maybe... I got a call this afternoon from Barb, and she let me know that there may be a living descendant to the family, not sure how, or the relationship, but her name is Allison Bettiger, and if she is still alive, she is in her 90's." I passed the name and information to the girls and they received it like a birthday gift, with surprise and excitement.

"We have some sleuthing to do!" Jenn said to Katie with a grin.

"Okay, before we get off on to much of a tangent, we need to get back to analyzing our audio." The girls agreed with me and soon we were all nerdily studying the recordings again.

As I searched through the audio I was interrupted by an email alert. I had received the photos from Barb. I paused the playback and opened the email attachments. The first photo initially appeared to be just a blurry picture of Katie, but the longer I studied it, I began to realize that only part of the photo was blurry. Squinting my eyes, I came to the realization that the blur appeared to be the transparent face of a woman very close to the camera lens. I was excited by Barb's discovery and was excited to see the second picture.

Opening the second photo, I noticed that it was also a picture of Katie. This photo was in the basement, and the only this unusual about the photo was an orb that hovered above her. I am extremely skeptical when it comes to any orb, and at first I almost rolled my eyes. Then something caught my attention, this orb was pink. That was a first for me.

"Ladies, take a look at these pictures." I said, and then as I showed them the photos, they dissected each one very closely.

"I see a face." Katie said while Jenn seemed puzzled until a look of realization came over her face.

"I see it now!" She exclaimed as she began to point out the jaw line, brow, and hair.

"That is cool, huh?" I asked and then continued with, "But this one is something I can't say I have ever seen before. A pink orb...and fittingly, it is over Katie."

They investigated the photo, and while Jenn and I were actually impressed with the picture. Katie studied it closely and a sharp look of disappointment showed in her eyes. Her hand went to her head, and she turned to Jenn and me.

"Sorry to disprove this one, but that pink orb is a reflection off of the face of my pink watch face." She explained.

"Don't be sorry. Debunking is just as important as finding evidence. I think you did a great job of disproving the orb in this picture as paranormal." I complimented her.

Though there was no clock on the wall, time ticked away slowly, minute by minute, hour by hour. Inevitably, we were all stopped again when Jenn interrupted us, with another possible e.v.p.

"Okay guys, I'm not sure if this is Del, or if this is an actual e.v.p. It's so clear, that I have to question it." Jenn said fore-warning us that we may be listening to a clip we can easily explain away. "I'm going to just plug the speakers in for this one. It's clear enough that you won't need the headphones."

Jenn plugged in the external speakers and turned the volume up. I immediately recognized the conversation. We had all been upstairs and while I was explaining to Barb about using the e.m.f. detectors to find the source of manmade energies. Then the recording played this, "Then, when I can't find a rational explanation for the energy, that's when things get interesting." The word interesting was overpowered by another voice, crystal clear and sinister saying "Exciting!", almost as if it were finishing my sentence.

"That was a creepy voice, huh?" I asked the girls.

"Yeah!" Katie agreed. "I don't think that was Del."

"No, definitely not." I added. "But, not only was it finishing my sentence, it was male, and sounded very sinister, or evil... even though what it said was just a single, harmless word." I thought for a second. "Okay, I think that is legitimate, and even though it doesn't give us any answers, go ahead and cut it down to a manageable clip and we will play it for the Owl's when we return." We returned to our scouring of audio and when Jenn finished her audio review, she began going over the photos, and video.

Katie listened intently to her recordings, and I could see her replaying a section of the recording over and over. A grave look of concern grew on her face and I wanted to break her concentration to ask if everything was okay. It was just about then that she drew a deep breath and sighed as she removed her headphones.

"Do you remember when I stayed upstairs in the stairwell alone?" She asked us.

"Yes, I knew I shouldn't have left you up there alone." I said.

"I remember, and you came running down the stairs like you had seen a ghost." Jenn joked. "Sorry... I couldn't resist."

"The reason I came running down the stairs so fast was because I felt someone over my shoulder and then heard laughter in my ear. Something was right behind me, and it really kinda freaked me out." Katie answered the humor with an honest and serious statement.

"That would be a very frightening thing, even if you weren't alone." I agreed with her.

"Well, it wasn't just my imagination." Katie said in a low somber tone as she unplugged her headset and plugged in the external speakers. She turned the volume up, and clicked the play button on the computer screen.

The static played loud and clear, and minor sounds of shuffling and the sound of Katie's breath were even obvious to us. The blaring sound of her voice whispered "Hello?" and was soon followed by a low and deep "Heh heh heh...", a chuckling sound so sinister, it made every hair on my body stand on end, and my skin crawl.

"Holy crap!" I blurted out. "That's what you heard in your ear?"

"Yeah..." Katie said slowly and quietly. "It really kinda scared me. I know it's not much, but it seems significant that I heard it and caught it on the recording."

"Don't discount it so quickly." Jenn reassured her. "It's very significant."

"Yes it is. It isn't often that voices are actually heard, and it's even more seldom that those voices are actually picked up on a recording. That's an excellent piece of evidence, and it's one that shows that there may be something less than friendly here." I added to the conversation.

We would discover one more bit of audio evidence that evening. During our time together in the old boiler room, when I asked for any entities present to light up the different colored lights, soon after I uttered the word 'red', a wicked sounding female voice, gruff and dry, painfully mocked me by saying, 'RED'. The thought that the ghost behind that voice was close enough and powerful enough to come across on my recorder louder than my own voice, which meant it was dangerously close to me. I knew all too well that when an entity came in contact with a person, such as myself, there was no telling how intensely horrific things could become... and how quickly it could escalate to that point.

We had finished with analyzing the audio and photographical evidence. Some of our review of the video had been completed, but the hour was late, and we all, unfortunately, we all had full-time careers that we would have to be well rested for. If only this passion were as fulfilling to our bank accounts as it was to our souls. The computers were powered down one by one, equipment was packed back into the appropriate cases, and once the girls had exited the room, I flipped the switch and put the office into a haunting darkness. There was a beckoning feeling as I closed the door. It felt as if I was missing something, but what it was had escaped me. I finished pulling the door to, and with a clicking-pop of the strike plate, I left the case and the mystery that eluded me, hidden in the inky darkness of night.

There were certain things that I was sure of, and those things caused an uncomfortable and unsettling feeling deep in my sinking heart. First, there was definite paranormal activity at the Owl's Nest #30. Second, Not only was there activity, but the Owl's Nest was genuinely haunted. Thirdly, the ghosts of the Owl's included several children, who apparently needed our help in some way, and our time was limited for an unknown reason. And finally, I knew that the most terrifying and wonderful spirit we had ever encountered, Ashley Sue- the burning girl, was taking an active part in our investigation... a frighteningly active part. These things alone kept me awake at night, every night... until exhaustion eventually took over, allowing me a few hours of much deprived sleep.

It was time to contact Theo, and I had a feeling we would need some serious help understanding all of the activity. More than that, we needed extra help... I had to put in a call to another friend, another Rick... Rick Hayes, who, in my opinion and many others, is one of the top psychic-mediums in the nation. I could only hope that he had some time available to join us soon...before it was 'too late'.

Chapter 7

GATHERING

FORCES

The following evening, once my typical after-work routine was finished, I sent a group text message to Jenn, and Katie.

Jenn, Katie:

I will contact the Owl's Nest and

set up the evidence reveal, and

contact Theo, and Rick Hayes to

get them on board to help us

and help the children of the Owl's.

Do you two mind going through

the documents and photos and

try to make some sort of time line?   -EVP rick

Sure, does Jenn have them?   -EVP kate

Got 'em! And no problem!   -EVP jenn

Cool. If either of you has a chance,

could you try to get any info on

Allison Bettiger?   -EVP rick

Of course. We'll see what we can find.-EVP jenn

I sat down at my dinosaur of a desktop computer and began writing and email to send to both Rick and Theo. I was opening the door to them, without too much definite information, mostly because I had very little 'definite information'. So, I typed my 'generic' email, and sent it to both of them.

***

Theo was finishing his day up at Barnes & Noble booksellers and about to clock out when he received an email notification on his phone. The familiar 'ding' was unmistakable. It had been a tiring day at work and all he wanted to do was to go home, relax, and unwind with a cup of Greek coffee, so he did not even check his phone until much later when he was sitting on his patio, enjoying the night air and the pale yellow glimmer of the waning moon as it rose.

He found himself gazing to the heavens, contemplating the spirit world which he was so closely connected to, the vastness of the universe, and the very essence of time itself. As he meditated on these things, in the peace and serenity of his quiet haven, he was startled out of his sub-conscious thoughts by the annoying beep of his phone again. He rolled his eyes to himself for forgetting to turn it off, or leave it inside where it wouldn't bother him.

Theo grumbled to himself as he pulled his touchscreen phone from his pocket. He had a text message from an old friend, and an email from 'E.V.P. Rick'. He quickly responded to his friend's text, and then moved on to open up the email. He immediately noticed it was sent, not only to him, but to another psychic-medium as well.

Good evening friends,

The team and I are working on an investigation at the Owl's Nest in Evansville, and we could really use your help. We feel pretty certain that there are multiple entities here, including several child spirits. I don't want to go into to too many details just yet, but I will say, we have good reason to believe that these children desperately need help. I will be setting up another night of investigating soon, and I would really like both of you to join us if at all possible. Please respond as soon as possible to let me know if and when you will be able to help.

Sincerely,

Rick Kueber- Founder, EVP Investigations.

(P.S.- Theo, it seems that Ash is somehow involved here...just an FYI!)

The breeze took a chill, and Theo felt his heart almost skip a beat when he read the lines about there being child spirits who so desperately needed help, and he nearly dropped his phone when he read the post script that mentioned Ash. His

71

mind raced as he recalled the transcendental dream, or vision he had experienced just a week or so prior. His pulse quickened and irrational thoughts and questions filled his mind. Struggling to add up the correlation between the Owl's Nest and Ash, he began to contemplate certain metaphysical things that I had not even begun to understand. Spiritual connections and astral travel, and how these things could tie Ash to Theo, the team, and the child spirits.

He sat soaking in the weight of the information he had received for quite some time, as the moon grew ever higher in the starry sky. Wisps of low clouds drifted by in the growing breeze, while Theo stared up to the sky wishing and praying for an answer to this paranormal perplexity... what help do these children need, and when will it be too late...and why?

He began to type a short response, and sent it straight away.

I would be happy to help you out again.

I am off every saturday night and sunday.

Just let me know when! And, BTW, I have

seen Ashley...she told me to 'help the child-

ren before it's too late.' does that make any

sense to you? i'm not sure what she means,

but I am anxious to find out

Always ready to help!

Theo

He sipped his now cool coffee, and the fears of another malicious entity began to consume his thoughts. Theo couldn't help but think that if Ash had become involved and these children needed some kind of help that was beyond her powers, it was more than intimidating.

He felt the need to meditate and connect with his spirit guides. With candles lit, he placed a smoldering sage stick in the half shell he had used during his smudging rituals. Though the breeze continued, the candles kept their flames, flickering wildly in some sacred dance of fire, and the billowing smoke from the sage filled the air with the scent of earth, the most ancient temple of all. Picking up a small cup, he poured out a thin stream of water, forming a circle around himself. Theo sat down in the midst of all of the elements... sage to represent earth, candles for fire, the circle of water, and the night breeze for air. Soon the ceremony would be completed by the spirit guides joining him.

Theo's meditation caused the harsh world around him to melt into a comforting fog, filled with dull colors of orange and mauve, chartreuse and teals, that all seem to swirl, layered against, or on top of, each other. He could feel the presence of the spirit guides drawing near. While many spiritual people have a spirit guide they follow, or ask for help and advice from, Theo had what he had always thought of as his spirit council, a group of a dozen beings which he could gain insights and direction from.

An unmistakable feeling came over him as the figures began to materialize, though never completely, in the swirling colors of the foggy mist. Some of these spirit guides took on a female persona, nurturing, gentle, and even sensual, in their own way... while others were more logical, strong, and defensive (when Theo had needed to have his guard up) and were obviously male. Other spirit guides that formed this council seemed to be neutral in gender, as if they had no need or reason to project anything as worldly as sexuality. Their appearance was another subject, and could fill a book all on its own.

As they gathered to him, he began to convey to them his needs. They could feel his questions and concerns about the spirit children that haunted a place he had never been, and was not even familiar with, though the spirits knew his most unsettling concern was focused on the ghost of Ashley Sue. Theo had brought her existence and malicious ways to their consciousness before, asking their help in ridding her of the shadow demon that she was plagued by.

The spirits didn't communicate as much with words as they did with feelings and ideas. As Theo thought of his questions and concerns the spirits answered him with only vague revelations. He knew in his soul that the children needed to be reunited with their family and pass on from our world to an eternal home, though they did not give him a reason for the urgency. There was also the undeniable feeling that Ashley was there to help. She would not cause trouble, at least not to him... not intentionally. His thoughts absorbed these truths while he built his own conclusions based on the wisdom of his guides.

There was another feeling that the guides had given to Theo. Though he knew Ash meant him no intentional harm, he could feel that there was a malevolent presence that he would have to guard himself against, perhaps more than one. He was also given the knowledge that this undertaking would require the help of many people... psychics, spiritualists, paranormal researchers, and everyday folks.... and love and compassion... most of all, love and compassion.

***

The passion that my team and I had for learning and researching the paranormal, and being able to help people (both living and those passed on), was a force that drove us from somewhere deep in our souls. There is a part of each and every person in the world that is pure passion, in some it remains hidden, while others have left it sleeping, afraid they will awaken a monster that will define who they are. Still, others let their passions out in whispers when they want to scream out to the world. We found that while life without passion may be easy, predictable, and painless, allowing our passion to flourish made our lives not only exciting and fulfilling, but rewarding on a level that most will never understand.

It was the mutual drive that everyone on my team shared, that made us great in our own ways in the paranormal field, and though I am undoubtedly bias, our combined passion as a team made us phenomenal. No egos, no slackers, just three or four team mates who worked together towards a common goal, like a well-oiled machine.

There was soon to be another cog in our timepiece, as the moments ticked away, another facet that would join us in our endeavor to understand the enigma of the shadow children, and gain the knowledge we would need to help them. I would have never thought that so many amazing people would unite to show these lost souls that they weren't as lost as they believed. They weren't lost at all...they were hiding. It was our task to find them, and to let them know they are loved, and not forgotten.

I soon received another email reply. The core of our team would be joined by Rick Hayes, and give our team five points of view, and five unique tools to uncover clues and hopefully understand our latest perplexity. Theo had committed to helping us on literally any weekend, and Rick was going to be available on possibly a few weekends. Though the schedules differed and at this moment nothing seemed to make any sense, I had this feeling deep in my heart that everything was about to come together. Like scattered yarns weaving themselves together, what was starting out as a few messy skeins, would slowly intertwine to become something useful and beautiful. Disconnected clues and disenchanted spirits would, hopefully, soon be on their way to a beautiful eternity, and Ashley seemed to already be showing us her desire to be helpful and useful.

***

It was Wednesday after work, when I made the first phone call of many. As always, Jenn was my first call, after all, she was my lead investigator, and my second in charge of the team. If we had three members, or ten, Jennifer was a cornerstone of the team, and I confidently put my faith in her.

"Hey there E.V.Prick!" She said gleefully answering the phone. "What's up?"

"Just wanting to set up an 'evidence reveal' for the Owl's Nest investigation... I haven't talked to them, or Katie yet, but I was thinking this Saturday afternoon would be good. What do you think?" I asked, genuinely wanting her input.

"Saturday's fine with me. Let me make sure Alan hasn't made any plans I don't know about, but I think it will be fine." She seemed confident that she would be available.

"Great. Let me give Katie a call, and if it works her, I will get in touch with Barb and see if that's good for them. I'll let ya know what time." I knew that whether it was just me, or the whole team, the Owl's would be amazed at the evidence we had caught. I also knew that seeing the amazement and disbelief on the faces of both the believers and skeptics was one of the highlights of an investigation, and I didn't want Jenn or Katie to miss out on that bit of gratification.

I ended the call with Jenn and immediately called up Katie.

"Hello?" Katie answered with a sound in her voice of curiosity or surprise.

"Hey Katie. How's things going?" I asked casually.

"Okay, I guess...typical work week. Nothing special. What's up?" She asked, fishing for a reason for my call.

"I was calling to see if you had any plans for Saturday afternoon." I paused and before the silence became too awkward, I continued with, "I'm trying to set up a meeting at the Owl's nest. If you can make it, that would be great. If not, I can try to find another time."

"OH!" she replied with enthusiasm. "I'd love to go! I don't have anything really planned, so I'll keep Saturday open for sure!"

"Great, I haven't set it up with Barb and Del yet, but that's my next call. I will shoot you and Jenn a text after I talk to them." I finished. After we said our good-byes, I took a moment for myself. I put my phone down and headed to the kitchen for a cold soda, Mt. Dew, of course. I took a few gulps of my Dew, and was back to my phone.

"Hello?" Barb's voice was on the other end of the phone.

"Hello Barb. It's Rick" I gave her a moment.

"Well, hi Rick! To what do I owe the pleasure?" I could hear a giddy sound in her tone. She and Del were true fans of the paranormal and were excited that we not only investigated the Owl's Nest, but that we all had some incredible experiences while we were there.

I laughed at her response. "I was just calling to see if you and Del might be able to meet with us this Saturday afternoon to discuss our investigation, and let you take a listen to a few e.v.p.s we caught during our time there."

"Oh, cool!" Barb sounded thrilled. "Yes! I'm here at the Owl's nest almost every Saturday and I can make sure Del is here too."

"Okay, that sounds perfect. We'll have everything ready and we'll see you Saturday. Is 4 o'clock good?" I questioned our arrival time.

"Yep! That's after the lunch rush is over. See you at 4." She confirmed.

I sent the text to Jenn and Katie letting them know we were on for Saturday at 4pm, and quickly received responses from them both agreeing that they would be there. I put my phone on the charger and stripped down for a steaming hot shower. Though it was barely half over, it had been a long week already. The steaming deluge flooded over me like a spiritual baptism, washing away all of worries along with the dirt and grime of my construction job. With a twist of the shower head, the water began to pulse in a rhythmic pounding that beat against my shoulders and back. I stood under its massaging powers, melting away the stress until the water began to lose its steam.

When I finally left the shower, I felt like a wet noodle. I toweled off and slid on a comfortable pair of shorts to lounge in. I chose a DVD from my collection on the rack and once it began to play, I kicked back on the couch with my second Mt.

Dew and a tub of peanut butter filled pretzels. It was time to relax and be a vegetable, or more accurately, a couch potato. I stayed there all evening until it was time for bed. The mind numbing movie (which I had seen more than once already) was just what I needed.

At nearly 10 o'clock, I began turning off the lights and electronics. Soon I slid myself between the sheets, and with the fan on high, I tuned out the real world and fell into a deep slumber. The time passed and the empty vacuum of unconsciousness ate away at the hours of my night, until I began to become aware of a new place of existence, a dream state in which I could exist for a few mystical hours, or minutes, until I would awaken.

As the fog and mists cleared somewhat, I could begin to see a group of four young boys playing in a room filled with handcrafted, wooden toys and stitched animals, an elephant, a lion, a bear, and an owl. I watched as if I was looking through a glass wall, I could not approach them nor could they see or hear me. I watched as the youngest, a mere toddler of two years, or so, sat on the floor, playing with the animals and hugging the owl, under his arm, as his imagination brought the other wild 'fabric' animals to life, in his mind. Without warning, sound or reason, the white, frilled night shirt he was wearing burst open in the front with a small explosion of woven cotton, flesh and blood. He turned his head in my direction and his eyes met mine. He saw me, and I felt the pain and fear in him. The confusion set in, as his eyes went empty and called out to me...hauntingly staring, and silently crying for help. The white cotton shirt now had a small hole in it, and a small area around the hole was stained red. Quickly, the red stain grew as the cotton fabric became saturated with the life of the small child. As the blood soaked through his clothing, and began to spill onto the floor, the boy began to transform before my eyes. Much like the layers of grime I had washed away in the shower, the solidity of the boy began to crumble away leaving only a translucent shell, a ghost of the boy who once was.

The three remaining youngsters froze in their places, stood still, and then eerily turned to stare at me with hollow, lifeless eyes and blank, expressionless faces. One by one they dissolved into specters of the children they had been, until all were ghastly, pale beings. The youngest stood and joined the others, and all were now facing me, side by side. I watched as their mouths fell open in silent screams and the once sparkling eyes turned black and empty. Like smoky vapors, the ghostly children who had stood frozen before me suddenly rushed towards me and their youthful innocence was replaced by a harrowing terror.

"RING! RING!" My alarm clock startled me from an all-too-real nightmare, so real in fact, that I had to question if I had been awake, or if I now was. I took a moment to absorb my alternate-reality experience, and then before it faded into foggy memories, I began to put pen to paper, and descriptively write every detail, yet even as I wrote, I could feel the images growing thin, transparent, and elusive.

Chapter 8

HISTORY

IN THE FOG

It was a sunless June day, gray and dull. The world was hidden in a cloudy, foggy shroud, and though there were still people going about their daily weekend lives, the town felt lifeless...cold and dead to the reality of the spiritual planes of existence within it. Jennifer and Katie had decided to spend their Saturday morning visiting our downtown central library, and the old Willard library (which sat less than two blocks from the Owl's Nest), searching for clues, answers, and the elusive Allison Bettiger.

They started out at the Willard Library, also known for its Grey Lady Ghost and famed as the most haunted library in America. The library's ominous pinnacles of its ancient architecture rose before them like a troubled castle, haunted and mysterious. The two women walked slowly towards the rising steps that led to the oversized double entry doors. As they neared the limestone steps, a cold drizzling mist began to fall around them, dampening everything it touched including them.

Jenn pulled at the heavy wood door, opening it slowly and then rushing inside just as the rain grew steadier, splattering everything with fat, cold, soaking drops...absorbing into things like the concrete, bricks and tree trunks and branches, darkening them. In sharp contrast, the wetness clung to the black painted handrails, grass, and leaves, unable to soak into them, and causing them to slightly shine and glimmer in an almost magical way. In life, it should be the opposite. We should each try to repel those things that darken us, and absorb those that make us shine. The difficult part is deciding which is which, in time to make the right choice.

The rain and mist in the air drew out the musty smell of dated fabrics, smoke-stained woodwork, and books...mostly books, and the smell of well worn, overly read, finger printed pages of, both ancient and relatively new, knowledge. Katie passed up Jenn as she entered, and with a smile, closed her eyes. She drew a deep breath, holding it in for a moment before exhaling an audible sigh.

"I love the smell of old books." She grinned at Jenn, and then looked around the familiar entryway, and stairwell.

"I know, right?" Jennifer laughed back to her. "We may have better luck finding information about Allison Bettiger down at Central, but I love this library, and when it comes to history, there is no better place." As if on cue, the two raised their eyes to the ornate carved woodwork, painted art of oil on canvas, and the rising stairwell before them.

Without a word, they made their way to the upper level, where the oldest collections, and personal records were kept. Dividing up, Katie began searching through the files on the computer for any books and documents pertaining to the Bettiger family, and the historical homes located on Evansville's First Avenue. Jenn underwent the same task, but she searched the physical card catalog. Willard Library still maintained an index card style collection of files that contained information that had not been entered into the computer system yet.

After making several notes, both women soon found themselves searching the Dewey decimal system notations on the book shelves and bindings. They collected books in their arms, packing them in ones or twos back to one of the long conference tables where they had decided to sit to do their research and note taking. Before long they had an assemblage of books, periodicals and newspapers that dated back to the 1870's, in several neatly organized stacks.

Short, brass desk lamps with green glass shades added to the air of the distinguished historical library, casting a friendly glow, and warming the gray filtered light of day that slipped through the tall windows that lined the walls. The girls plundered through the pages of old books both worn from use and yellowed from age. A few of these books had a spine so crisp, it would make one wonder if they had ever been opened since the day they were systematically put on their shelf, and when opened, made a near silent cracking sound which caused Jenn and Katie fear the bindings may actually crumble and the pages fall from the covers like a deck of cards that got loose during a shuffle. Their eyes poured over the pages, intently searching for any clue that may shed even the dimmest ray of enlightenment on this peculiar investigation.

"I think I might have something here." Jenn whispered across the table to Katie, never raising her eyes from the rather large, red cloth covered book.

"Whatcha got?" Katie returned the whisper, filled with curiosity, peeking her nose over the edge of the literary work she was dissecting, and looking very much like a bookworm version of 'Kilroy'.

"This book is full of family photographs from Evansville, circa 1870-1920. I found a Charles E. Bettiger in the index...and this is what I found under his name. She turned the book to face Katie holding it open by the top. The book was opened to a page that was nearly half covered in a brown tone family photo. A man stood on the right end of a Queen Anne style sofa. Across the sofa sat three small boys and sitting on the far left was a woman facing away from the others, holding a young child, only a couple of years old, in her arms.

Katie scanned the details of the photo carefully, and read the names listed across the bottom caption, whispering out loud. "Charles, Donald, Timothy, Brian, Jonathon, and Amelia Bettiger." Studying the details of the photo, Katie's eyes grew wide and her mouth opened slowly. "Is this what I think it is?" She quietly asked Jenn.

"Family Photo?" Jenn asked back, puzzled slightly by Katie's expression.

"Well, yeah, but I think this is a 'postmortem' photo. Look at the boy she's holding." She directed Jenn. "Look at the little boy's head and face."

Jenn turned the book back to herself and scanned the young lad in his mother's arms. "Shut Up!" She said in a voice much louder than a library voice. She swiftly looked back and forth, but it seemed that no one had paid the girls much attention. "His hat is on crooked, eyes are closed, and he **does** look kinda like a rag doll, now that you mention it."

"Might as well photo copy this page, huh?" Katie said rhetorically, and Jenn nodded back to her.

The afternoon trickled by and the stacks of history, slowly melted away, revealing their hidden treasures, secrets, and clues. Though the sun grew higher in the sky, the day outside only grew darker, and more gray. Index searching and page turning, note taking and photocopying, were the order of the morning until noon had come and past. Eventually Katie and Jennifer made their way through all of the piles of information, and began to whittle away at it, taking one or two pieces at a time back to the librarian's cart to be returned to their dark hiding places on the shelves where they were discovered.

"I'm hungry." Jenn whispered to Katie as she took one of the last books to the cart.

"I know, right? Me too..." Katie smiled. "My stomach has been growling for the last half hour. You wanna go grab something before we go to Central Library?"

"Heck yeah!" Jenn's voice rose slightly. "We're only a block from the Owl's Nest, and Barb said they have great plate lunches and it's almost noon."

"Perfect!" Katie grinned to Jennifer, thinking it was *perfect*, since they had been researching information on the family that originally owned the Owl's Nest #30 property.

Jenn carefully carried the old newspapers and periodicals back to the librarian's desk for safe keeping, while Katie finished writing a few final notes from the last remaining book on the table. When she had finished, she placed it on the monstrous pile atop the book return cart. The two (momentarily nerdy) girls then closed their notebooks and organized the photocopied papers. Once everything was squared away in its place, the two left the upstairs room, and began their descent of the old wooden stairwell.

Leaving the foreboding old library, they noticed the rain had all but stopped, though the day had not grown any brighter. It was quite unusual to have such a gray, foggy day in southern Indiana in June, but then again, the weather in the Ohio Valley was completely unpredictable. Neatly storing their research in the back seat of the Jennifer's Camry, the two made the short drive, just a block and a half north, to the Owl's Nest.

Exiting the car, the two trotted quickly up the handicapped-accessible ramp, as the drizzle had once again emerged from the darkened sky. With their hair and clothes slightly dampened, but not their spirits, the two shook off the cold wetness upon entering the front door of the club. This wasn't their first visit to the club, but it was their first uninvited visit.

"You do realize we aren't members here, right?" Katie asked nervously.

"Crap... I didn't even think of that. Well, maybe Barb or Del will be here and can sign us in as guests." Jenn tried to think of how they might get around not being members. She smiled a comforting smile to Katie. "Worse case, maybe one of us will just have to join."

Looking around the entry and hallway, memories came flooding back. Slowly, and silently they emerged into the open room. A thickset woman of about five foot nothing, wearing blue jeans, a Corona t-shirt, and a half-apron came bustling by with an empty glass and a bar towel in her hands. She glanced at the two girls as she blew by them, and within seconds, returned empty handed.

"Can I help you?" She asked politely. "You two here for lunch?" Placing her hand on her hip, she awaited an answer to her questions.

"We aren't members." Katie blurted out, wanting to get that out in the open quickly. "But we were hoping to have lunch." She stated with a concerned look.

"You don't have to be a member to eat here today. Sit anywhere you want and I'll go grab you some menus." and as quickly as she had appeared, the whirlwind of a barmaid disappeared.

Jenn and Katie found a seat near the back wall where they wouldn't draw too much attention to themselves while they discussed their discoveries. The waitress took the orders, brought the cold sodas, and slipped away again, back to the kitchen to drop off the orders she had collected. The girls sipped the soda through their drinking straws, and bubbled over with excitement as the bits of history were tossed back and forth between them. Just as something in their chatter caused them to giggle simultaneously, a figure appeared unexpectedly at their table.

"Hey, you two! What brings you here so early?" It was Barb, who was expecting the team to arrive much later to reveal the paranormal evidence we had found.

"Well hey Barb, we just dropped by for a bite. We were doing some research at Willard's, and since this is so close, thought we'd stop in." Jenn said casually, trying to contain her laughter from the prior conversation.

86

Katie minimized her smile and added, "Yeah, we'll be back after-while with Rick, so no teasers... he wouldn't be happy if we let you in on anything without him here."

"Yeah, he's funny like that." Jenn said, but this time she and Katie couldn't hold back the laughter. They knew I was always proud to reveal any evidence. It always made me feel like the person who had the best gift at the birthday party...and as wrong and selfish as that may sound... it was true.

"I understand." the words came slowly, and the disappointment in Barb's tone was far beyond obvious. The waitress brought Jennifer's 'gluten free' lunch choices, and Katie's bacon cheeseburger and fries. "Well, I'll leave you two to your lunch, and I'll see you in a few hours." Soon Barb was back to bustling around the room and the girls watched as she made her rounds. When one of her conversations with the lunch crowd turned to the building's ghosts, the eyes would all turn towards Katie and Jenn.

Soon enough, lunch was finished, and with the bill and tip paid, the two overly stuffed girls headed back to the cold misty day outside. "Remind me to split a lunch with you next time we eat here." Jenn groaned as she rubbed her tummy.

"Yeah, no doubt...That was delicious, but way more than I needed to eat." Katie spluffed, but with a smile.

A few blocks through downtown Evansville and the diligent duo were pulling into the new Central Library, the largest collection in the metro area. Quick work was made of the enormous vault of information held within its doors. Before long, they had located several addresses for Allison Bettiger, and found records showing her parents to be Charles and Amelia Bettiger.

"Why do you think she kept the Bettiger last name, you know...?" Katie questioned.

"Not sure, I was kinda thinking that there wasn't a female in the records Barb and Del had. Isn't it odd that Linda knows her or knows of her, but there aren't many records of her, and no photos?" Jenn's reply wasn't an answer, but another question, and that is the way of these investigations... too many questions that sometimes are never fully answered.

The search continued until nearly four in the afternoon, but the success was minimal, and incredibly disappointing. Very little was uncovered besides a few good leads on how to find the Bettiger's elusive, final living relative. From the moment they stepped from the car until they had completely finished and were once again opening the car doors to leave, the mood was melancholy at best. The atmosphere of the new structure, the smell of new carpet and paint compared to the total Willard experience, lacked the feel of having its own history. The library itself was fantastic, but from a paranormal investigator and historical researcher's point of view... well, it was like the difference between hearing a classic Beatles song on CD, or digital download versus hearing the scratchy white noise of a needle on an old vinyl L.P.

Chapter 9

SPIRITS

IN A

MIRROR

The time passed swiftly, and soon it was time to meet up at the Owl's Nest as planned. The gray mist and drizzle had turned into a fog filled, late afternoon. The day only grew more dismal and dark as the hours wore on. I turned off the rhythmic 'tap, rub, tap' of the windshield wipers, and with a turn of the key shut off the motor of my convertible. Reaching to grab my laptop bag, I noticed a drip near where the passenger side window and the rag top met. The dreary day now seemed exponentially more depressing. I put the hood up on my E.V.P. hoodie and stepped from the car. Carrying my laptop bag carefully, I trudged up the ramp and waited outside for the rest of my team to arrive. The cars grumbled by slowly with their headlights on dim in the minimal light of the cloudy afternoon. I watched as each one passed looking for the familiar black Camry, or black pick-up. Breathing in the damp air, I wondered where this case was leading us, and how we would be able to help so many spirits, as well as the staff and members of the Owl's Nest #30.

The silver scorpion logo on the rear of the black Toyota that pulled into the parking lot caught my eye and clued me in that Jenn was here, and when the car doors opened, I realized that both of my team mates had arrived. Though the sun was still somewhere, high in the sky, it was masked behind numerous layers of charcoal gray clouds, giving the overcast day an oppressive feel. The three of us scurried to the cover of the front awning as the raindrops began to splatter on the pavement once again.

"Geez! Is it ever going to stop raining?" I asked, grumbling about the dreary weather we had been recycling for months.

"Yeah, about two days from now... then you won't be able to buy a drop of rain until September." Jenn said semi-sarcastically. Her tone was mocking, but the statement was true enough. You couldn't count on the weather in southern Indiana for anything, except a few months of near drought every summer, and being a horticulturalist, Jenn knew this well.

Katie chuckled at the comment. "Well, let's get out of the weather and get this party started." I smiled back at her as I opened the door for the two ladies and followed behind them as they entered the dimly lit corridor.

We took the path down the corridor, passing the card room where three elderly gentlemen were poking fun at each other's poker skills, and into the open bar room. I quickly spotted Del, who waved to us and then disappeared around the corner and into the dance hall. He emerged again within a few moments with Barb at his side. The smiles on their faces could be seen from across the room. The five of us walked towards each other and met near the middle of the smoky room. An old Patsy Cline song played on the jukebox as we shook hands and greeted one another like long lost friends.

"It's a little noisy in here." Del said leaning into the circle of friends. "We can go into the dance hall, or what do you think?" he said turning to his wife, Barb.

"Probably the quietest place would be upstairs, and there wouldn't be anyone else around... but there aren't too many places to sit up there." She thought about what she had said, trying to come up with a better alternative.

"Upstairs is fine with me." I replied, looking back and forth to Jenn and Katie, who readily agreed.

"Okay, let me tell Fred and then we will head up." Del said to us all and then turned to disappear once again. Fred was the current president of the Owl's Nest #30, and though he agreed to our investigation, he was also one of the club's biggest skeptics (which was saying a lot).

We followed Barb, though we knew the way to the upstairs door. As we turned the corner and inched closer to the door, Del appeared from the opposite corner. When we all reached the door, with a turn of the key, Del opened it for us and turned on the light switch. The lighting at the top of the stairs brightened up the second floor landing, but only cast a dim glow onto the steps themselves. It was enough to see by, and more than we were used to, as paranormal investigators.

Once at the top, we entered the room to our left. Once inside, the ladies took a seat on an old church pew-style bench that ran along the left hand wall of the room. I searched for a nearby outlet where I could plug in my laptop and Del swiftly aided and directed me to the closest one. I knelt down to slide the plug into the outlet and noticed something I hadn't before. There was a large painting of a creepy and angered owl leaning against the wall. I pulled it from the dust covered cob webs to show Jenn and Katie, who agreed it was a very unique and ominous portrayal of an owl, and then Barb proceeded to snap a photo of me holding the piece of art.

"You *have to* email a copy of that picture to me, please." I hinted to Barb.

"Of course, and I was thinking of putting it in our Hoots news-letter, if you don't mind. Speaking of emailing photos, what did you think about the ones I sent you?" She asked timidly.

"Be my guest." I said as I returned the painting to it home among the layers of dust and webs. I was ready, and I'm sure everyone else was also, to get on with the evidence reveal, and our interpretations of what it all could mean.

I pulled the photos up on my laptop and began to show and explain how the orb was merely a reflection of Katie's watch face, but when I pointed out the outlines of the face in the other photo, Barb and Del were fascinated.

***

The four spectral siblings huddled together in the darkened corner of the room, listening to us, as if *we* were the ghosts, and *they* were frightened of us. To them, our voices were muffled and hard to hear and understand, like trying to hear the words spoken on a television from another room...no matter how loud, still hard to discern every word. And our plane of existence was shrouded to their eyes. They peered at us through the distorted veil of parallel realities, curious and frightened...but mostly curious.

The children strained their ears to hear through the fog that lay between them and the living human beings that shared their home. The sentences were mostly garbled and difficult to distinguish, only one or two words, here and there made any sense to them. Watching and waiting to understand anything they were experiencing, they saw one of the people open up an unusual book like object, silver and black. Staring more intently, it appeared to be some sort of flat typewriter with no paper. Much to their amazement, the upper half of the unusual typewriter lit up and made a faint musical sound. The ghostly children covered their mouths and giggled silently.

They watched as the man pecked away at the odd typewriter keys, and the colors on the upper portion changed, and then changed again. Then something happened that they did not expect. A woman's voice came across loud and clear to them, saying, "This was in the basement, remember when we heard the bang?" Followed by other female voices, in bits and pieces with the voices of men intermingled in the conversation. To the spirit children, the voices of the women were comforting, and more discernable than those of the men that spoke.

"Listen closely." They heard another female voice say. Suddenly the typewriter that had made the whimsical music, began to emanate a sound, high pitched and static-filled. Hollow and blackened ghastly eyes opened wide, as they could not believe what they were hearing, something they had never heard before. A memory from the past confronted them, though they had no sense of how long ago the memory was. They actually had no real sense of time at all.

"....I want to talk to the children that are here..." said the memory, and it spoke to them from the magical typewriter light. And then after moments of white noise and static, they heard the voice of their new found friend Ashley, replaying the words they had heard her shout before. "You can't find us!" The moment her voice appeared, so did young Ashley. The young spirits looked up to her for her older appearance and her unmistakable power. To the shadow children, these magical voices were like listening to a mystical mirror of themselves, amazing, confusing, and disturbing in a way.

***

"Oh wow!" Barb exclaimed. "That's incredible!"

"Awesome! Can you play it again?" Del said through the huge grin on his face. "Can we play that for Fred?"

"Sure, you can play these for whoever you want." I said as I began the recording again. The snippet and the incredibly clear e.v.p. were played over and over again, but there came a point where I was too anxious, and had to move on.

"Okay, now this one is just one word, but I'm sure you will remember our conversation upstairs when we were talking about e.m.f.s and how I like to use the e.m.f. detectors to try to

93

find the source of the energy, then when I can't find a source, that's when it gets interesting." I began to explain the story behind our second electronic voice phenomenon, or e.v.p. as we typically call them.

"Yes, I remember it well." Barb said. "We were over in that room over there," she pointed 'through' the wall towards the other large upstairs room, "You and I were at one end, and those three were at the other end." She said to me, and gestured to Jenn, Katie and Del.

***

Ashley wrapped her spectral arms around the youngsters and whispered to them. "Take me to your secret hiding place." The boys agreed, smiling to the beautiful and powerful, young ghost girl with her flowing blonde hair and glowing red eyes. Ash hunkered over and the children all drifted, ethereally, through the walls and into the secret place we had yet to discover. The five souls gathered together in the cramped quarters and played the quiet mouse game, fearful and listening for the voices from beyond the physical walls, which gave them a sense of security, a hiding place from years gone by, that had always made them feel safe.

The spirit of Mikey found its way into the room just in time to see the mysterious typewriter-thing begin to make sounds all on its own, like some sort of otherworldly Victrola. He watched as five shadows gathered around it, listening to the scratchy static that is played, until suddenly he heard a voice coming from it.

"That's when things start to get interesting-exciting." The strange object spoke to him and he was amazed to hear his own voice and recalled saying the sarcastic remark. To Mikey, it was puzzling. He had never heard a recording of himself, but he knew right away it was his voice that he heard. The shadows gathered around and the mumbling sounds they made were only broken up by the repeating sounds of the magical talking typewriter, as it replayed the words, "interesting- exciting." over and over. He began to not only become comfortable with hearing his own voice, but soon he felt almost proud that these shadows were intrigued by it also, and a sinister grin grew wide across his scarred face. His grin soon turned, and his mouth dropped open as he began to think of what this must mean. 'Somebody, these shadows, they know I'm here. They prolly even know Martin and Nick's here too.' and that thought troubled the ghost of the long-ago gangster. 'Maybe they can send me someplace worse than here, maybe...maybe they're gonna help them miserable kids and put us someplace....' his mind drifted off to his childhood days of Catholic church and school, where he learned of Hell and purgatory, the waiting place for damned and lost souls... he thought to himself, 'Could I be in purgatory now...they gonna send us to hell?' He didn't want to go anywhere at that point. He wanted his revenge on the souls of the children. He and his partners had been taunting them for decades upon decades, and he was enraged at the thought that someone was here to help them and what else could happen caused his wicked soul to shiver.

***

"I remember exactly when that happened!" Barb exclaimed, and my team and I thought she was going to jump from her seat on the old church pew.

"Me too... I wonder what it means." Del interjected.

"Damn good question. The voice doesn't sound threatening, but there is no telling what it really means... other than perhaps someone was listening to us so closely, they tried to finish my sentence for me." I said, not having an answer, which always frustrated me.

"I'm not sayin' it sounded threatening or anything, but it did have a sort of sinister-sarcastic tone... just my opinion." Katie said bashfully. Even after more than a year with the team, she still felt like she had to gain our approval, which was far from the truth. Jenn and I held her in the highest respect as an investigator, especially after our experiences at the Helmach house. There are many people who would have turned their backs on the paranormal field after that haunting, but not these girls!

"I have to agree with you Katie, and speaking of sinister, let's move on to the next one." I spoke up, drawing the attention of Barb and Del. "This clip was when we let Katie stay upstairs on the landing by herself for a few minutes, and the fascinating thing about this one, is that Katie actually heard this voice...Katie?" I looked to Katie to explain the situation.

"Yeah, looking back, I know it was a bad idea to be alone upstairs, but I wanted to try to see if there was any activity that might reappear. I felt very alone up there, and when I said 'hello' to try to get a response, I felt a cold chill on my back and neck. I almost felt like someone, or something was leaning on me, and then I heard this whispered voice in my ear." Katie said recalling her experience and with a smile said "...and roll 'em."

I had already cued up the audio clip and on Katie's word I turned the laptop toward Del and Barb and played the audio. When Katie's *hello* had passed and the menacing voice chuckled deviously, the room went silent. Not a word was said, and even though it was a very obvious and chilling clip, it wasn't questioned, and no one asked me to replay it. I decided to move on and break the awkward silence.

"Okay, we have one more...again, a single word, and once again, I'm afraid I have no idea what this one means." My words were solemn, but honest. I preferred to at least have some connection to make when it came to e.v.p.s. Other evidence, such as photos or video of shadow figures or apparitions usually only provided proof of the existence of a haunting, and rarely gave much insight about the situation, or reason behind it. E.v.p.s, on the other hand, often times gave us a glimpse at the other side, what they are trying to communicate, something that helps glue the paranormal puzzle pieces together... and then there were some that didn't answer anything other than the fact that something is communicating on some level beyond our own understanding.

My fingers caressed the keyboard as I thought about the last e.v.p. I was about to play. My mind pondered the simplicity of the word, how it echoed my word, and the eerie tone. Zombies don't talk, but if they did, this is the voice they would have. Being an avid fan, I have seen literally every horror film ever made, but this voice equaled or surpassed the creepy factor of any horror villain's voice. I have to also say that even though sometimes the voices are probably accurate, there are other times when they can be dangerously deceiving. I moved the mouse, chose the file, and opened it. Even the graphic of the audio track looked ominous, to me. I explained to Barb and Del about the scenario around this capture, with input from Jenn, filling in and details I had left out. I placed the mouse over the play button and clicked it. The static was not as noticeable on this particular audio clip, and our voices were quite clear, as was the voice echoing "RED!"

"Oh wow!" Del burst out, and their eyes popped open, as Barb rubbed her bare arms.

"That was so creepy, it gave me goose bumps! The last few were not what we expected, and they kinda make me a little uncomfortable" Smiling back at one another, Barb and Del seemed more than pleased at our captured audio clips.

"Do you mind if we have the president and some of the club's officers come up here and listen to these?" Del asked.

"They most definitely can." Jenn answered for the team. She was well aware that the approval of the officers and trustees of the club was the reason we had been invited to investigate the Owl's Nest. Without their blessing, we would have never had these amazing experiences.

Though Ashley wanted to keep the children away from the malicious spirits of the mobsters, she and the children huddled together in the corner of the room to hear their mirrored voices once more. Across the room the three men, members of the organized crime family, also gathered to hear the voices, wanting to figure out what we were planning to do, and if they were in any danger of being found out and sent away to a possibly worse eternity.

Del jumped up as soon as we had given him the okay, and soon returned, followed by four men and one woman. They had all gathered around the laptop as best they could with arms crossed and looks of skepticism on their faces. The mood of the crowd began to swing in the opposite direction when I was asked for the third time to play the e.v.p. that answered Jenn with 'You can't find us.'

"And none of this was set up, right?" one of the officers asked in disbelief.

"We were there the whole time with them, and you can hear us all reacting to the metal banging sound. So, no, this is as legitimate as it gets." Del answered back, supporting our team efforts in proving the haunting of the Owl's Nest.

It was then that a woman, tall, blonde, and probably in her late forties spoke up. "So besides these voices, have you found anything else?"

"We have done a ton of research that we built by starting with a lot of great information that was provided to us by Barb and Del." Jenn began to explain as she passed the photocopy of the postmortem photo that had been discovered in the old Willard Library. She and Katie went on to explain who was in the photograph and some of the other interesting discoveries they had made.

"As best as we can tell, there is still one living direct descendant of the Bettigers. She would be over 90 years old now, and we are doing our best to track her down. We think she may be able to shed some light on the family history that was never really recorded." When Katie exposed the fact of there being a living descendant, several of the listeners perked up, and the woman who had asked the original question mouthed to Katie, 'See me later.'

"I appreciate everyone here allowing us to investigate and research the activity here, and I would like to ask that you all consider having us return for further investigating. We firmly believe that there are mysteries here that need to be uncovered and solved. With that, I would once again like to thank you very much for having us, and I would like to become a member of the Order of the Owls, if I may." I addressed everyone, but the president spoke up in response.

"You have all conducted yourselves in a very respectable manner, and I don't think there would be a problem at all with having you come back out. In fact, we may have a proposition for you, if you are interested in helping to educate the public, our members, and helping us with a fundraiser...and of course, we'd be glad to have you as a member of the Owl's."

"Thank you!" I said enthusiastically. "I'm not sure what you have in mind, but I'm pretty positive you can count on us to help you out with the fundraiser."

While the president of the club and I spoke, the blonde woman took Barb by the arm and whispered into her ear, staring at Katie and Jenn while she did. Barb then motioned to the girls to come and follow her.

Jenn leaned over to me and with a bit of confusion and sarcasm in her voice, said, "We'll be back in a minute... I hope." and then she and Katie followed Barb and the blonde woman into the stairwell.

"Jenn, Katie, this is Linda." Barb began the introductions. "Linda and her husband, Fred, live next door."

"You live in the house with the spire on the corner?" Jenn asked with excitement in her voice, like a child walking by a candy shop, hoping for the chance to enter and pick out a tasty sweet. "Is it haunted too?"

Linda smiled. "I don't know, and I don't wanna know! Barb has already asked me if you guys could check out my home, but I really like it just the way it is... if there is a ghost there I don't want anyone to find it."

"Awww... that's too bad, it's a beautiful home." Katie said respectfully.

"Well, the reason I wanted to talk to you in private is because I think I might know how to find the last Bettiger, Allison Bettiger. She never married, and lived in my home for many years until we bought it from her about 20 years ago, but I have still tried to keep in contact with her. She was living in a small town just outside of Indianapolis, maybe twenty miles south. As far as I know, she is still there. I can get you a phone number and an address if you want."

"Yes! That would be fantastic!" Katie exclaimed.

"Do you think you could contact her for us? I mean... I don't know how well she would react to a complete stranger calling her out of the blue." Jenn added, knowing how awkward it can be to try to get anyone to open up about their past.

"Sure, I need to call her anyway. I haven't talked to her in months. I hope she is still doing okay." Linda agreed. "I'll tell you what, give me a number where I can reach you, and after I talk to her, I will let you know what she said about you calling."

Jenn agreed and returned to the room where we were all still gathered. While I filled out the paperwork for my Owl's membership, Jenn wrote her phone number and email address on a piece of notebook paper and returned it to Linda.

"I can't thank you enough, Linda. Without your help, we would have run out of avenues to pursue, I'm sure." said Katie.

The crowd of a dozen or so people, including officers, the EVP team, and Del and Barb, casually talked amongst themselves while the girls and I gathered up our laptop and informational folders and prepared to head back to our homes. We shook many hands and were invited to come out to visit anytime we wanted, and were assured by the Heerdinks and the Owl's officers that we would soon be given a date on which we could return for a second investigation.

The rain had come to an end, but the gloom of the evening was overwhelming. There had been such an incredible amount of activity at this place, and most of it only caused more questions and concerns to grow. Many times we had investigated a home or business only to prove that it was not haunted, or to quickly provide proof that the activity they were experiencing was either the spirit of a loved one, or a benign entity that meant no harm and only existed in the same space with no intention of causing any trouble, or of leaving. This was completely different. The mere numbers of spirits that occupied this one place was mind boggling and with Ashley having joined the shadow children and asking for help, we knew this was more than a prove or dis-prove situation. This was what I had coined as a 'Para-Mystery' that we felt compelled to solve.

We wandered quietly through the damp parking lot to our cars and with quiet waves good bye, went off in our own directions. I had a feeling that Jenn and Katie were having similar thoughts to mine...we have found ourselves in the middle of another one of 'those' cases.

Within days of our reveal, I was contacted by Del Heerdink, who invited us back as soon as possible, and passed along a little more information. I had been approached about helping the Owl's with a fund raiser, and was not only open to the idea, but excited to help them out. The idea I had was to host a seminar, with psychic readings, and a ghost tour. There would be a cover charge at the door for anyone who wanted to join us, along with that we would offer up to twenty everyday folks to join us for a few hours at midnight for another investigation. This would hopefully raise some decent funds for the local Owl's Nest, as well as raise awareness of what the EVP Investigations team did. Del and I discussed possible dates, and we had decided that this Friday night would be a great time to have a second investigation, and it might be best to wait two or three weeks before having the fund-raiser, which would give plenty of time for advertising through social media, and the Owl's newsletter.

Chapter 10

A BURNING QUESTION

Having us back as soon as possible translated into another investigation on the following weekend. Apparently our discoveries were well received by the officers of The Owl's Nest. There was undeniable proof that something paranormal was happening, or from the point of view of the Owls, they were haunted, and it was a haunting that was shrouded in mystery. The puzzle of the missing history surrounding the family, and why it was missing, was something that everyone involved was eager to learn, and we were devout in our search for answers. I contacted Theo, the team's psychic-medium, and asked him to join us for the investigation Saturday night. Theo knew this invitation was coming, but he was still excited to receive it, and a quick invitation turned into a long conversation about what he already was feeling and seeing that he thought was related to the Owl's Nest. His insights were not only interesting, but also helpful. The words and thoughts that he conveyed not only gave me some information, but a different perspective on things. In order to put the puzzle together, I was going to have to look at things in a new way, and I already understood what fate was bringing into play.

***

The team and I spent our weekdays as usual, and looked forward to the weekend's investigation. It was amusing how some people thought of us as having 'alter egos' as if through the week we were mild mannered everyday folks, but on the weekends, when the sun went down, we transformed into something completely different. We weren't viewed like a superhero who enters and exits a phone booth, and was cheered on by the general public. We were viewed more like Jeckle and Hyde... avoided, misunderstood, and unapproachable. It was a shame, but it did not discourage us or dull our passion.

***

Most Wednesdays I had my son, and that father and son time in the middle of every week made my life alone, bearable. He and I were the best of friends, and so much alike it was downright eerie. The most difficult moments in my life have always been when I had to say good-bye to him. I missed him from the moment he left my sight until we were reunited. It was always the night after he went back to his mom's house that I would sit, awake and alone, contemplating the value of my life and what purpose it served. The only answer I could ever find was that I was put on this earth to be a father to the most amazing boy in the world, and that was good enough for me.

I had been married to his mother for over ten years, and though it always felt like we were meant to be together, that was not the case. In the years since our divorce I had met many wonderful women, but though I went on numerous dates and even had a few relationships, I could never really find my soul mate. I am very particular in whom I date, but I am also quick to 'fall in love'. Once I am smitten, it is only a matter of time before it is over.

I suppose *that* was my curse... to repeatedly fall in love, only to repeatedly have my heart broken. I suppose with my unreliable schedule, and my passion for the paranormal, I was just not quite 'relationship material', and though I call it a curse, I believe I find myself single for a reason. Perhaps a hopeless romantic and lonely soul, such as myself, can connect with those distraught and tortured souls who have left the physical world. Perhaps we can sense each other's pain and anguish. Are we somehow drawn together and connected by our sadness and our regret?

Once my son had gone, it felt like my sun had gone. The rest of the week drug by until the weekend had finally arrived. I had the unexpected surprise of another visit from my son Saturday morning. It wasn't my weekend to have him, but his mom had some things to do and I was more than happy to keep him, in fact I volunteered to keep him anytime she needed or wanted me to. When it was time to say so-long, it wasn't as saddening as usual, and I believe that was because his visit was an unexpected joy, and therefore how could I be sad? So, when we hugged and said our good-byes, though there were the usual tears, there was also a smile. He remained in my thoughts for the rest of the day, and time passed swiftly until it was time to meet up with the team.

Instead of meeting for coffee at the Barnes & Noble before the investigation, we had decided to meet up at The Owl's Nest. It was agreed that we would meet between 11:30 and 11:45. I had arrived early. I strolled through the doors around 11, about an hour before they would close down for our investigation. I perused the bar room, eyeing the ladies, and greeting them with smiles. Approaching the bar, I was suddenly met by Del.

"You want a drink?" he shouted over the music that was playing in the dance hall.

"I wasn't going to, but it's early enough, I think... can I get a Crown and Coke?" I asked.

"Yep... give me a second and I'll bring you one." He shouted once again, and I nodded in response.

I found a tall round table with four bar stools, sitting alone in the corner of the room as if it were patiently waiting for my arrival and had shunned all others who may have chosen it. I sat down with my back to the wall, as I always did, not in fear of someone behind me, but because I loved to watch people, and it also gave me a good vantage point to catch the team as they arrived. A few minutes later Del showed up at my table with the beverage as promised. I reached for my wallet, but he quickly stopped me.

He leaned over close to me so he wouldn't have to yell over the crowd and music. "This one is on me." He smiled. "Barb and I are running the bingo game downstairs so I can't stay, but I'll see you as soon as we start to close up." And with that he waved good-bye and disappeared into the crowd.

I sipped at the drink in front of me, but I drank in the sea of people before me. One by one, I sized them up, imagined who they might be once they left the club, if they were single, married... it was just something I found myself doing in most public places. I didn't judge anyone, or assume I knew anything about them. I was only making up a story in my head of who they might be, if this place were just a scene from a fictional story in my mind.

The sweet syrupy taste of Coke was diluted by the warm burn of the whiskey, as I slowly enjoyed my one drink. Guilt kept knocking on my door, knowing that it was never a good idea to investigate after having anything to drink, or while taking any medications that could alter my perception. My nerves would always answer the knock with its own excuse... just one drink to calm the nerves, and with the numerous spirits here, not to mention that Ashley Sue, I felt justified. I took another drink as I spied the bustling people and my foot kept time with the music.

My drink was all but gone when Jenn and Katie arrived together at 11:40, and just as they sat down at the table, the music went suddenly silent, and the bar tender shouted out "LAST CALL!" It was nearly closing time, and I watched as the

106

patrons and guests prepared to leave, some left in pairs, some hand in hand, while others left alone and tugged at my heart. I could see the loneliness on their faces as they looked around the room for one last chance to make a new friend, or for the spark of a predestined, and doomed, romance. I knew exactly how they felt as those poor souls left the bar room and headed home alone, disappointed again and wondering what was wrong with them, why they couldn't find love and happiness like so many others they had seen leave together that night. It was a cruel and twisted thing, this emotion we call love, and though often times it feels as if it will kill us, we know we can't live without it. Such is the conundrum for so many good-hearted people. I have learned a few things in this life. I have been taught far too many times, that karma takes her sweet time, life has no loyalty to fairness, and love does not play well with others.

***

We watched as the club emptied out rather quickly until we were the only ones left in the building besides Barb and Del, and a couple of the staff who were cleaning up, and beginning to turn off the lights. Soon the building, for all intents and purposes, would be ours. Theo rushed into the room and made a bee-line for the table we were still sitting at.

"Sorry I'm late. There was a wreck that had traffic tied up." He apologized.

"It's fine, you aren't late. In fact..." I began to think more rationally, "we haven't even brought in any of our equipment. So, in that respect, you are right on time." I smiled.

"Yep, good point there E-V-..." I cut Jenn off mid-nickname.

"Hey now!" I smiled.

"We better get everything brought in before they lock the doors on us." Jenn laughed.

"Right!" Katie agreed and jumped up, along with Theo, Jenn and I, and the four of us hastily headed to the cars for our equipment cases. In one arm-loaded trip, we had managed to carry in everything we would need for the night. I quickly set up the DVR in the basement, covering the room where we had heard the 'bang', the old boiler room, the large room were we had been rushed by three shadowy specters, and one that covered the upstairs bar and part of the dance hall. The last of the lights were turned off, and only the faint glow of the exit signs lit our way, as we all reassembled in the main bar room. We unpacked the rest of our hand held gear and our next risky undertaking commenced.

Del and Barb were making their rounds, checking the outside doors to assure they were locked and secure, while we made our way down the hallway towards the main entrance, and in the direction of the stairs to the second floor.

***

The twisted old specters searched the second story of the old home for the poor young children, grumbling back and forth at each other for their flagrant inabilities. They drifted from room to room searching for the four young spirits who refused to leave their home. The anger grew and manifested itself in the form of papers flying across the emptiness with the only wind being that which they created in their movement. In a fit rage the three haggard old souls burst through a closed door causing it to open in the physical world.

From the hallway of the first floor, we heard the banging open of a door. Jenn sprung up and darted through the unlocked door and up the stairway in just enough time to see the door slowly swinging to its final resting point. Theo, Katie and I rushed to the foot of the stairs just as Jenn called down to us.

"It's the door to the room here on the left, here. I saw it moving." The excitement bubbled in her voice.

"What do you want? You aren't welcome here." Theo said to the emptiness, and the three of us gave him a look of bewilderment.

"Who are you talking to, and why aren't they welcome?" I asked out of curiosity as well as necessity. As the

108

team leader, it was my place to know what was going on, and why.

Just then a warm sickening feeling came over Jenn, and Theo's eyes opened wider. I watched as Jenn tried to keep her footing and placing her hand on her stomach, let out an uneasy groan.

Just then, a few bits of old paper and a tattered yellowed ribbon were caught up as if in a sudden gust, lifting and then settling back down on the steps. Theo took a step back and immediately that warm nauseating feeling overcame those of us at the bottom of the stairs. It took us all a moment to regain our senses, and as Jenn started making her way down to us, Theo began his explanation and the answer to my question.

"Three male figures came out of that area to the right." He pointed to the opposite side from where Jenn had seen the door move. "They were searching for something or someone, and they were *not* happy. I felt that they did not really belong here, but I believe that they were claiming ownership of this place and didn't want to share it. They rushed down the stairs and passed us."

"This sounds like a feud, to me." I pondered the potential scenarios that could be in play. "Could they be after the Bettiger children? I mean, really, what would be their motivation?"

"Huh...I suppose there could be some connection, but I don't know what it would be." said Jenn, perplexed by the thought of it all. "I guess we need to do some more research, and by that I mean some serious digging in the dirt."

"Sounds perfect. I like a little gritty sleuthing." Katie replied with a wink. "Time to find Allison."

"Could you tell which way they went, Theo?" I asked.

"It was so quick. All I could tell was that they went down the hall that way, but I lost them." Theo answered back with a slight disappointment in his voice.

"I wonder if that's the same shadows we actually saw downstairs last time?" Jenn interjected.

"Could very well be." I answered back. "Let's take a quick tour through the upstairs so Theo can get a feel for the layout of the house."

I began climbing the stairs to meet Jenn. Katie followed close behind, but Theo lagged a bit. When my trio had stopped on the landing we found Theo had stopped on the stairs, and when I pointed my flashlight in his direction, I could see a look of bewilderment on his face.

"This is like deja-vu." He mumbled to himself, but the sound echoed up the empty stairwell. "I've been here before." He thought hard and peered left and right trying to place it, and then suddenly, like he was hit with a surge of memories, it came to him, and even caused him to check his footing.

"I know..." His voice trailed off. "This place has changed so much, but this is the stairs in my dream. When Ashley told me to help the children." He stammered. "I felt like I was being chased... kinda like what just happened... those shadows were chasing the children, or something...I'm almost positive of it." He continued to climb the stairs, until he reached the top and rejoined us.

"You know Theo... that makes sense in a crazy, new age, paranormal, psychic kinda way." I grinned, and was swiftly smacked on the back of the head by Jennifer.

"Sorry!" I digressed. "I didn't mean any disrespect. You know how I am. I meant that it did make sense, but to the average person, they would think we were all kooky." I grinned once again, and quickly cringed, but there was no slap, just a dim glimpse of smiles and rolling eyes in the midst of this dark nightmarish haunting.

We toured Theo through the upstairs and though I could tell he was sensing things, he never spoke up about any of them, until we reached the odd shaped, large rectangular room with the adjacent non-closet that was still a mystery to us. When we neared the 'whatever' room that wasn't a closet, Theo paused and backed up to one of the windows. In fact, he had backed up to the only window on that side of the second story that was boarded up.

"I feel a pressure on my chest and a dizzying rush, like I'm falling." He stepped away from the window. "I believe someone was pushed out of this window, a woman...maybe on accident, but I also feel hostility. It's a bit confusing, but I'm almost positive that something like that happened."

"Yeah..." Katie said quietly, remembering back to our first visit, when she had thought she caught sight of a ghostly woman falling from the building, out of the corner of her eye, but she did not bring it up. The very thought of it filled her heart with remorse and she was ready to think about something else...anything else.

We finished the tour upstairs with very little conversation, and found ourselves back in the stairway. There was an odd feeling in the air, and we all sensed it... like that feeling you get when you know something is about to go terribly wrong, but you can't pinpoint what it is, until it happens, and then it's too late. That feeling that connects the pit of our stomach to a place deep in our consciousness, to warn us, even though we rarely heed the warning. I had to do, or say, something. Each second we stood there was another second for this uncomfortable feeling of despair to grow. I turned toward the stairs and without a word began my descent. The other three followed close behind and we found ourselves huddled at the bottom landing of the stairs, still feeling this awkward sense of confusion. Something was going to happen; I could feel it in my very bones, something bad.

"Do you all want to split up in pairs and cover more area or all stay together?" I finally broke the silence.

"I'd say split up, at least for now." Katie spoke up.

"Yeah, I think so too." Theo agreed, and so we paired up and went our separate ways.

***

While Katie and I had decided to head upstairs to investigate, Jennifer and Theo took their search for answers to a much lower level. Back in the old basement area of the home, the unlikely duo found themselves drawn to the old rickety stairway to nowhere. While Theo planted himself on one of the bottom steps and began a brief meditation to become in tuned to the spirit world around him, Jenn was drawn into the old boiler room and without even knowing why, began snapping photo after photo, more than a hundred in fact.

There was a force driving her decision that she did not even realize existed. While taking the pictures, she simply assumed she was doing it because that is what her subconscious investigator was telling her to do. When she sat down in the old wheelchair to quickly review the photos, she soon found out that there was another will that had been directing her.

She scanned through each picture, using the digital display on the back of her camera, looking for anything out of place. She had reached the section of about three dozen photos taken in the direction of the wheelchair, when she stopped. There was something off about one of them. She studied the screen, but saw nothing unusual, so she decided to compare it to the previous shot. Nothing... and the one before... nothing. She dissected each one in turn looking for oddities and irregularities, picture after picture, looking back through all of the wheelchair shots. When she backed up to the sixth photo, she paused, once again picking the photo apart, pixel by pixel, when it hit her. There, in the cutout opening in the wall, just up and to her right (because she was now sitting in the wheelchair) was a face. The outline of the old hairdo, a high and frilled collar, and the shoulders that seemed to fade into the background of the picture appeared to be an old woman, and it was all too familiar. She had seen this face before.

Without warning the batteries in the camera went dead, and the blackness engulfed her. A stinging pain grew stronger in her head, and she could not bear it any longer. Jennifer stood up from the wheelchair, pressing her fingertips against that small, indented spot, just where the nape of the neck meets the skull. She stumbled forward a few awkward steps in the dark, and her foot slipped over the edge of the rectangular cut out in the floor. It was less than a foot drop, but it was enough to throw Jennifer forward, and being unable to see at all in the unlit room, she could not catch herself. In one quick motion, she stumbled forward into the corner of the pit. Her shin hit, and scraped, against the corner of the shallow pit. In that same motion, the instant pain caused Jenn to reel backwards, contorting as she fell until she struck the crown of her head against the uneven brick floor of the cut-out pit. The world of pain that she was experiencing went uncomfortably numb and quiet, and the conscious world around her ceased to exist.

The sound of a roaring fire awakened Jennifer. Somehow she was standing upright, and to her it felt like a dream or some near death, 'out of body' experience. The room she was in was the same, and yet it had noticeable differences. The electrical wiring that had been stapled to the rafters and the dusty cobweb covered insulation that had been hanging from the ancient pipes were no longer there, and the brick lined cut out in the concrete floor was now filled with a huge pre-1900's coal fired boiler, which was burning at full steam.

One thing that had remained was the wheelchair. Much to Jenn's bewilderment, the chair now had an occupant, a terribly macabre occupant. An old woman with her hair up, wearing a high collared black dress and boots sat in the chair. In her hand she held a bouquet of red roses that had such a crisp and dry appearance; it seemed that even a slight wind could cause them to turn to dust. The old woman's legs bent awkwardly to one side as if they had been useless for a number of years, or decades, and her head was bowed, giving the impression of sleep, or worse, death.

It was just as Jenn had summed up her surroundings, that a man in an old time officer's uniform and another man in business attire (minus a sport jacket and tie) entered the room. The uniformed man backed into the room first, hunched over and struggling with a heavy burden in hand. She knew immediately what she was seeing. He was dragging a limp and bloody body into the room with her. The business-man followed behind him with the same posture and dragging yet another lifeless cadaver.

Jenn glared across the space between her and the wheelchair in horror, but the horror hadn't even begun yet. As the men teamed up to drag yet a third body into the now crowed room, she noticed a movement across the way that grabbed her attention like a train wreck that she could not look away from. The old woman, whom Jenn had almost assumed was dead, slowly raised her head. Second by agonizing second, the pale grayish flesh of her wrinkled and weathered face was revealed, until Jennifer noticed something was amiss. One of her eyes was as gray the billowing smoke from a burning pile of damp leaves, and the other was a black abyss, and the blackened blood that ran from its socket, was now dried and stained the monotone skin of her cheek.

The businessman rolled up his shirt sleeves and donned a pair of leather gloves. Stepping over to the oversized door of the boiler he grasped the lever-arm and lifted it, unlatching the hinged door and spewing forth a blaze of heat into the small room. The two men the cautiously lifted the first corpse and with a 'one-two-three' swing, tossed the body into the roaring flames of the coal fire. Much of the cadaver landed in the white hot coals, while an arm and both of his legs dangled out of the opening, like limp branches sticking out of a bonfire. Grabbing the charred coal shovel that leaned against the wall, the uniformed man began to poke and prod, pushing the body completely into the furnace. The man in the dress slacks and shirt swiftly closed the door, and opened the damper, causing the fire to roar like some medieval, mythical dragon.

Just as they performed this heinous act, the old woman opened her mouth and jerked her head towards them. Jennifer could hear a shrill, raspy voice calling out "RED!" and was drawn to the sound and movement like a moth to the flame. She now knew the source of the eerie voice on the recording, but what could it mean? When her eyes met the old woman, the flame light illuminated her distorted features even more. Much to Jenn's horror and disgust, she could see the non-existent eye socket and beyond. In fact, she could now see the dancing-yellow-flame lit wall behind the invalid woman through the hole in her eye socket that went completely through her head.

The men did not take notice of the nightmarish woman, nor did they notice Jennifer. They simply continued on with their morbid task of filling the belly of the old boiler with the three murdered men, one by one, and then shoveling even more coal on top of them to ensure the flames reach their peak intensity. While the two men carried on with their task, Jenn noticed the old woman was somehow fading, becoming slightly translucent, and then somewhat transparent, fading from her sight. She could feel her own self beginning to feel hollow and growing emptier from within, until the woman was a mere shadow, and brightness of the room faded, as did Jennifer's sight. All was dark.

***

Theo sat on the stairs in a trance-like state, meditating and trying to get in-tune to the energies of the house. The once newly remodeled place just a few steps from where he sat, was now old and worn with years of use by the fraternal club. Years upon years of occupation had left many imprints on this historic structure, and Theo felt the connection with the location and the energy it held. Slowly, he began to open his eyes, only to find that the time battered stairs and surroundings were now replaced with a newer feeling, yet antiquated look. As he took in his surroundings he began to hear the voices and laughter of children playing. A coolness in the air appeared and seemed to brush past him, and almost through him, when he saw a string of youngsters, hand in hand pass him, trotting ad skipping into the room before him. He watched as the ghosts of three children past, all boys, playing happily in what was once their home. Theo began to speak to them, hoping to find answers to the questions that were confounding him.

"Hello..." He paused and waited for a response, but the children did not seem to notice his presence. "Are you all okay? You seem happy, but are you frightened by anything? Is there anything I can do to help you?"

Two of the boys continued to play, as boys will do, but the oldest one, (only seven or eight years old) stopped, dead in his tracks, (as the fitting cliché goes) and stared directly into Theo's eyes. His face became darkened and twisted; his eyes

115

grew completely black, as did his mouth when he opened it to let out a blood-curdling screech. As the sound left his lips, his features physically contorted and twisted in an inhuman way that left Theo not only shocked, but utterly disturbed.

A distant echoing sound 'popped' from another level of the house followed by the hollow and muffled thundering sound of footsteps. A fourth child ran into the room, a young girl who was a few years older than the boys. She shuffled them all quickly into the cubby hole under the stairs. It was only when they were all hunkered over and hidden in the safety of the darkness, that the girl wandered across the room, away from Theo and the boys under the stairs.

"You should follow them and hide little girl." Theo prompted her, before realizing she had an ulterior motive behind her presence.

"Time is running out. Save them! Save the children before it's too late!" She called out desperately to him, and as she began to crumble and fade away with the rest of the scenery, Theo cried back to her.

"ASH! Is that you?" He tried to get his words out before she was completely gone. "Help me save them." he called out to her, but she was gone, and he sat alone again in the dark of the stairs, rubbing his face and head, trying to make sense of what Ashley's pleas could mean. From what did these children need saving?

There was a shuffling sound and a brief series of dull, blunt thuds that came from the boiler room area. He jumped up to investigate what series of events may have caused these noises. Still 'waking up' from the daze of his interactions, he entered the boiler room with flashlight in hand.

His light flickered across the decrepit old wheelchair and from wall to wall, and scanned the floor when he realized that Jennifer was lying unconscious in the shallow brick lined pit in the center of the room. He approached her distorted body carefully. She looked unnervingly still, and Theo feared the worst, but only for a moment.

116

Nervously, he checked for her pulse. It was strong, and rapid. That was a good sign. His light flashed Jenn's face in sporadic and frantic movements as Theo tried to check for any bleeding wounds. He gingerly ran his hands and fingers behind her head and though her hair, noticing a large goose egg of a knot on the back of her head. She started to groggily come to.

Moaning under her breath, she muttered, "What the hell happened?"

"I'm not sure. Did something push you, or maybe, did you miss a step and fall into the pit?" He questioned. "I heard this noise, and came in here... that's when I found you, just lying there."

"I don't know how long I was out, but I seemed like a long time. And I had this weird dream, thing... I dunno what it was, but it was freaky. It started off when I was sitting in the wheelchair..." Her sentence trailed off and Theo cut her off.

"Maybe you should write it down, before you forget, and we can all talk about our experiences together... come to think of it, I have a couple of experiences that I need to get on paper, before I forget any of the details."

"Yeah, okay... I really want to tell Katie and Rick about it anyway, so, I might as well get all the details out now while it's fresh in my aching head, you know, before I get... what do you call it?." She grumbled, but it caused Theo to smile. Jenn was acting just like Jenn should, and though she had a nasty knot on her head, a skinned up shin, and a few minor bruises, it was a comfort to know she hadn't been seriously hurt.

"Amnesia?" Theo answered and laughed at the silly joke Jenn had made.

"Yeah... I think that's it." Jenn barked out sarcastically.

A face in the window

Chapter 11

A Chill in the Air

While the Heerdinks were taking a break from investigating on the main level and Theo and Jenn were scouring the sub-level, Katie and I had returned upstairs, where Katie had been spooked by the maniacal laugh of a devious entity on our first visit. We had slowly made our way to the top of the steps where Katie pointed out the exact spot next to the banister where she felt the presence and heard the voice. We both sat quietly for a while with no real activity to speak of, though we both had an uncomfortable feeling, like we were not welcome and were being watched. Who was watching and why they didn't want us there was something we desperately wanted to find out. When we couldn't take the eerie stillness anymore, we ventured into the rooms to the right of the stairs.

That side of the upstairs had a restroom, which was originally a large storage area, and now, years later was no longer even a functioning rest room. Next to it was a kitchen,

121

that was also a re-purposed area, and no longer functional. Both of these rooms were entered from the large, somewhat rectangular room at the top right of the stair way. We did not spend much time in these areas, though each had its own personal 'creepiness' about it.

In the larger room, we searched once again with our meters and kept our digital voice recorders running. There were several instances where we would 'catch' a rogue e.m.f. that seemed to be free moving and had no connection to anything electrical that we could explain.

"Do you hear that?" Katie asked with the hint of a quiver in her voice.

"Yeah... I hear it. Sounds like people on the stairs, trying to be quiet. No worries." I answered silently with a grin, and in a half dozen long strides had placed me back into the upstairs landing.

I poked my head back around the corner where I could see the light from Katie's e.m.f. detector.

"Nobody." I whispered in the dead silence of the night.

"Cool." Katie said.

"Yes, it was cool." I replied quietly.

"No." She whispered sternly. "It's getting cool in here."

I strained through the darkness where I could barely see the outline of Katie's face in the dim green light of the K-II meter. I could also see the light reflecting off of her breath, now billowing out like wisps of smoke. Her heart raced, for she knew what this meant. Something was pulling every particle of energy from the atmosphere around us, leaving it frigid and barren. But this feeling was an illusion, because it was far from empty. Whatever was collecting the energy was in close proximity, and what was more alarming was the truth that the energy was being accumulated for a reason, and that reason was to perform some paranormal act that we could not anticipate.

"I'm f-f-freezing." Katie murmured, as she began to physically shiver. I rushed back to where she was and found myself stepping into an arctic blast of bone chilling air.

I wrapped my arms around myself and rubbed them, trying to create heat from the friction. An obvious thought came to mine and I reached into the darkness, grabbing Katie by the arm, I tugged. More than tugged, I nearly pulled her off balance, and pulled her out into the stairwell landing. It was much warmer, and a more comfortable feeling was in the air around us.

"You don't need to be that close to any possible negative energy." I said, feeling like an overprotective, big brother.

"You're probably right, but we've all been exposed to the spirits here already, and we did do the protection ritual with Theo before we started." She stated confidently.

"Fair enough... those are good points, but I don't see any reason to take chances... ya know?" I insinuated about her pregnancy.

"I know, I know... hey, look." She said as she tuned on her flashlight and held it perpendicular to her side, shining it across the 'bump' of her belly.

"Oh my gosh! How cool!" I truly was excited for her, but also concerned. She had wanted to be a mom for quite some time, and now that she was going to be, I wanted nothing to put her or her unborn child in any danger.

In the glare of her flashlight, I noticed the relaxed smile leave her face, and her eyes slowly wandered over my right shoulder towards the coldness we had just escaped. My head turned ever so cautiously and slowly, looking over my shoulder, and then slowly turning my entire body to face a growing darkness that not even the brilliance of Katie's l.e.d. flashlight could penetrate. The black and massive shadow moved independent of the movement of the light. It increased in size, filling the entire corner, and then transformed from a single black mass to three individual shadows that were so unexplainable dark, they were like spiritual black-holes, pulling in every bit of light and energy in close proximity to them. We could begin to feel the very energy of life being coaxed from us, despite our ritual of protection.

"Let's go!" I said in full voice.

"I'm one step ahead of you." Katie called out to me from the stairs. She had already made it nearly half way down when I reached the first step. In an instant these formidable shadows seemed to give chase. I stumbled on the steps and tumbled half way down before catching myself. In an icy gust, the shadows passed over me and disappeared from my site out of the doorway at the bottom. Fear gripped me, and all I could think was, 'they weren't after me'. In disregard for my personal safety, I scrambled, and half tumbled to the bottom of the steps. I had to catch Katie, but how could I protect her from things I couldn't even begin to fathom.

I burst through the doorway and into the hallway to find Katie cowered down in a corner just a few feet ahead of me. I couldn't see the shadowy figure anymore, though she seemed to be staring off into a blank nothingness. Squatting down beside her, I placed my hand on her shoulder. My touch pulled her back to our reality, her head jerked towards me, and she looked straight into my eyes.

"I saw them." was all her quivering voice could muster.

"Who... the shadows? I saw them too. I thought they were after us." I said trying to ease the tension, but I did not understand.

"NO. I saw THEM. It was the three shadows; they took form right in front of me. Their faces were withered and cruel, and I watched them thin out, and then in a burst of black flames, they were nothing but bones, and then...nothing. They were just gone." Katie collected her thoughts. "I get this feeling that they were the same skeletal remains Jenn and I saw in the boiler room, maybe."

I stood up, and helped her to her feet. We stood there quietly in the hallway, hidden in the night's cowl. I thought, in depth, about what Katie had just explained to me, and about what the potential dangers could be with the public event we were planning. Then something dawned on me, these shadows had not been seen by the patrons before, they had only appeared when the place was closed or nearly empty... when there were only a few people around. Perhaps there **was** safety in numbers.

***

Just above Theo and Jennifer and below where Katie and I were, Barb and Del Heerdink were on the main floor of the Owl's nest, taking a bit of a break in the dance hall and enjoying a cold Coke under the dim, green glow of the exit signs.

"I wonder if the team is having any luck." Barb casually asked her husband.

"I'd be surprised if they don't find anything... you know how often we experience things here that we can't explain... and they have already caught some great e.v.p.s and had activity here on their first visit." He reassured her.

"Yeah, I'm sure you are right. I would just really feel bad if they came here, spent the whole night and didn't get anything." The corners of her mouth turned down in a slight frown, worried that the haunting they knew existed would not show itself and leave them feeling let down.

"I would too, but I don't think..." Del stopped in midsentence, staring over Barb's shoulder and across the eerie green of the room.

"What??" Barb said as she turned to shoot a glance in the direction of his glare, just in time to see the fading figure of an older gentleman in a yellow button down shirt, dancing his way across the stage.

"Did you just see what I think I just saw?" She grinned back at Del.

"Maybe... I saw our friend in the yellow shirt, dancing up on the stage." He confirmed her experience with his simple statement.

125

"Well dang it!" She said, snapping her fingers in disappointment.

"What? That was pretty darn, cool! What are you so upset about?" He asked bluntly.

"Why couldn't at least one of the EVP guys been here to see that too?" Barb sounded disheartened.

"We'll tell them about it, and I'm sure they will believe us... and, hey, at least we know there is some activity tonight. Maybe there's activity in other places too." His words gave her the comfort she needed, and they went back to their conversations, just as they would have on any other night when they had a random supernatural experience. This was something that they had grown accustomed to in the ancient building. Much of the life of this place was filled with joy and happiness, but there was also an older, more sinister past, and this structure, past and present, was home to such a colorful and varied history.

"Are you ready to find some more spirits?" Barb asked enthusiastically.

"I'm ready when you are! Maybe we should try to find the team, and investigate the rest of the night with them." Del suggested.

"Good idea." Barb agreed, and so they got up from their table and grabbed the meters they had borrowed from the team, and resumed their investigating. The happy couple didn't waste a lot of time in the large areas, except for where they had seen the apparition of the man in yellow. Once they had finished, they worked their way towards the stairwell that lead up.

Katie and I rounded the corner of the first floor hallway, and nearly ran right into the Heerdinks.

"Holy crap!" Katie nearly screamed, still skittish from her run in with the terrifying entities. "Thank goodness it's only you."

"I'm not quite sure how to take that." Del remarked with a smile.

"You two didn't see and shadow activity, did you?" I asked cautiously, not wanting to cause a fright.

"No. But we did see the man in the yellow shirt. Both of us! And I think he was dancing." Barb answered.

"Oh, okay. That's really cool! I still haven't seen the man in yellow. I'm jealous!" I acted disappointed, but in all reality, I was relieved. "We were pretty sure we saw some shadow people going down the stairs. They are fairly common in the paranormal field, and we thought maybe you had seen them too."

We grabbed our gear and headed down to find Theo and Jennifer. As we wandered down the darkened stairs and into the large room, where everyday folks had been playing bingo just a few hours before, some-thing caught my attention.

"You hear that?" I whispered. "It sounded like people talking."

Everyone strained in the silence to catch the sound of a ghostly conversation. The four of us stood quietly, and the longer we waited, the more deafening the silence became, until that annoying high pitch tone that we all hear when things are too quiet, began to hurt my ears so badly that I was ready to speak out just to end the silence. When I was at my breaking point, it happened. A voice came from across the room, muffled and indistinguishable, but it was unmistakably a voice. The words it mumbled echoed quietly in the large empty room, but ended quickly, only to start again, only this time the voice seemed to have mustered up its strength and was now louder, yet no more discernible, than before.

"Sorry." Katie spoke out loud, and the silence and concentration were broken.

"Sorry about what?" I quickly asked.

"Sorry to have shattered the silence, and sorry to have to tell you I know that ghost. I'd recognize Jennifer's voice anywhere. She and Theo must be down here somewhere talking." Katie was correct, the voice grew louder yet again, and this time, I could tell it was definitely Theo.

From the cobweb filled room, that was usually hidden behind a locked door, I could begin to see a dim glow, green in color, and knew it must be the back lighting from the Mel-Meter Jenn had taken with her. It almost danced in the darkness as Jennifer and Theo came walking conservatively through the old forgotten place, trying to see through the blackness, to not make any missteps that could land either one of them in the same predicament Jennifer had been in just thirty minutes earlier. We stayed our position, and let them come to us.

"Hey guys." Jennifer moaned slowly.

"What's the matter? You sound like you aren't having much luck... boring night?" I asked.

"Anything but!" Jenn quickly shot out, in an aggravated tone.

"You'll have to excuse Jenn." Theo began. "She had a bit of an accident earlier, and she hit her head pretty good."

"I'd say! You should feel this damn goose egg I've got!" Jenn leaned over gingerly touching the spot where her head had abruptly met with the boiler room pit.

I reached up and ever so gently put my fingers where hers had been, and as my fingers ran through her hair, I felt it. "Oh my god!" I blurted out. "You need to have that looked at."

"Do you feel dizzy or nauseous... or is your vision blurry?" Barb quizzed Jenn, knowing a bit about the medical field and having gone to nursing school.

"Hell, I don't know if anything's blurry, were standing here in the dark." Jenn spouted off.

"True." Katie tried to calm Jenn's irritated state. "What about the other symptoms? Do you feel dizzy or sick?"

"No, I'm going to be fine, my head is pounding, though." Jenn said, sounding less moody, and more like herself.

"I'll be right back." Del said and shot up the stairs, spanning two steps with each stride.

"Me too!" I said loudly and sprang up after him.

I had no idea where Del was going, but after our experiences at the Owl's Nest, and especially Katie's experiences, I wasn't about to let anyone go anywhere alone. I caught up with Del just past the doorway at the top of the stairs. A few strides into the bar room and I was nearly beside him. We talked as I followed his lead into the large industrial style kitchen, full of stainless steel workstations, deep fryers and every utensil imaginable hanging from hooks over various tables and cook stations.

"Hey... Whatcha doing?" I asked casually.

"I just thought I'd get her some ice for her head." He answered as if we were just having an everyday-sort-of conversation.

"Good thinking... But just so you are aware... not to scare you, or freak you out... We have had some pretty aggressive activity tonight, and I really would rather no one went anywhere in here alone." I hoped he would take my word on it and be understanding. I was half right.

"Sure, make sense. I just wasn't thinking...in a hurry you know?" He pulled a quart sized zip-lock baggie out of the cabinet and then headed towards the ice machine, which was isolated from the rest of the kitchen, probably to keep it away from the heat of the ovens and grill. Then, filling the bag half full with ice, closed the lid on the machine and zipped the baggie closed. Having been disturbed, the agitated machine started up with a whir, and once again, I followed Del back downstairs.

"Here you go." He said kindly, handing the ice bag to Jenn.

"OH!" she sighed. "Thank you, thank you, thank you!" Appreciative of his actions, Jenn gratefully took the ice and, using both hands, carefully eased it into place.

"I know it's a little earlier than normal, but I think we need to go ahead and wrap things up." I said, knowing Katie and Jenn both were probably ready to get home, or at least away from here in Katie's case. "So, I was thinking, if you wanted to go ahead and go, Jenn, we can pack everything up."

"Naw, just give me few minutes and I'll help round everything up." She almost smiled.

"Well," Katie stretched out the word and then continued, "you just have a seat for a few and we'll get started, and then if we aren't finished by the time you feel up to it, you can help." I smiled at Katie for always having such a big heart, even though I knew she couldn't see me.

"Deal." Jenn groaned as she took a seat at one of the cafeteria style bingo tables.

Before we began, Theo suggested we all huddle up around where Jenn was sitting, and then he began telling us how to repel any negativity that might want to attach itself to us, and said a prayer to St. Michael. And though I don't follow any particular religion, I had to admit, there was something comforting about hearing the words of the prayer. It was like a chanting of some mystical spell that called to the very depth of our souls and brought us an incontrovertible feeling of peace. When Theo had finished, we all stood quietly for a moment, and then as if someone had pulled the trigger on a starting gun, Theo, Katie and I took off to get everything put away while Barb and Del instinctively stayed with Jenn, knowing she could be particularly vulnerable if left alone.

Before long, we were saying our good-byes, and still holding the bag of now ice-water to her head, Jenn passed out her hugs, almost instinctively, or as if it were built into her DNA... brown hair, hazel eyes, hugs. We then parted ways, not knowing exactly how soon we would be seeing each other again.

Chapter 12

A TIME TO BELIEVE

       Once again, we had found ourselves passing the time of our everyday lives, elbow deep in paint, dirt, books, or financial paperwork, respectively, and though the haunting of the Owl's never left our thoughts for long, we had to maintain ourselves and our non-profit group through our careers. A few days had passed when Jennifer received a somewhat unexpected phone call. Driving home from work on Tuesday evening, with the radio blaring out a solid drum and guitar based rock-n-roll song, Jenn happened to look over and notice her cell phone in the passenger seat lighting up with an incoming call. Though she did not recognize the number, she quickly muted the radio and answered the call.

"Hello? This is Jennifer." She had tried to sound professional, just in case it was one of her business clients who would often call her personal phone with questions or concerns about one of their prized plants, or trees.

"Why, hello there Jennifer. You don't know me..." Jennifer put up her window and strained to hear the quiet voice of a very elderly woman on the other end of the call. "...but I'm Allison Bettiger." she struggled to clear her throat. "Linda asked if I minded to call and talk to you about my family's history in Indiana."

"Yes! Thank you so much for calling." Jenn pulled her car into the first parking lot she could find and shut the motor off. She grabbed a pen a note pad and began to ask the first in hopefully a series of questions. "My friends and I were doing some research on the Owl's Nest in Evansville and we found out that your parents used to live there. Is that correct?"

"Oh, why yes, and that is quite an interesting tale of how I became the last Bettiger born to that family. It is a very long story, and I would love to tell it, but I am not one to talk on the phone for any length of time. What I do like is having company to talk to, and I haven't told this story before. I used to tell myself that I never would, but now that my years are running out, and I have no children to pass this tale on to, I would be very happy to tell you if you promise to pass my story along and 'keep it alive' as they say." Allison's voice had grown stronger as she spoke, and its gentle sound had drawn Jennifer in, heart and soul.

"Ms. Bettiger, I can't say when, but I'm positive we can make some kind of arrangements to come for a visit and to hear your story. I can also promise you that we will make sure your story is told, and that your family name lives on. My team mate Rick, may even want to write your story down in a book, with your permission." Jennifer was almost choked up as she spoke. She could sense the urgency and the shortness of time that dear Allison had.

"Thank you deary. Let me give you my phone number and my address and you just call whenever you want to and you let me know when you can come for a visit." The kindness in her voice told a story of its own, a story of love, kindness and a loneliness for family that had been missed for far too many decades.

"I'm ready to write it down whenever you are." Jenn said politely, knowing she didn't need to write down the number, as it had shown up on her caller ID, but also knowing that was probably not something a 90-something year old woman would think of. She graciously wrote down the information, exchanged good-byes, and after ending the call, sat in her car in the parking lot for a few minutes with a smile on her face and thought that the answer to this mysterious haunting may be easier to find than we had all thought. With her optimism renewed, she resumed her drive home and made a few phone calls along the way.

***

I sat on my couch, waiting for the pizza delivery guy to show up with a steaming hot pie covered in every meat on the menu, plus onions, olives and mushrooms. True, I didn't really like mushrooms, but I was feeling daring this evening. It was going to be pizza, Mt. Dew, and a marathon of as many of the Harry Potter movies as I could stay awake for. It was a night to be lazy. The doorbell rang and I hopped up to answer it.

"That'll be $12.97." The pizza delivery gal said with a smile and an overly perky demeanor. Feeling generous this evening, I handed her a $20.

"Keep the change." I said smiling back at her, and taking the large pizza from her. It was heavier than I had expected, which made my smile even more grand, and as I closed the door I said to myself, "looks like I have dinner for tomorrow too."

Placing the pizza on the kitchen counter, I grabbed an ice cold Dew, a few napkins and a plate. With perfect timing, as my hands were overly full, my phone buzzed from the front pocket of my jeans.

135

"Grrr..." I growled as I emptied my hands to retrieve the buzzing piece of technology. Jenn was calling, so I quickly answered to find out what had urged her to call on a Tuesday evening.

"Hey Jenn! What's up?" I said cheerfully, having put my 'growl' away.

"You'll never guess who I just talked to on the phone!" Jenn's voice was filled with emotion.

"Um... the president... that guy from the vampire movie, or that guy who gives away the door to door sweepstakes?" I jested with her, knowing I wouldn't be able to actually guess.

"Pshhh... I wish!" she laughed. "No... Allison Bettiger!" She paused and awaited my reaction, which was probably exactly what she expected.

"No freakin' way! Are you serious...How?"

"The blonde lady from our reveal, Linda, actually knew her, and had her call me."

"No kidding! I remember Barb introducing me to her when we first went there. Doesn't she own the building or something?" I asked.

"No, she and her husband live next door... which just happened to be the former home of Allison. The only problem is she wants to talk in person, and she lives just south of Indianapolis now." Jenn's voice went from elation to dispirited.

"That's great though. I mean, seriously! How awesome is it that we might actually get to talk to her. That has to be the closest thing to a first-hand account of the Bettiger family's life and tragic deaths, if she is willing to talk about it." I tried to reassure her. "We made it to West Virginia twice; I think we can make it to Indy."

"Keep in mind that she is over 90, so we don't know how long she will be with us." Jenn said soberly.

"True enough. I have a thought, let me make a phone call or two and see what I can do." I actually had a few thoughts, but there was one that jumped to the front of the line, and I was very optimistic about the possibility.

"Okay, just call me back if you figure anything out... remember, I am free on Sundays." and with that, the call was ended, and I quickly made another call.

As I searched through my contact list on my phone, I ambled my way through the maze of my apartment. I found my way back to the couch and, sitting down, sent a call to my dear friend, Psychic Medium Rick Hayes. The phone on the other end was ringing and I thought about the voicemail I would leave.

"Hello, this is Rick." The voice on the other end answered.

"Rick! It's Rick Kueber. How are you?" I was thrilled that he was able to take my call, and not in the middle of a session or something. I had always tried to send him a message and ask that he call at his convenience, but I was far too anxious to wait.

"Hey buddy! I'm super! How have you been?" I could hear the happiness in his voice. There was something about Rick Hayes that was always uplifting. He had a certain aura about him that simply brought everyone around him up to a higher level of peace and happiness.

"Pal, I need your help. I know you have already committed to coming down to help us at the Owl's Nest. This is related, but different." I opened with a request for help. Rick is one of those compassionate people who would rarely, if ever, turn down a plea for help.

"You know I'll help you if I can. What do you need?" He answered honestly.

"We have a chance to talk to one of the children of the family that used to live at the Owl's, back when it was a residence, but she lives just south of Indianapolis. Did you tell me the other week that you were giving some life classes in Indy?" I threw it all out on the table.

"Yes, I am...next Friday and Saturday evening. What can I do to help?" He asked genuinely.

137

"Could you meet Jennifer about twenty miles south of Indy on Sunday, maybe mid-morning?" I cringed as I asked the question, and hoped that Jenn would be okay with traveling alone.

"You know what... I have to check out of the hotel by 11am. Can I, maybe, meet her at noon?" He asked.

"I'm sure that would be fine. I'll email you Jennifer's phone number and the address where to meet, if that's okay?" I was incredibly relieved. "Thank you very much, in advance, for all of your help, brother!"

"That'd be fine, and like I always say, 'Us Ricks have to stick together'." and then he chuckled a very cheery chuckle and said, "Okay, well... I'll keep an eye out for the email. Keep living life supernaturally and I'll talk to you soon."

I sat my phone down for a moment, and breathed a sigh of relief. Once I absorbed the idea that Rick Hayes would be able to meet Jennifer, I felt immensely better. I took a few breaths, picked my phone up once again, and called Jenn.

"Hey there E.V.Prick, now what's up?" She sounded less down than earlier.

"Okay, here is the deal. I have my son this weekend, so I am completely out for making a trip to Indy, or anywhere. I don't know what Katie's plans are, but if you are able to go, I can help cover the gas, and Rick Hayes said he would meet you there to talk to Allison and get her story." I had hoped that she would find comfort in not having to interview a complete stranger alone, even if she had to make the drive by herself.

"Really? You aren't just saying that are you?" Jenn quizzed me.

"No seriously...he said he was in Indy this Friday and Saturday and would be glad to meet you around noon on Sunday. I am going to give him your number and the address where to meet you, with your permission, of course." I felt like I could hear her smile through the phone and that gave me a warm feeling inside.

"Of course that's alright." she said.

138

"...And if Katie can make it, I'm sure that would be fine too." I added

"I'll call her and see if she can, and I'll call Allison to make sure she is able to have us visit. Thanks for setting that up. This is going to be great, I can just feel it in my bones!" and as the words left her lips, she was immediately pulled back in time, remembering the chilling vision of the skeletal remains in the basement of the Owl's Nest, and then like a rush through time and space, the memory of finding Ashley Sue's remains flashed in mind.

"I gotta go. Thanks." Her tone had gone dead, and I was a bit concerned, but I knew if there was a problem, or if there was anything I could do, she would have told me. As a team, and as friends, we held nothing back, and that helped us to work together more like a family, solving problems and having the genuine desire to help each other in any way we could.

I sat there silently for a moment, contemplating the fact that I would not be there once again for the discovery of more answers, much like when the girls researched the local libraries. It was a rare occasion that I would miss any part of an investigation.

I thought about compiling all of the pieces of information and putting this puzzle together. Up until now, we had been taunted by the apparition of Ashley and the shadow children, rushed by three seemingly malevolent shadow spirits, caught at least three different voices on our recorders, and nothing seemed to make any sense at all. If Ashley wanted us to 'Help the children', why would she say 'You can't find us'. The confusion had set in from the first experience and grew with each additional encounter and discovery. Why was there no date of death for Amelia Bettinger, and why was it so hard to find that there was a Bettiger sister named Allison... and who was this man in the yellow shirt? I could only hope, and pray, we would find these answers and be able to help all of these spirits find peace. It was an overwhelming task, to say the least, but that was our collective goal.

I reached up and turned on the television, and mindlessly scrolled through the channels, hoping something would grab my attention and distract me long enough to put these mysteries out of my mind for a while. I had surfed through many of the channels when I realized that I had planned on a Harry Potter movie marathon tonight. 'Well crap!' I thought to myself, I had totally forgotten about my pizza, but cold pizza was better than no pizza. I thought about warming it up in the microwave for a brief moment, but I found it to still be slightly warmer than room temperature, and that was good enough for me.

I filled my plate with a couple of healthy pieces of pizza and headed for the couch. I sat the plate down long enough to put the DVD in and press play. I plopped down, stuffed my mouth with the biggest bite I could take, and as the flavors began to tantalize my taste buds, my phone rang once again. Was I never going to get to eat? I looked at the display to see that it was a call from Rick Hayes and so I chewed and swallowed as quickly as I could and answered the call.

"Hewwo..." I mumbled through the half swallowed mouthful.

"Hey Rick! Did I catch you at a bad time?" He asked and I could hear the laughter in his voice.

I took a drink of my Dew, and responded. "No, just had a bite in my mouth, is everything alright?"

"Oh yeah, yeah... I was just trying to get my things together for this weekend and I kept being distracted. Does the name Charles or Charlie mean anything to you?" He asked nonchalantly.

"Yeah, it means a lot. It's a key person in the latest investigation. What does it mean to you?" I couldn't wait to hear his reply.

"I keep seeing this man, in old styled dress clothes, and I'm pretty sure his name is Charles. It feels like he is lost and looking for someone, maybe family." I could tell by his distant sound that he was deep in thought.

"I wish he were at our next investigation at the Owl's. I have a feeling it might be good to have him there." I said to him, hoping he would have a positive reply.

"Once I've connected with a spirit, it makes it easier to make contact again...but I also see him being trapped there at his home, reliving the deaths of his family over and over. For some reason, I think he feels responsible." Rick spoke sincerely, and honestly. It

140

wasn't exactly the answer I wanted, but it wasn't a bad answer either. "I know this is going to sound crazy, but can we get into the Owl's Nest tomorrow night for an hour or two after they close."

"I'll have to ask, but I bet we could, if it's just for a look around, and to get the feel of the building. Hey, does the name Allison mean anything to you?" I asked even though she was still alive, I thought perhaps Charles was also looking for his daughter that hadn't passed yet.

"Maybe... but I was getting the name Amy, or Amelia, which is kinda similar, but Allison doesn't feel right. I feel like either Charles is looking for Amelia, or she is looking for him. Does that make any sense to you?" He explained.

"It might... Amelia was his wife's name. The records we have don't have a date of death on Amelia, which is a conundrum. Allison is the name of the woman you will be visiting with Jenn on Sunday. She is Charles and Amelia's only daughter and the only living family member." I informed Rick of the basics, but he had always asked to keep the facts to a minimum. It helped him to focus on what he sees and feels if he wasn't distracted by what he thought he should be seeing.

"That is all very interesting, and I will keep that in mind when, and if, I reach Charles again." Rick said, though I wasn't encouraged by the way it sounded.

"So far, with this investigation, I'm a bit overwhelmed." I wasn't proud of the fact, but I was always honest to a fault. "There is so much going on there, and so many unanswered questions. I hope there isn't so much going on that it's confusing to you when you join us."

Rick Hayes laughed a genuine, belly laugh, and when he finished, he said, "There is almost always confusion. Don't you worry about a thing, Rick. If we can't figure it out, it isn't meant to be figured out. You just have to believe."

"You're right, and I do believe." My confidence and surety grew as the words left my lips. "Theo Kostaridis is going to be joining us too. He is on my team, and comes out with us on a lot of our investigations. He is also a psychic medium. I figured between the two of you, we'd have to get some answers."

There was a silent pause before rick replied with, "Is he Greek, by chance?"

"Do you know him, or was that your psychic intuition?" I was impressed by his accuracy.

"That name sounds familiar... but mostly, it just sounds Greek." He said with an obvious tone.

"Oh...yeah, I guess it does." I was glad it was a phone conversation because I'm sure my face was beet red from embarrassment.

"Okay buddy, I gotta go and try to get back to preparing for this weekend. If you need anything, send me a message or call me." Rick not only had to pack, but had a lot of mental preparation that he needed to do before a long weekend of seminars and readings.

"Alrighty pal, talk to you later." As I sat my phone down, I realized I had a lot of good people who were ready and willing to help me. I had genuine friends, and that was worth more than anything in the world. I also realized that I had missed a good bit of the movie and my pizza was freezing cold... oh well, I could live with that. I could restart the DVD if I wanted, and I owned a microwave. It wasn't tragic, but it was kind of 'par for the course' that evening, in fact, I was almost afraid to pick up a slice and take a bite because I knew if I did, someone would call. 'Oh Yeah', I thought, 'I have a call to make.

"Hello?" said the voice on the phone.

"Del? It's Rick Kueber." I said.

"Oh, hey Rick. What can I do for you?" He asked politely.

"Funny you should ask...what are the chances that Rick Hayes and I could get into the Owl's Nest tomorrow night after closing, for just an hour or so?" I nervously awaited his answer.

"Sure, that's not a problem at all. Barb and I are here to close up tomorrow night anyway...and since it's a weeknight, we will be closed by eleven." Del's answer was perfect.

"Okay, thanks! Rick and I will show up about a quarter till if that works for you?" I was relieved.

"Yep, that's fine. I'll see you then." Del said and with that we ended our conversation.

I sent a text message to Rick, letting him know that we were 'on' for tomorrow night, and what time to meet me. Within seconds I had a reply that simply said, 'super, I'll see you then'.

I lounged on the couch, propped up with over stuffed pillows and nibbled at my cold dinner, not even half watching a movie that I already knew by heart. Almost in a daze, I began to contemplate the haunting, the mystery, and the enigma that my life had become. The encounters and the investigation of the spirit of Ashley Sue Helmach, our last investigation, had taken us completely by surprise. It had crept up on us and, with only a glimmer of clues, ambushed us. We had walked blindly into a situation we would have never expected, or even dreamed of. This time, we had learned a great deal of the history first. We thought we knew what to expect, and we walked in with our chins up and our hearts, eyes, and minds wide open, and still these spirits caught us completely by surprise. We found ourselves in a mystery that would be much easier to walk away from, with some amazing experiences, than it would be to continue on. Hours and days were spent searching and researching, and digging up the past like a crew of supernatural archeologists, but that was something that was beyond our control. The history simply is. It cannot be altered, nor can it be completely known. The best we could hope for is to uncover enough of it to explain the haunting, and possibly help those misguided souls to find their way.

The field of paranormal research and investigating was a passion that none of us could deny. We spent countless hours driving to and from 'haunted' locations, reviewing photos, video, and audio evidence, and researching histories...not because we thought it was 'fun' or because it was cool, but because we needed to, and we wanted to help people who truly needed it. Sometimes those people no longer had a physical body like we did, but to us, they were people just the same.

143

Some of our friends, family and complete strangers thought we were weird, or eccentric at the least, for staying up all hours of the night and spending all of our spare time immersed in something they did not even believe in. They couldn't figure out why we would sit, or search around, in some dark, dismal abandoned place, and be 'anti-social'. Truth of the matter was that we were very social. What they failed to understand was that sometimes we preferred the company of the dead more than the living. The dead were far less scary and certainly less dangerous... for the most part.

There were four of us on the team, plus Del and Barb helping us investigate and research, and now Rick Hayes was fully committed to the cause...seven in total... lucky number seven. Now if the clues would continue to surface and come together as well, we just might have a shot at solving this one, and helping several others in the process. It was a long shot, but I always enjoyed being the underdog. It made our victories ever so sweet.

***

The next day and evening flew by. Once again I found myself standing in the Owl's parking lot, and waiting on a friend to show up. I had always been accused of having a bit of OCD, which is probably why I arrived everywhere no less than fifteen minutes earlier than planned. My mind wandered as I waited. Where was all of our investigating leading to? Had we been thorough enough with our research? Could we help these spirits? Who was that cute girl who just left the club? ...as I said, my mind wandered.

Just as I watched the attractive woman pulling out of the parking lot in her shiny red convertible, I saw Rick Hayes pulling in. I got out of my car and walked over to greet him.

"Hey pal!" He exclaimed.

"You ready to get a blast of activity?" I asked him bluntly. "It's very blatant activity."

"Let's go check it out." He smiled.

We found our way into the empty bar room, and ordered a couple of cokes. Sitting at a table, we discussed having a public event, and what our options might be. While the staff closed everything down, and punched the time clock on their way out, Barb joined us at the table. Del had followed the crew out to lock up behind them.

"Do you want us to start turning the lights out?" Del asked upon his return.

"No. We just want to talk a walk around and give Rick a chance to pick up on anything, before he and the girls meet up with our elusive Ms. Bettiger." I explained.

"Okay, that works." He said.

"Lead the way." I prompted.

"Alright, how about we tour upstairs first." Barb suggested. Rick agreed, and once upstairs, he began to name the rooms we entered.

"I think this room," He said, speaking of the odd rectangular room, "is where the children slept" Rick stopped close to one of the windows, and stood in silent meditation for a minute. Del, Barb, and I stood by in anxious anticipation. The seconds seemed like hours, as we watched his every move and expression that crossed his face. "There was a bed here." He placed his hand out, palm down, towards the wall. "I get the feeling a child died in his bed here." We listened intently, and half wondered, half knew, how precisely accurate Rick was. "But...I'm also getting the same feeling in a couple of different places. There may have been several children who actually died in this very room."

From the shadows, Ashley Sue kept the spirits of the children at bay. They watched us closely, but mostly, they watched Rick, knowing if anyone were to see them, it would be him. Though our voices were muffled and distorted, Rick's voice came through to them clearly, and to their amazement, he was disturbingly accurate. Ashley pushed them back deeper into the shadows, as we began to wander the upstairs.

In the opposite room, Rick immediately spoke. "This was the gentleman's room, where the father conducted business, and the children weren't allowed in here. Women probably weren't either... No offense, Barb."

We followed him through the room, pausing occasionally to try to pick up on the energy that surrounded us. "We're being watched." Rick said with a smile, and then made a bee-line for the locked door.

"This place is important. You haven't been in it, have you?" He asked.

"No one has been in that room for decades...maybe not since the Owl's bought the place in the twenties." Barb explained. "We don't have a key."

Rick grasped the red-glass doorknob. "It's here. I think the key is here somewhere, maybe in this very room." From the other side of the door with the red-glass knob, the children gasped, and wondered what else this man might know.

We moved our tour to the main level made only one stop. "This room used to be the parlor, and I feel that there were two tragic deaths in here. Mother and child, maybe... I don't want to seem over-dramatic, or make anyone uncomfortable, but it feels like one death was intentional, like a murder, and the other was accidental."

When he spoke, he looked at me with a seriousness in his eyes that filled me with intimidation. Rick saw much more than he admitted to, and I knew it, but he kept the details of his second sight to himself. After a rapid walk through, Rick suggested we move to the lower level. Barb and Del lead the way, and when Rick and I were a few steps behind, he touched my shoulder and leaned in to whisper in my ear.

"There is a lot happening here. We'll talk later." His words left an empty feeling in the pit of my stomach.

Finding our way around the maze that was the downstairs was much simpler with the lights on. Rick took a brief walk around the large 'bingo' room, while the three of us huddled together near the stairway doors. Upon his return, he had a slightly concerned look on his face.

"I sense three males here, but they aren't showing themselves. For whatever reason, they are intentionally hiding from us." He looked about the room, trying to find any clue of who they

146

were, but nothing stood out as an obvious answer, so he remained quiet.

Next we entered the pool room, just to our left, and once again our stay was brief, but I believe Rick was very dead-on in his conclusion that the children liked to play in this room, but weren't there now. So we made our way through the rest of the basement, with very little reaction or emotion expressed by Rick, and no paranormal activity was experienced by the three of us, Del, Barb, and me.

Our last stop had been saved for last intentionally. Immediately upon entering the creepy, web and dust covered boiler room, Rick stopped.

"This is the room." he paused. "There were some unusual things that happened in this room." Once again, he held back the knowledge he was receiving until a more appropriate time and place. "May I sit in the wheelchair?" He asked gesturing to the old wooden and somewhat frail looking, antique.

"If you think it will hold you, go right ahead." Del slightly cringed unaware of the degree of deterioration and rot that the old chair had undergone over its many decades of storage in the dank old boiler room. The truth was that the chair hadn't moved since it had been placed there by the Bettiger family.

We all held our breath as Rick turned his back to the chair, and gripping one of the gritty, dirty arms took a seat. With a collection of pops and creaks, he settled into the chair. After a moment, he closed his eyes, and began to rub the back of his head. Then, leaning forward, covered his face with his hands, and rested his head there. He remained silent and motionless for minutes, before raising his head, and with eyes still closed, he spoke.

"There is an old woman, stern, but not mean, that is here. I believe this was her chair. She is saying something about the children needing their parents... they all need to be saved. It feels like it's some sort of a warning, but I don't think she is the problem...I think she has been trying to protect the children." He rubbed his face like someone waking from an uneasy sleep, and ran his hands through his thick wavy hair. He reached his left arm out towards the pit as if he were warming his hand by a campfire. "Something took place

147

here, maybe not a death, but something that expelled an exuberant amount of emotion, and I feel it is attached to the three males who are not revealing themselves."

Rick leaned back in the chair and took a deep breath. Waiting a moment, as if he anticipated another revelation, he slowly stood. Shaking off the mental cob-webs of many years past, he looked directly at me and I knew that more information had been revealed, and I would know, soon enough, what that was. It had only been about forty-five minutes since we had embarked on our tour of the building, but we were already coming to the end. No 'wrapping up' this time, no gathering of equipment, just a quiet walk back to the main entrance. Rick paused briefly at the door and shook Del's hand, thanking him, and then he took Barb's hand and held it for a moment.

"Your father is proud of you, and says you and Del make a wonderful couple... I hope that means something." He smiled at her.

"It does." Barb squeaked out, unable to hold back the tears, and truthfully having no desire to hold them back. "I never felt like my dad approved of Del and I, and he passed away before we were married. I have always wondered if he looks down from heaven and what he thinks of how I have turned out." The tears streamed down her cheeks and she wiped them as best she could on the sleeve of her shirt.

"He not only looks down with pride, but he comes to visit you sometimes too. I am just the vessel, and I tell what I am asked to tell." He said with sincerity.

Her watery eyes were smiling, and she reached out and gave Rick a warm hug. "Thank you so much."

Rick smiled and we said so-long to the Heerdinks. Walking away, I could hear Barb elated, still talking to Del about how wonderful that message made her feel. I am certain that the validation of her father's pride in her, and his approval were life altering, and a burden that Barb would no longer carry in the back of her mind.

Rick and I parted ways in the parking lot, but before he left me, he said, "I want me, you, Jenn, Katie, and Theo to all get together one evening next week. Bring all the info you have, and I'll bring what I've learned tonight, and we will figure out what happened here. Oh, hey... can you text me Theo's number. I'll reach out to him, if you'll call the ladies."

"Definitely! That sounds like a great idea." I was genuinely pleased with the plan. "Maybe we will order some dinner for delivery or something and brainstorm all evening." I imagined how we might put the data we had into a more compendious time line, but I never thought for one second how difficult that would prove to be, and how much we really didn't know yet. What I did know was that I was beginning to believe that I could get a handle on what was going on here, and that we still had to discern how we were to help these desperate children.

Chapter 13

CIRCLE OF FRIENDS

Once the workday had passed, and my routine of a shower, a microwaved dinner (leftover pizza), and a few minutes to relax and read a few emails was finished, I sent out a group text message to Jenn, Katie and Theo.

'Meet me at Barnes & Noble for coffee at 8pm if you can'

The texts came in like clockwork every few minutes, with confirmation from Katie followed by Jenn. Then shortly after, a message popped in from Theo saying:

'That's perfect, I work at B&N until 8'

151

I had been relaxing in a pair of gym shorts and nothing else, and it was nearly seven o'clock when I decided I had better actually put on some clothes if I was going out in public. Donning some khaki docker shorts, a white polo shirt and some well-worn canvas and cotton, frayed flip-flops, I headed out early to the bookstore to get my dose of caffeine started.

***

Business was slow at the bookstore this evening, which was unusual, but Theo didn't seem to mind having the extra time to straighten the shelves and wander around assisting the few customers that were there. After receiving my text, he began thinking about his spirit guides and the form of wisdom and advice they had given him. The thoughts wandered through his mind as he wandered the store offering help to those who might need it, much in the way his guides offered it to him; sometimes directly, but other times only pointing him to the path, where he needed to search.

Turning the corner of a long row of shelves somewhat secluded in the back area of Barnes & Noble, in the history non-fiction section, he noticed a woman looking around. Theo's first impression was that this was one of the Amish customers who would occasionally come in to pick up a few books to read for entertainment or education. She was dressed in a long sleeved, light blue, cotton dress and had on leather boots that were a woman's, but definitely lacked the style one would find in today's shops. Her hair was up, her skin- pale, and she lacked any makeup, a sure sign of the Amish or Mennonites. She searched, but seemed to pay little attention to the books, or to Theo.

"Can I help you find anything?" and as he spoke the realization came to him. This woman was not a customer, she was a soul, and what she searched for wouldn't be found in any bookstore...unless she had been searching for someone to help her...unless she were searching for Theo.

"Ally-girl, where are you?" The hollow, voice seemed to echo as if it had called out through a long tunnel or across a large empty room from some cold and distant place.

"I will help you if you let me try." Theo thought out loud.

"Charles!" She called out as her posture slumped, turning to face Theo. He could now see the emptiness of her expression and her harrowing, barren, white eyes. "Charles... I am ever so sorry, Charles." Her hand and arm reached out toward Theo from only a few feet away, and then in a blur, she quickly turned, and in a vaporous mist, disappeared, falling backwards through the wooden book filled shelves. The experience stuck in Theo's mind, and he absorbed every detail, stunned for a moment until a real life, flesh and blood customer turned the corner and ran directly into him.

"Oh! I'm so sorry! I wasn't paying attention." exclaimed a young woman with eyes that had an unfathomable depth and beauty which hid a sadness behind them that only she understood. Then, in a moment of realization, the attractive, young woman spoke again. "Oh, hey Theo!"

"It's okay Tabitha. It takes more than that to take me down." Theo smiled at Tabitha, a woman who often came to his seminars and classes. "Well, is there anything I can help you with?"

"Not tonight," she said offering a beautiful smile, "but I'll see you soon, and then we can talk more." The strawberry blonde curls of her hair bounced as she turned back around the corner and took her selection to the register to pay, and then headed home for some good reading.

"Okay, see you soon." He said, retrieving his phone and checked the time. It was nearly 7:30, and he was anticipating the arrival of his friends and teammates. He was also relieved to know that his long work-day would be ending soon. He carried about his business, and for the remainder of the evening, every corner he turned, he turned with caution. Theo found himself unusually startled whenever he rounded a corner and entered an aisle, to find someone searching the shelves. Before he knew it, eight o'clock had rolled around and it was time to clock out.

***

Finding my way into the Starbuck's coffee shop around 7:45, I ordered my usual, a French vanilla cappuccino. I chose a seat and contemplated everything we knew, and how much we still had to learn, or discover. Soon Katie arrived and our conversation began with going over some of the history we already had been given or

153

discovered, and what we still needed to find out in order to put this case to rest. A few minutes into our conversation, Theo joined us. It was just about the same time when Jenn rushed in, assuming she was late.

"Hey guys, sorry I'm the last one here." She said apologetically.

"Somebody had to be." Katie stated the obvious in a humorous way that made us all smile.

"Yeah, I know." Jenn agreed. "But it seems like I'm always the last one to show up."

"No worries, Jenn. You're right on-time, and we haven't really started talking about much yet." I said, and then immediately jumped right into the purpose of having the meeting. "Rick Hayes wanted to meet with us all, but he isn't available. That meeting will have to wait for another day, but I wanted to try to piece together what we could. So... what we know is we have had a very intense first and second investigation. We have some history, and are hoping for a lot more details when Jenn and Rick Hayes meet up with the last living Bettiger in the family line this Sunday. Theo, Katie..." I glanced at the two of them, "You are welcome to join Jenn Sunday, but it is near Indianapolis, so I would expect a full-day trip."

"I'd love to, but I can't." Theo said regretfully. "I have classes scheduled, and I really don't want to cancel with such short notice. If something changes, though... I will definitely call you."

"Well, Sean is working Sunday, but I'm off, so I don't see why I couldn't go. I'd love to go, it'd be like a mini road trip, and I haven't ever met Rick Hayes, so that would be extra cool." Katie was exuberant, and the tone, rhythm, and some of her wording, at times, was directly from her twenty-something vocabulary. She was very intelligent, but her unique style and occasional 'silliness' were refreshing.

"Alright, now that we have that out of the way...ladies, if you don't mind to fill Theo and myself in on what we have as far as the known history, 'to date'." I then turned the invisible microphone over to Jenn, but only because Katie was never one to choose to speak, especially to a crowd of three or more.

154

"Okay kids... here is what it looks like right now." Jenn began.

"Mr. Charles Bettiger bought a large piece of property on 1st avenue which included three large houses and two carriage houses in 1878, a very pricey purchase. He lived in one of the houses alone for several years and had placed his mother in the house next to him, shortly after her husband had passed away...probably of natural causes.

Charles was a shrewd businessman, and along with his legitimate business dealings, he also had alleged ties to some shady real estate deals, and reportedly had ties to a Chicago based crime family. Charles was known by the Evansville locals as the gun and ammunition supplier for all of Chicago and probably St. Louis, though it was mostly hear-say, and no one really had the 'guts' to confront him about it. You know, afraid they'd be swimming with the fishes at the bottom of the Ohio River. The story goes that he ran illegal weapons for nearly eight years before buying the 1st avenue property, and continued to do so for a several more.

Well, after living there for about ten years, his mother, there was an 'accident'. One of the 'business associates' apparently knocked Mrs. Bettiger down the stairs, breaking her back. It was very possibly an accident, because the men remained partners, but Charles' mother never recovered and was confined to a wheelchair for the remainder of her life.

So, what did ole' Chuck do? He 'fell in love' with the young and lovely Amelia Croft. Now whether or not it was really love or not, I don't know, but it seems that the two were soon married, and they moved into the house with his mother, which is now the Owl's Nest. My guess is that Amelia was partly a marriage of convenience. She looked after mom, while Charles conducted his 'business' from one of the neighboring houses that was also part of the property purchase. It is even speculated that there were tunnels running underground connecting the houses, so he could easily move from place to place without suspicion, but... if they exist, no one has found them yet." Jenn paused in her storytelling to take a drink of the Dr. Pepper she had brought in with her.

The topic remained the same, but moved in a less concrete direction, away from the documents, newspaper articles and the photographs. Theo rubbed his forehead, deep in thought and

155

memory, and spoke. "Just to catch you up a little bit, I connected with the spirit of a woman earlier. She was searching for someone or something, and she called out for someone named Charles, Bettiger I'm guessing, saying she was sorry, and she also called out for an 'Alley-girl'. Now, I'm not big on turn of the century terminology, but would an alley-girl be, maybe a little homeless girl, or something more sketchy, like a street walker?"

"I've never heard of the term myself. Alley-cat, yes...Alley-girl, ummm... no." I said in all honesty.

"Maybe it's a nickname." Katie interjected. "...for Allison." It almost sounded like a question the way it was stated, but she had picked up on the correlation before any of the rest of us.

"Theo, Allison Bettiger is apparently the Daughter of Charles and Amelia, and the last living Bettiger that Jenn and Katie are going to see Sunday with Rick Hayes., and I have known a few Allys who were either Allisons, or Allysas" I clued him in.

"Interesting. I wonder if the woman I saw was Amelia." Theo grinned feeling as if he were already deep into the dirt and gritty history of this investigation, yet on a different plane of investigating than the rest of us.

"I don't know, Theo, was it?" Jenn asked with the slightest of sarcasm, as she pulled out the photocopy of the postmortem portrait.

"Yes...." Theo said, almost under his breath, as his eyes grew open wide, studying the picture.

"Well, this is certainly a fascinating situation we have, but Jenn, do you mind to carry on?" I asked. She and Katie shared the tales, filling in and taking over for each other, almost peaking as one person.

"Most definitely!" she said. Jenn was usually very outspoken, energetic, and typically excited when given the opportunity to take the lead in any speaking situation.

"So, a few years passed, as did the turn of the century. 1900." Jenn gestured with her hands like she was setting an invisible box on the table. Jenn, like Theo, talked with her hands emphatically,

I did somewhat, and Katie... well Katie was a bit more reserved. "Then they started popping out babies. In six years, they had four boys, and when the oldest was almost eight, the youngest was barely two, that's when things start to go south."

"Yeah, things get pretty dark for the Bettigers right about then." Katie added quietly, with a solemn look on her face. In retrospect, she may have been thinking of her own child whose birth was still almost seven months away.

"That's very true. In the fall of 1909 the youngest son died with the description of 'sudden trauma' listed on the death certificate. Only a few weeks later Charles' mother passed away from apparently 'natural causes' and I guess it must have been a rough winter, because by spring of 1910, Charles had lost his mother, and all four boys, two to influenza, and one to whooping cough. We don't have much else, other than the largest house on the property was bought by the Order of the Owls in 1922. The home on the corner stayed as a private residence, and still is today. Hopefully Sunday we can find out how, where and when Allison came into the Bettiger family picture."

"I don't want to get too far off subject here, but the night we all left Dr. Covand's house, I had a visit or a vision of Ashley Sue. We were in this beautiful Victorian house, and I was being chased." Theo continued on in detail telling us all about how he found himself hiding under the stairs. "Ash said to me 'Save the children, or help the children, *before it's too late*.' and she sounded almost desperate. I'm sure it was the Owl's Nest stairwell." He emphasized the key words: 'before it's too late', and his description of how she crumbled and disintegrated into thin air, as if she had turned to dust or ash herself was hauntingly visual.

"Yeah... we sorta had the same thing happen during the investigation last weekend." Jenn began.

"Uh huh, we were in the basement of the Owl's Nest and there was fire, and bones, and Ash, well Ashley... telling us the exact same thing, and then it all just sort of went away." Katie spoke with a glazed look in her eyes and a blank expression on her face as if she were somewhere else, deep in the confines of her memories.

We sat around the table passing the documents and photos back and forth, each of us taking our own perspective on what we were seeing and reading. The conversation had no order to it and was filled with broken bits of sentences and questions that were fragmented. All in all, our friendship circled the table filled with clues, and our friendship contained the glue we needed to put these pieces together. All that remained was to gather as many of the missing pieces as we could find and the try to fill in the holes. Once we could do that, we could use our pieced together puzzle to make a plan of how we could 'help the children', before it was too late.

"I think what I'm going to do, is scan all of these documents into the computer, and send them all to Rick Hayes. He can look at them before or after you all visit with Allison Bettiger. That way, if he connects with any of the passed Bettiger family while he's there, maybe he can put together his own ideas of what the whole tale is." and that is exactly what I did. I thought it seemed like a good idea, but only time would tell. We wrapped up the evening, headed our separate ways, and to our diversely separate lives.

***

It was Saturday morning, just after 11am, when Theo's phone rang. He was on his way to work, and answered his phone while he drove down Green River road.

"Hello?" He said, not recognizing the number on the caller I.D.

"Hey, is this Theo?" the voice on the other end was effervescent.

"Yes it is." Theo said, still puzzled, but beginning to recognize the familiar sounding voice.

"Well, hey Theo, it's Rick Hayes. I was wondering if you had time to talk with me next week sometime. I wanted to talk about the spirits at the Owl's Nest."

"Oh, hi Rick. I knew I recognized your voice." Theo chuckled at himself. "Yes I can do that. I am off most mornings and Wednesday evening, so whatever works for you."

"Great! I'll be meeting Jennifer and Katie at Ms. Bettiger's home on Sunday, and I thought we could all try to work as a team to put together a history, and then we can work out what we need to do about the spirits there." Rick suggested to Theo, who was more than willing to work with him.

"That is a fantastic idea. It's so refreshing to find someone who's willing to work together. I don't know if you have had the same experiences that I have, but there are a few people in our field, who are so jealous and unwilling to even be at the same events, that it really disturbs me." Theo said, thinking of the lack of unity amongst some of the others in the paranormal field.

"Yes, I have seen it. We always talk about us all as being a family...sure would be nice if everyone felt that way." Rick agreed with Theo wholeheartedly. "Okay. How about I call you the first of the week, and we will figure out if we need to meet up, or if we can do this over the phone. Talk to you soon."

"Sounds good. Bye." Theo said and as he returned his phone to his pocket, he thought back to when he first met Rick.

His thoughts wandered through the mists of time to many years ago when Barnes & Noble Booksellers had a special guest author, Rick Hayes, in to do a seminar about being a psychic-medium and sign his book about the supernatural. Theo, having grown up with the gift, and having a long history of psychics in his family, decided he should attend. During the seminar, and one of the readings, Rick turned directly to Theo and said, 'What do you see?' as if it were common knowledge that Theo was also a psychic. For Theo, it was a wonderfully gratifying validation of his gifts. He found himself left with a fond memory and a smile as he strolled into work.

Chapter 14

WORLDS APART

The weekdays were filled as usual, and my evenings mostly consisted of going over the researched histories and all of the audio, video and photos we had taken at the Owl's Nest. The weekend was coming quickly and that meant my son was coming to stay with me. To me, those were the greatest moments and memories of my life. The days we spent at the swimming pool were priceless, and our 'movie nights' on our hide-a-bed couch, with popcorn and candies we had picked out, were some of the most enjoyable hours we spent together. It wasn't so much the movie itself, as it was the company we kept, and being able to be our goofy selves unlike at the theater. We could 'boo' and throw popcorn at the screen, laugh out loud, make fun of the movie, or talk through the parts that didn't hold our interest. Plain and simple, it was father and son time, and that was golden to me.

Our weekend was filled with ten year old boy fun. Daniel and I spent the mornings playing spies, and saving the world. The afternoons were warm, and we spent hours playing our own version of volleyball in the pool. We had lunches at McDonalds, and dinner was delivered, just in time for movie nights. For the weekends that we were blessed with the magic of father and son time, my son and I lived in our own world, away from the harshness of reality.

***

While Daniel and I spent hours and days in our land of make believe, somewhere a couple of hundred miles away, in some alternate-reality universe, Jennifer and Katie were nearing the home of Allison Bettiger from the south, and a bit farther out was Rick Hayes, approaching from the north.

Slowly driving up Wright lane, the car was silent save for the sound of tires, slowly grinding against the paved road, while the girls searched house numbers looking for Ms. Bettiger's address. Suddenly Katie pointed, and nearly popped Jenn in the nose.

"There it is!" she said excitedly.

"Whew!" Jenn sighed. "Adrenaline is pumping now!"

"Uh huh, funny how I can meet a ghost I've never met and I'm just fine, but when it's a living person, I get all jittery and nervous." Katie divulged her inner fears to Jenn.

"Well, just breathe chica. She's ninety-something and *she* invited us... just think of her as somebody's grandma." Jenn comforted her team mate. "It'll be fine, I promise."

Katie's face went pale and she blankly looked at Jenn. "Unless she's dead... or dies while we're here." She had

162

imagined the worst possible scenario and was not helping herself calm down one bit.

"Okay... shut up!" Jenn laughed. "Let's go kid."

The two casually walked up to the small front porch of the white sided, single story home and, finding no doorbell, tapped lightly at the storm door. A few moments passed and just as Jenn was about to knock for the second time, the door opened and a woman with short wispy gray hair, and tiny dark eyes said to them, "Hello, can I help you?"

"Are you Ms. Bettiger?" Katie spoke up.

"Yes, I am." The woman seemed almost puzzled, which began to worry the two girls who had just driven three hours to speak to someone who didn't seem to remember they were coming.

"Hello, my name is Katie Collins."

"And I'm Jennifer Kirsch... we spoke on the phone. Do you remember?" the two said in turn.

"Oh yes, I remember... I had a feeling that's who you were, but one can never be too careful these days. Come in, come in." Her voice lightened, and rose in tone as she invited the two in, motioning with her hand.

The girls could see her fingers were bent and disfigured from years of debilitating arthritis, and her skin was thin... frail and wrinkled, like a crumpled piece of white parchment. The old woman hobbled through the front room as Jenn and Katie entered the home. Though it was a warm summer day, she pulled at her quilted housecoat, wrapping tight around her, as if warding off a chill.

"Come in and have a seat." Her lighthearted voice crackled with the wear of her years. "Can I get you something to drink? I have water, tea, milk, or I could put on another pot of coffee, if you'd like."

The two girls looked at each other, not wanting to put the woman out, but not wanting to be rude either. "Tea would be nice." Jenn said.

"I would like some water, if it's not too much trouble." Katie said, and then thought about the poor woman's hands. "Let me help you."

"Thank you dearie, but it's no trouble at all." The kindly old woman waddled back towards the kitchen, and Katie promptly followed, being 'shewed' by Jenn, who mouthed 'go on, it's okay.'

Jenn absorbed her surroundings, and noticed that there was a bible on the coffee table, and a print of the last supper on the wall. There were also, stacks of DVDs sitting on top of a small entertainment center, which held a player and a small, box style TV, not too old, but not one of the newer flat screen types that had become so popular. The old woman reentered the room carrying a cup of tea, followed by Katie, carrying two glasses, not plastic cups, but real glass glasses... something that was a rarity these days, outside of a restaurant.

Jennifer was still standing when they came in with the drinks, but when the old woman took a seat in a comfortable looking chair, the girls followed suit and had a seat on her pale, flower printed couch. The simple, wooden coffee table in front of them had the appearance of something one might find in the Sears and Roebuck's catalog, circa 1967, but was as crisp and clean as if it had just been unpackaged. Her entire house, what the girls had seen of it, appeared much the same, simple, but well taken care of and neat as a pin.

"So you two are wanting to find out about my family history in Indiana, is that right?" Allison Bettiger said with a smile on her care worn face.

"Yes, and actually, we have another friend who will be joining us, hopefully soon. His name is Rick, and I'm sure you will like him. I don't think I have ever seen him without a smile on his face." Jenn said, hoping not to upset her with the news of an unforeseen guest.

164

"Oh, that's right." said Katie, looking at the pink dial of her wrist watch. "He should be here any time."

"That will be just fine, I have nothing but time today." Allison smiled and relaxed a bit in her chair.

"I don't want to get off subject here, and I don't want you to think I'm kooky, but do you believe in ghosts Ms. Bettiger?" Jenn interjected, and caught Katie off guard.

"Please, call me Allison, or Ally." she said, smiling again. "If you mean spirits here among us, then, yes, yes I do. Why, sometimes I even get a visit from my mother at night when I am just about to fall asleep. How can someone believe in heaven and not believe in spirits?"

"That's a very good point Ally." Jenn smiled back at her, and though it felt odd to call such an elderly woman 'Ally', it seemed to make her happy, and that gave Jenn and Katie a warm feeling deep in their hearts.

"The reason Jenn brought that subject up, is because we have experienced some spirits in the building that used to be your home in Evansville, Indiana, and we think they may be some of your relatives... at least some of them." Katie added to the topic.

"Really? That's fascinating." Allison began. "You know I have often..."

'Knock, Knock, Knock' came a rapping at the screen door.

"Would you like me to answer it?" Katie asked, being the one sitting closest to the door.

"Yes, thank you." Allison sighed, not wanting to get up again so soon after getting comfortable.

Katie opened the door to find Rick Hayes, patiently waiting with his permanent smile adorned. They said their greetings, and she invited him in. He said his hello to Jenn, and then his eyes met Allison's. She jumped up, and Rick rushed

165

across the room. The two hugged, as if they had been reunited after years of separation.

"You look wonderful!" He exclaimed. "How is Ms. Ally feeling today?" Rick's smile had almost out grown his face, and his eyes had begun to water.

"Today is a good day. I feel much better than I have in quite some time." She paused awkwardly as a tear broke free, and found its way to her chin. "You have seen my father, haven't you?"

Rick nodded. Allison covered her mouth with her crippled hands and began to cry tears of joy, and they both laughed almost silently, yet uncontrollably.

"Strange as this may seem, I am the happiest right now, than I have been in such a long time...thank you for coming, from the bottom of my heart." said the teary eyed woman to the now teary eyed Rick Hayes.

"The pleasure is all mine. My friend Rick Kueber is the one who had me meet you here, but he is at home spending the weekend with his son." Rick choked the words out through his smile and the tears that left a salty taste in the back of his throat, and were beginning to cause his nose to run. Katie handed him a box of Kleenex tissues from the coffee table. Rick took one before replacing the box. Allison soon took her seat again, and Rick took a seat in the only open chair left in the room.

Jenn and Katie then opened the file folder that had been placed on the table and began to divulge all of the information to her. As the stories went back and forth between the girls and Allison, with the occasional question from Rick, a presence grew in the room. The clouds caused the sunshine to hide, and the front room to dim, but everyone present sensed an uplifting feeling in the air, though Rick was the only one who realized what it actually was.

"Ms. Ally, I don't mean to upset you, but there is something I have to say." Rick started out, and rubbed his hand across his mouth. "There is someone here with us today. Right

166

there in this room, her name is Amelia, and he wants to tell you she is so sorry, and he misses you more that you know."

Allison began to weep openly. "Oh mamma! I miss you too." There was no question, and no hesitation. She knew without a doubt that her mother was with them.

"I just tell people what I am asked to tell, so if this doesn't make any sense, don't 'shoot the messenger' please... I'm supposed to tell you something about 'big red'. Does that mean anything to you?" Rick was puzzled, and could only think of the fizzy red soda pop of the same name.

Allison sat back, deep in thought and memory, and with her hands on her pale, spider-veined cheeks, said "That was my father's nickname ... from his mother, but that was long before I was even born... but oh, I used to hear the stories all of the time from my mother. All of my brothers died before I was born, but the youngest of them, little John, had fiery red hair like our father, and grandmother nicknamed him, 'Little Red', so, it was Big Red, and Little Red...and they were going to take on the world together. I think he must have had a special connection with little John. You have no idea how long it has been since I have even thought about those nick names, let alone how long since anyone spoke of them...probably not since I was a young woman in her twenties. That's when my mother and I parted ways, but now I'm getting ahead of the story. Let me just tell you my family story from the time my father moved to Indiana."

And so, she began. The pens scratched at their notepads and the digital recorders ran on and on, while she recanted her tales, the history of her family, and the tragedies that plagued them. The storytelling was very well done, concise and complete, with hardly a moment of thought put into recollection. Well into her nineties, Allison Bettiger's mind was as sharp as a tack. The memories flowed from her lips like warm, bitter-sweet honey, and at times, so did the tears. Allison's heart ached over the memories of the lost family, even though most of them she had never met... and though a vast amount of the tales took place before she drew her first breath in this world, she had a passion for the story as if it were her own, and the feelings she shared felt more like they were from personal emotion and experience than just some hand-me-down memory.

Allison's tale was so emotion filled and flawless that it brought the three strangers to tears, and gave them an unusual feeling of belonging to the story, which Katie conveyed to Allison.

"That was such an incredible story, and brilliantly told." Katie paused to clear her throat. "You made me feel like the story belonged to me, or like I was somehow a part of it. I am just overwhelmed. Thank you."

Rick Hayes glanced at Allison and then the other two women and smiled his smile of agreeing and knowing, while Jenn chimed in with a perplexed tone. "I agree with you Katie. I feel like I'm almost part of this family... not that it's a bad thing at all, but it is kind of an unusual feeling that I just can't explain."

"Now what is there to 'not understand'? You are here with me, to hear my stories, the first to hear them since I was your age." Allison said, nodding towards Katie. "And you said you would tell my story, right?"

"Most definitely. Our team will find a way to tell your story, and the story of your family. The Rick that we left back in Evansville is pretty good at that." Jenn smiled, knowing she had to contain herself and not call me by her 'term of endearment', E-V-Prick.

"Well, there you go... I tell you my story, you tell Rick the story, you all find a way to tell others the story... it now becomes your story too...there is the connection you said you didn't understand. When you genuinely care, and genuinely want to help someone...that's family. I don't care where you go to church, or *if* you go to church (she said the second part under her breath), what color your skin is, how old or how young... family is caring, and you've all shown me how much you care. I don't really have any blood family left, but I have my visiting nurse Penny, and I have my friend Linda in Evansville, and I have you all... that's all the family I have, and that's all I guess I really

168

need." Allison Bettiger's voice cracked at the end, but she smiled and choked back another tear.

She finished her stories of her life with her mother, and its tragic ending. Her voice seemed uplifting when she spoke about how she met Linda, and eventually sold her house in Evansville to move north, near Indianapolis. She didn't want to leave, but she needed, and wanted to be, closer to her cousins, who eventually passed on too, and their children, some of which had also passed, and those that hadn't died, had moved away. It was a sad tale filled with many heart-broken, lonely years, but also some tales of happiness and even love, though she had never married or had children of her own.

Afternoon began to creep into evening as the four new friends chatted and queried each other about all sorts of different topics. But eventually they had to part ways. Many hugs were given, and phone numbers were exchanged with those who did not have them, just in case there was another question, or someone just wanted to say 'hello'.

"It was wonderful meeting all of you. Tell Linda I am doing fine, and I will try to get down there to see her sometime soon. G'bye now." She said, waving to her new friends, as the storm door closed. The three waved back to her and then the two girls said their good-byes to Rick Hayes, and they all began the long journey home.

Rick had spoken to Theo already about meeting up to discuss the story that we knew, the parts that all of us had experienced, and those things that only Theo and Rick Hayes had seen, or felt. As it turned out, we had worked it out with Barb and Del to all meet up on a Tuesday evening at the Owl's Nest #33, where we would recant all of the stories, the history, piece together the documents and use Rick Hayes' and Theo's intuitiveness to fill in the underlying tale that most of us would never know...and that is precisely what we did.

Chapter 15

OUT OF MANY, ONE

It was a beautiful day, and not terribly hot for this time of year. The sky had been as pale blue as I believe I had ever seen it, like it had been painted by God himself, just for me. There hadn't been a cloud all day, not the big, puffy, cotton ball, cumulus clouds...not even the hints of shredded stratus clouds that were nearly see through, like cotton candy as it is being spun at a carnival. It was a perfect summer day.

A picturesque day had turned into an evening that only Shakespeare himself could describe, and even then the words would be like dribbles on a page compared to the culmination of senses that this evening had bestowed upon the good people of Evansville. I smiled at the beauty of it, and thought to myself, 'what a shame that there are people in this world who won't even notice the awesome gift that nature gives us every day'.

There was something more about this day... something almost magical. I felt better and more positive than I had in quite some time. Soon we would be meeting at the Owl's Nest and working our puzzle. I just hoped we had enough pieces to get a good idea of what the real picture was. I did, however, feel that it would be a good night. How could it not be, after the seemingly flawless day I had experienced? My hopes were high, and my spirit was higher.

7 pm had arrived and so had the five of us. We had straggled in, but in the magnificence of the evening, we had decided to gather outside until everyone was there. I didn't want to leave the day outside, but I knew we had some serious work to do, and some gaps in our time line to fill in. I was intrigued by the thought of what I was about to learn. The stories that Allison had told were like candy on a shelf just out of the reach of a child. I wanted to know, but I had waited, however impatiently, for this night, and it was finally upon us.

"Hey guys, let's head inside. Barb and Del are probably waiting for us." I urged them on, and our group found its way inside, where Barb and Del were attentively standing in the hallway, awaiting our visit. With only a quick "This way, please" from Del, the lucky seven ascended the stairs to the second story...in hopes of putting together a story of a different kind.

Del had brought some comfortable chairs upstairs, the kind that have cushioned backs and seats and stack for easy storage. He had also set up two folding tables for us all to sit around. They were the old style, card tables, with four folding legs and a fake brown wood grained top. It reminded me of my child hood and 'Bunco' nights, when all of my mother's friends would choose a house to meet at to play 'Bunco', a dice game much like Yahtzee. They were fond memories, and it only added to my already positive attitude as we gathered around the two tables snugly. There was a sudden flurry of sounds... notebooks shuffling, papers being sifted through and the sound of scooting chairs on the gritty wooden floor. It was time.

"Okay, Jenn or Katie, do you want to catch Rick, Barb and Del, up to speed on what we have learned so far?" I asked to get things started.

"Sure." began Jenn. "So... Charles Bettiger was a shrewd businessman, but according to the stories we have heard, he had a darker side... Rick," Jenn said, looking at Rick Hayes, "You've heard most of this from Allison herself, so feel free to chime in at any time..." and so the stories rambled on aimlessly at first, like Lego blocks strewn across a floor, but block by block, bit by bit, arranging and rearranging, we began to build, until we had assembled the many pieces into one cohesive story.

***

The story that unfolds before you now, is constructed from those tales we had pieced together. Though it is written as a descriptive narrative, instead of a documentary, I believe it covers the story from everyone's point of view. It took input from the documentation to the imagination and from the natural to the supernatural, to complete this tower of blocks that I call ... the Story of the Children of the Owl's.

***

Life was good for young Charles Bettiger. By his mid-twenties, he was already one of the wealthiest business men in the mid-west. There were speculations that it was an inheritance...old money, and that he hadn't truly earned it. Others thought he must have hit a vast amount of oil on a large piece of land and sold out to an oil company. Many wondered, few knew, very few.

Charles was born and raised in Chicago, and his family was large. The members of his 'family' weren't entirely related, but they were a family none the less. Often labeled as mobsters and gangsters, Charles grew up tough, ruthless, and very keen on the way business in the family was run. When he was only in his teens he began to work for the family, and began running one of their more profitable companies, as well as one of the most profitable smuggling rings in all of Chicago.

Chicago wasn't enough for Charles, he wanted to expand, and he told the head of the family of his plans to move south to where he could take over the mid-west, from St. Louis to Cincinnati, and Chicago to Atlanta. As he laid out his plans to the head of the family, he placed a map of the U.S. on the table, and drew lines from city to city, east to west, north to south. Those lines intersected near a small river port town named Evansville, and with the river port, and its central location it would be perfect for his new venture.

Charles began by starting an expansion of the family's already successful and legitimate business, in Evansville. He had the company set up, and an official office space where he would occasionally work, but this was just to get himself established as a respectable business-man in the area before his shipments of raw supplies began hiding illegal goods. Those goods came mostly in the form of fire-power, guns and ammunition. Business was grand, and just as he had figured, soon he had cornered the black market in the three cities he had tied to Chicago. It was said that he even began to handle all of the guns for Chicago too.

Charles' father had died at an early age, when Charles was just a boy, and he had grown close and protective of his mother, so naturally he had brought her to southern Indiana to live with him. Nearly a year had passed when Charles felt that he was established enough to make a major purchase without raising too many eye brows, and so he began looking for a nice home just outside of the bustling little city, but still close to the port.

The first road that went north from downtown was named, for obvious reasons, First Avenue. It was on this road, only a half of a mile from the business district, and only a block from one of the nicest and newest libraries in the mid-west, Willard library (which would later be known as one of the most haunted libraries in America) that he stumbled across a large piece of land for sale with three grand homes, with lovely and spacious carriage houses behind them. He set up a tour of the homes and without blinking an eye, he bought them right there on the spot. He set his mother up comfortably in one home, with a full time maid, while he lived next door.

174

It was nearly comical to think that these three huge homes were occupied by only two people. But then, his mother's 'accident' had left her unable to even walk without assistance. At that point, Charles moved his mother, and her full time maid, in with him. He also hand- picked a live in nurse to care for his mother, and whether it was love or convenience, no one can be certain, but he and the nurse, Amelia, began to take a liking to each other, and in only fourteen months, the two were married.

With his new bride being a nurse, Charles was able to continue on with his business, and though Amelia knew there was more to his dealings than he let on, she didn't want to know the truth. He had already built a small fortune and a thriving empire with a perfectly legal business. Life was good for the young couple, and soon the children began to come, four boys in only six years, but while life seemed to be going so well, Charles mother was worsening. He had made up his mind. It was time to retire from the illegal gun running and focus on his family. And so it was that when the Chicago boys dropped in to pick up the latest shipment, he broke the news to them, but it was not well received.

***

"I'm out." said Charles Bettiger. "I can no longer do this. I have four young children and an ailing mother, who is in a wheelchair now, that need me to be here for them."

The displeasure on the faces of Mikey and Geno Alanzo and Martin Smitty was obvious to Charles, but he was a well-respected, upstanding business man in the community and intended on standing his ground.

"How you gonna take care of these urchins of yours without workin' with us? You know we can ruin your chances with any business in town, right? All we gotta do, it flex a little muscle, and you won't be able to buy a cup of coffee in this town." Mikey growled at Charles with his thug rhetoric.

"My connections here run much deeper and stronger than the fear of you and your 'mob mentality'. My mind is made up, and there is nothing you can do to change it. If you still want

175

it, just take this last shipment and be done. Otherwise, you can leave my home right now." Charles' stern tone did not strike the correct chord with the tough guys.

Mickey leaned into Martin and muttered something under his breath, and then nodded to Charles and said, " 'Scuse me." and turned to walk out of the door and into the stairwell.

"Where are you going? This is my house!" Charles called out angrily. "Well, why don't you follow him and the three of you can just leave." He was a bit worried about trying to get rid of the black market weapons he had acquired for them. It wasn't just that he needed the money, but he did have a sizable investment in the guns and ammo that he couldn't afford to just lose. The sweat quickly began to bead on his brow. He started to step past Martin and Geno to go after Mikey and see what likely devious act he was up to. Hopefully they weren't planning to take the shipment without paying... or worse, take it and then take Charles for a ride, never to return. Martin pulled back his overcoat to reveal his revolver tucked in its holster under his arm, and gave Charles a sinister grin.

"You ain't goin' nowhere pal!" He spat forth, and his words hit Charles like the rank smell of his uncleansed breath.

"Pop!" the sound of small caliber shots echoed through the house and Charles shot forward screaming "NOOOOOOO!!!" Just as he passed Martin, he heard the thud and felt the simultaneous cracking of the hilt of Martin's revolver on the crown of his skull. Charles heart sank, and his world went black.

When Mickey exited the room, he stumbled upon Donnie, and chased him down the stairs, drawing his gun. Donnie had fled far faster than Mickey, and when he reached the bottom of the stairs, he met two of his brothers. He quickly herded them into the storage cubby under the stairs and silently closed the door. Reaching the bottom of the steps, Mickey had lost the boy. He listened intently for only a moment when he heard the voice of Charles' mother. A sinister thought grew in his demented mind. He peeked around the corner and into the parlor, where he saw the elderly woman sitting with her back to him, in her wheelchair, and reading a book aloud.

Creeping closer, he quietly aimed his derringer, and pulling the trigger, fired a shot that even his insensitive soul regretted. The bullet instantly killed the woman, but it also hit a second target that was most unfortunate.

Charles had no idea how long he had been unconscious when he heard the small voice in his ear. "Daddy... Wake up daddy. Can you hear me? Please wake up." He recognized the sound of his oldest sons voice intermingled with sobs and sniffles.

"Ohhhh... Donnie..." Charles groaned and opened his eyes, struggling to focus on his young son, who was only eight. His head pounded and he could see that the daylight was dimming. "Where is your mother?"

"She's not home yet. That bad man chased me down the stairs. He had a gun, daddy. I was scared, so I ran and hid under the stairs with Brian and Timmy. We stayed hidden for a long time, but you never came for me. When I came out grandmother and baby John were sleeping, sort of like you were." His innocent statement punched deep into the pit of his stomach and he jumped up and his head swam, almost to the point of vomiting.

Charles looked down to the floor where he saw the pool of nearly dried blood where he had been laying and then noticed the rusty dried stain on the shoulder of his crisp white cotton dress shirt. Reaching up, he felt his hair, matted and blood soaked, and a rather nasty goose-egg that had risen where he had been pummeled by the toughie's gun handle. He slowly, painful step by step, made his way to the stairs.

"Your brothers, where are they now?" He asked his son as he began his slow trod down what felt like an endless set of steps.

"Under the steps still, father." He answered sheepishly. "Except for little John... He is lying with Grandmother, in the parlor.

Every step grew more diligent and each passing second, Charles found his strength returning, and with the words of his frightened son burning in his ears, his pace quickened. He exited the stairway door, and headed left, down the hall to the small first floor parlor, where he saw them.

Grief stricken, he called out to his eldest son, "Donnie boy, go and collect your brothers. Take them to your room."

"Yes father." Donnie replied respectfully, though his stomach ached from not having any lunch and it now being nearly dinner time, he said nothing and did as he was told.

Charles stood in the parlor doorway and the warm salty tears began to dampen his cheeks. There directly in front of him was his mother, slumped over to her left side, pale and lifeless, still sitting in the wheelchair she had been confined to. He walked over to where she sat in her deathly silence, the children's book, 'Red Riding Hood', lay on the floor at her feet, appearing to have fallen from her outstretched arm. Closer now, he could clearly make out the single bullet wound to the back of her head...execution style. The vase, on the small end table next to her, had fallen over and shattered, spilling its contents of water and red roses on to the floor next to her.

Kneeling down he felt the cold of the watery blood saturating the fabric of his trousers. Charles gathered up the roses, now soaked and stained with the mix of blood and water. Carefully he placed them and the book in her lap. "Red Riding Hood." He almost smiled. "Red was always your favorite color, mum." He rubbed his eyes, leaned forward and kissed his mother's icy, pale gray forehead.

Turning as he began to stand a second horror overtook him. Though he knew it in depths of his heart, nothing could have prepared him to see little John lying silent as the dead, still in his night shirt, the pool of coppery crimson surrounding him.

"Oh no, dear God, please no!" The words gurgled in his throat through the snotty, tear-filled breaths, and seemed stuttered, with their sounds emerging with each short gasp of air. Charles' heart was breaking to degree of being irreparable.

He crawled over and scooped up the limp, cold, tiny body of his youngest child, little John, the ginger haired little man, who was barely a toddler. The cruel wetness of his nightshirt penetrated the sleeves and midriff of Charles' own shirt as he held his son tight against him kissing the soft, fine hair of his head and pressing his cheek to the cool expressionless face in his arms, rocking him instinctively as he wept.

"Oh little Red" he said, calling him by the nickname his mother had given her youngest grandchild because of his dark red hair. "Red, I am so sorry son... this is entirely my fault." His words were stuttered by his sobs and barely understandable, but there was no one there to hear him. With one single shot, one bullet, a single execution to convey the hierarchy of the mob family, two had died. The man had stepped up behind Charles' mother, and as she looked down, reading the book to little john, he pulled the trigger. The bullet had passed straight through her from the back of her head and exited her eye, but then quite by accident, the bullet's path met with the toddler who sat on the floor playing with his toy animals.

His wife returned home from her visit with her parents later that evening to find Charles and his good friend and second cousin, Thomas, the local constable, in a deep discussion. She immediately saw the blood stains on his shirt and the redness that still swelled his eyes. Without even having a chance to ask for the truth, she fainted and collapsed to the floor. When she did regain consciousness, she felt as if she too would die, of a broken heart. She bawled endlessly, as she held her child, begging him not to leave her, and cursing God and her husband for this tragic slaughtering. For days and weeks after that fateful night, Amelia carried her grief outward for everyone to see, and also carried little John's tiny blue knitted blanket, either in her arms or over her shoulder. She could not let him go: her heart would not allow her to.

Charles had made the decision to bury his son with a closed casket on the following Tuesday, but he thought it best to wait a few weeks to lay his mother to rest. He thought that with her already failing health and the loss of a grandchild, that most people would just assume it to be natural. He would have to have a closed casket for her as well, especially if she were going to be buried weeks after her demise. Though it seemed

179

terribly morbid, Charles moved his mother's wheelchair into the boiler room, where no one ever went, and placed her in it. He laid the blood stained roses in her lap, and placed her hands across them.

In the days and weeks that followed, the constable and the governing bodies of the county found ways to proceed with the funerals and documentation to make the entire situation appear as if it had been accidental, and not murder. This did not ease the stress or tension between Charles and Amelia. The two hardly spoke, rarely ate, and when they did, it was out of necessity and because of the three remaining children.

Each day, the distance grew between them, and each day Thomas would make his rounds to check on the family and to ask if the men had returned or threatened them again in any way, occasionally staying for hours to visit and play with the children.

Young Donnie had developed a nasty cough, and had become confined to his bed mostly, and when the constable would stop by, he would read a few pages from the Red Riding Hood book to the lad. One afternoon when Thomas was over reading, there came a loud knock at the front door. He sat the book down and rushed into the foyer drawing his sidearm and looking to Charles wide eyed and nervous, who drew his own weapon, and holding it hidden behind the door, proceeded to open it ever so slightly.

"TELEGRAM! for a Mister Charles Bettiger." The man in the uniform called out.

"Yes, I'm Charles." He replied with a sigh of relief.

"Sign here please, sir."

With the scratch of a pencil, he signed for the telegram, snatched it from the young man, and with a short "Thank you." closed the door abruptly. Thomas dropped his pistol to his side, wiped his hand across his brow, and looked to Charles.

"Gee whiz. That about gave me a heart attack." but as he spoke he could see the color leaving Charles' face. "What is it?" he asked with concern.

180

"It's from the Boss, Martin's Boss." He proceeded to rip open the telegram and read it out loud to Thomas.

Mr. C. Bettiger,

Allow me to convey my deepest condolences on the passing of your mother and young child. We have every intention of continuing to do business with you. Now that you no longer have to care for your ailing mother, and you have one less child, we hope you will reconsider your choice to end our business relationship. If you choose not to, I hope that should anything happen to the rest of your family in the near future, you will, once again, reconsider our business proposal.

Regrets, Antony Capelletti

"Aw, geez. Looks like I'm gonna tell Betty not to expect me home for a while, and I'll tell the boys at the precinct that I'm on a special assignment. I'll stay here with you and the family for a while just in case those thugs show back up."

"Thank you Thomas. My family..." he choked the words out, knowing the word family now included two less souls, "appreciate everything you have done, and continue to do." And with that Charles reached out to his cousin, and embraced him with a truly heartfelt hug.

Days passed without incident and it began to feel normal for Thomas to be there. He not only stayed throughout the day, but he would run the errands for them, and even sleep there. When almost a week had passed,

"Looks like it's a man's day here, just you, me and the boys." Charles said, patting Thomas on the shoulder.

181

The two men made their way to the upstairs business room where Charles poured them both a stout brandy and they began to recant the days of their youth, remembering the typical things cousins do, hunting, fishing, teasing the girls, and skipping school to have childhood adventures, pretending to be civil war soldiers, and fighting over who would be the Yankee and who would be the Confederate. The conversation ran and the two men laughed at the innocence of their youth that was now long gone.

A sudden noise came from downstairs. Someone had entered the home unannounced. Charles dropped his brandy glass and it hit the floor hard with a loud crack. Thomas and he rushed to the doorway, and through it only to find Martin, Mikey and Geno already coming up the steps, with pistols drawn. Thomas dove across the second floor staircase landing and drew his pistol, firing at the men through the banister spindles. Charles darted across the hallway and into the room where his boys played.

"RUN! HIDE!" he shouted at them and the frightened children fled to the back of the room, and the secret closet passage to their father's business room. Reentering the stairwell, with pistol drawn and a vengeance he did not even realize he harbored, Charles squeezed the trigger repeatedly, and with purpose. Thomas and Charles, and the three men on the stairs exchanged a flurry of dozens of gunshots. In mere seconds it ended. All three cronies lay in a motionless, tangled heap at the bottom of the stairs.

Catching his breath, Charles turned to Thomas to congratulate him. "Dear God man! You've been hit!" He cried out.

"What? I have?" Thomas asked and frantically looked himself over for a mortal wound. "Oh, this?" he calmly said as one hand pulled at the opposite upper arm to reveal a tear in his shirt and fresh blood darkening his blue constable uniform. "This is just a scratch. I don't even think I need to get sewn up." He smiled back at Charles, "We showed those Confederate bastards, didn't we?" He jested about the childhood tales.

182

"I suppose we did, my brother in arms." Charles smiled back.

Their smiles turned to grimaces as they forged a morose plan to 'get rid' of the slain thugs. The ideas and random bits of thought spewed out between them attempting to come up with a fool proof way to dispose of three bloody, bullet hole filled corpses without raising the suspicion of the neighbors.

"Well, whatever we do, we have to get 'em off this landing and out of your foyer. Last thing we need is for somebody to knock on the door right now, what with a collection of dead goons in your entryway and all." Thomas' voice had a tinge of worry, and Charles knew he was absolutely correct.

"You make a strong point Tom. Let's drag them down to the cellar, and then we can clean up the mess here. That will buy us some time, maybe."

"I hope so. Maybe we can sneak them out in the middle of the night, if we're careful. We just have to figure out what to do with them once we get 'em out. It's a long way to the river from here." Charles was growing more concerned by the minute.

The two men made short work of dragging the three cadavers to the tiny and dank basement of the oversized house. Once the bodies were lumped into a grotesque pile of lifeless flesh, the two returned upstairs to the scene of the shoot-out.

"You go tend to your little ones, and I'll start mopping up all of this blood and the broken picture glass. We can fix the frame, and get your walls patched another time." Thomas offered to Charles.

"Thank you, Tom. I should check on the boys and make sure they're alright." Charles said, and then scurried up the steps and into the large room.

He found the boys still hiding in the secret passage between the closet, and their fathers 'business room'. Though quietly sniffling back tears, the boys were fine. When Charles opened the door, the three youngsters rushed him, grabbing, and hugging his legs and waist, as if they had feared they might never see their father alive again. After spending some time with his boys, Charles returned to the downstairs where Thomas had just finished cleaning up. Charles thanked him many times over, as they found their way to the basement of the home and bodies that awaited them.

"Into the boiler, I say." Thomas said grimly.

"Probably best..." Charles agreed. "No evidence and no risk... much better than trying to drag them out in the middle of the night, and toss them in the river."

So, Charles chucked a few more shovelfuls coal into the boiler, and Tom pumped the billow, to fuel the red hot coals. Then came the task of burning the cadavers. They carried the first one in, and tossed him through the massive door. When they pitched the first body, it didn't fully go in. The two men found themselves prodding and pushing with the shovel and fire irons to stuff the man fully into the chamber so they could fully close the door. The second and third bodies were even more challenging with the boiler already having extra coal and a full grown man inside, but eventually they managed to stuff all three corpses into the fire and the putrid smell of burning flesh filled the air.

"I must thank you yet again Thomas." He said as the two men ascended the stairs to the main living level of the house.

"We are family, and that's what family does, we look out for each other." The solemn voice of Thomas was beginning to show the strain and weariness that he had been feeling since this whole ordeal had begun. There was a feeling of relief, and Charles thought for a moment that life might return to normal, but like so often, feelings can be misleading, and even betray us.

***

Time passed slowly, and Donnie's condition worsened. The local doctor made regular house calls, but his diagnosis was not promising. Charles and Amelia Bettiger watched as their oldest son, only eight, became shallow and hollow. Less than

184

two months after the brutal slaying of his grandmother and youngest brother, young Donnie left this physical world behind, passing in his sleep one cold winter night.

Though he had left the physical world, he did not go far. When his physical body ceased to function, and he drew his last breath, Donnie felt renewed, and amazingly, unexpectedly, alive. He stood beside his shell of a body looking on as his parents wept. The light through the window grew ever brighter and called to Donnie.

'Come, be one with us, become a part of the eternal universe, where you can be anything and everything you can imagine and things you are not yet capable of imagining'

They were not words, but feelings with compassion and purpose, and he longed to go to the eternal light, but there was an otherworldly feeling that caused him to turn from the light. Looking away from its beckoning warmth, Donnie felt the tug of little hands at his side, and looking down he saw the spirit of little John pleading silently with him.

'Don't go bubby...don't go. I don't want to be alone. I want to stay here with Gramma and momma and daddy. Momma begged me not to go, and I promised her I wouldn't.' Looking beyond little John, Donnie saw the smiling face of his grandmother still sitting in her wheelchair, holding a bouquet of disorderly and withering roses that she would never let go of.

Donnie had a hard decision to make, though he did not understand completely the consequence of his actions. He hugged his little brother tightly and turned back to the beautiful white light of the window just as it faded along with the voice of the universe calling him, and so, Donnie and little John stayed behind with their family, and grandmother.

Over the next year, Charles felt his life unraveling like the sleeve of an overly worn sweater, unnoticeable at first, but eventually to the point of being unwanted and pointless. Before the winter's end, his remaining two boys died naturally as well... Brian at the age of six from pneumonia, and Timmy at four from scarlet fever.

Only months after the death of their last son, the couple, now not quite as young, tried to rekindle their romance, and love for each other, but it was not the same, too much had happened and they had both changed. Amelia had met Charles at the bottom of the stairwell, and unable to understand her confused feelings, had made a decision.

"I am going up to the children's room to think, and to read. I have to gather my thoughts, Charles... but I think I may have to go away for a while until I can clear my head." She couldn't even bring herself to look him in the eye and she had found herself unable to cope with living day to day next to the man whose 'business' choices had caused the beginning of the end of her happiness.

It was on that fateful day when Amelia was upstairs reading, that Charles had come up to join her, and plead with her not to go. They had discussed all of the problems they had, and the wonderful memories too, and when the topic of family came up, it became awkwardly silent. They stood facing one another trying to find the words to begin again, when the sound of an opening and closing door distracted them from their misery.

Charles had reached the doorway to the steps, when a stout man in a gray suit pushed him forcefully back into the room. Amelia was terrified, and hid behind her husband.

"It's been a year now, Chucky..." He snidely said. "The boss says you ought to be ready to do some business by now."

"I have already said it too many times. I am through, and you aren't going to change my mind." Charles puffed up his chest, and stepped nose to nose with the man.

"Is that a fact?" He snorted. The two men were about to come to blows. Their breathing was heavy and noisy, hearts raced, and nostrils flared, but the man was not going to be intimidated. He quickly drew a pistol from under his jacket turning it swiftly upward. Charles could feel the cold steel of the barrel pressing uncomfortably hard against the soft spot below his jaw, where the neck and chin meet.

"Now what?" He snarled. "You gonna get back in the business or you gonna end up as a mess? You gonna make this dame to wipe your brains off the walls?"

Amelia was ravaged with emotions. Fear and anger and dismay overtook her, and she darted out from behind her husband and tried the separate the two men. This only infuriated the thug, and he with all of the force he could muster, he shoved Amelia hard, away from them. Then the world changed. The glass shattered, Amelia screamed, and her body plummeted from the second story window to the earth below. In that moment of passionate fury and adrenaline, Charles grabbed the gun and twisting it hard, pointed it at the man and fired two rounds into his chest, and then standing over him, he pulled the tiger once again, hitting the man in the eye, an act of vengeance for his mother's death.

People were beginning to gather around Amelia's body, as it lay there unnaturally contorted, and lifeless. Thomas was passing by when he saw the commotion and rushed into the house. He found Charles upstairs, gun in hand, still standing over the body.

"Oh, for the love of God, man! A fine mess you're in now. No easy way out of this one." Thomas rubbed his forehead as he spoke.

"Should we... you know...take him to the boiler room?" Charles voice was shaky as were his hands.

"Heavens no!" Thomas exclaimed. "You are going to tell everyone that this man broke in to your home, pulled a gun on you, and in the midst of a scuffle, he pushed Amelia out of the window. You were so distraught, that you took his gun from him and shot him. A crime of passion" It was a good plan, he thought.

"That is almost exactly what happened." Charles explained.

Amelia was rushed to the hospital as a protocol, and the authorities questioned Charles. He was taken to the county jail that night, and went before the judge the very next day. After his time in court and a long evaluation, Charles was told he had two days to get his affairs in order before he was to be taken to the state hospital when he would go through psychiatric treatment until which time they deemed him safe to rejoin society.

Charles kept his mental state clear for a while, and was becoming well respected. He thought, surely, he soon would be released. Becoming too comfortable with some of the staff, he began to tell them that the ghosts of his mother and his children haunted his home, and he would often times hear them calling out to him. The attending psychiatrists found his stories fascinating and thought perhaps a more invasive therapy might be what he needed. Experimental, mind altering drugs along with the power of suggestion were used for weeks, but he refused to deny the ghosts were real. It came to the point of shock therapy treatment, and soon after they began, Charles knew he needed to just play along with their game, and say nothing more about being haunted by his family, in fear that a lobotomy could be their next course of action. He had expressed such vivid tales of the spiritual visitation, that Charles was eventually committed to the Indiana state hospital, where he lived out the rest of his life. Though he may not have actually been insane when he was committed, he certainly was after several years of confinement. He would frequently cry out, asking to go home to his mother and children, which would only reaffirm the staff and doctors of his mental instability.

***

Amelia had been rushed to the hospital and the doctor on staff that day found her to be miraculously alive. She had broken both legs, cracked several ribs, dislocated her shoulder, busted her head open, and broken her jaw. There was little chance of her survival, but the doctor worked feverishly trying to mend her limp and broken body. She lay in stitches, casts and bandages, in a near comatose state for over a week. Slowly she began to use some of her motor skills, first blinking her eyes, moving fingers, and so on. Her stay in the hospital was nearly eight weeks.

When she was finally released from the hospital, she was torn between moving on or staying in the home that had so many horrible memories. She had decided to stay in the home next door, and sell the house that held so many dreaded memories and nightmares.

After settling in, Amelia began to find herself growing ill. She would feel fine most of the day, but every morning she became nauseous, and so she requested the doctor to make a house call. When he finished his examination and his tests, he picked up his black leather bag to leave and turned to Amelia with a smile, and said, "My dear, you are a miracle. Not only did you survive that horrible fall, but I firmly believe your baby did too." And with that he tipped his hat and exited her home. "I will be back to check on you in a few weeks."

Amelia was in shock. She had left her husband, most everyone thought she was dead, and after losing all four of her children, she was suddenly expecting another. She lived next door to the old family home for many years, in the home that was originally set up to be Charles' mother's home. The old homestead was put up for sale, and the Board of Directors for the local social club, The Order of the Owls-Nest #30, purchased the property from her. The deal was struck, and though the club didn't occupy the building for nearly five years, it was as if a weight had been lifted, when the deed was finally handed over.

She decided to keep a low profile, and did so for most of her life, and though she did not change her name, it seemed that no one really knew her or her past, which she found liberating. She began to make new friends, and to go to the church that sat just across the street from her home. It was almost as if she had been given a chance to be who she wanted to be, and not be the controlled housewife of a businessman with beyond questionable associates.

The time came, and Amelia gave birth to a beautiful baby girl, which she named Allison. The two of them lived and loved happily together for many years. When she became an adult, Allison began to question her mother relentlessly about her father, and her mother's life before Allison was born. She was nearly twenty-eight years old, and her mother was nearly sixty, when Amelia finally felt it was time to tell of their family's dark past.

Allison listened intently to every syllable of every word, hanging on at the end of each sentence for the next one to begin. When it came to the end of the story where Amelia had been pushed out of the window, and Charles had been placed in the state hospital psychiatric ward, Allison grew angry and felt as if her mother had cheated her all of these years. She could have at least met the man who was her father. She had grown up with the vague story that he died in an industrial accident that her mother refused to talk about. The anger began to overtake Allison, more strongly with each passing day, until she couldn't hold it in any longer.

"I can't live here any longer. I hate you for keeping my father a secret from me for all of these years. Crazy or not, I had the right to meet him, to see him, to get to know him. I hope you have a happy life mother." She spat out the words like venomous poison, and grabbing her things, she made her way across town with only a suitcase filled with clothes and a few of her favorite books and memories.

Allison had a sizable bank account and lived modestly, but without worry for many years, and each year when the holidays would come around, both Amelia and Allison would spend them alone, often crying. Allison never married, and her mother never married again. It wasn't until Allison learned of her mother's passing, that she truly felt deep regret for her actions, and for the life they did not share. It was also then, that Allison inherited the Bettiger Property on First Avenue.

Allison lived her life out in that beautiful home next door to the Owl's Nest until one day she felt she could no longer be this lonely. She put the property up for sale, and soon had a few prospective buyers. A young and prosperous couple named Fred and Linda Sammet, bought the property. Linda Sammet became close friends with the now elderly Allison, and when she eventually moved north, near Indianapolis, Linda helped her pack up, and even unpack and arrange her new home. The distance did not hinder their friendship, though. Both women would frequently call, or send cards and letters to each other. As the years passed, the time between phone calls and letters grew longer, until it was only on holidays, and sometimes, not even then.

***

Though the story was told from several different people, and from several points of view, that was the 'gist of it'.

"...and that pretty much brings us up to date." Katie said when we had reached the end of the puzzle.

"Wow..." I paused. "That's a lot to absorb."

"Yes it is." Theo agreed.

"It's time to formulate a plan." I said. "I'm just not sure where to start."

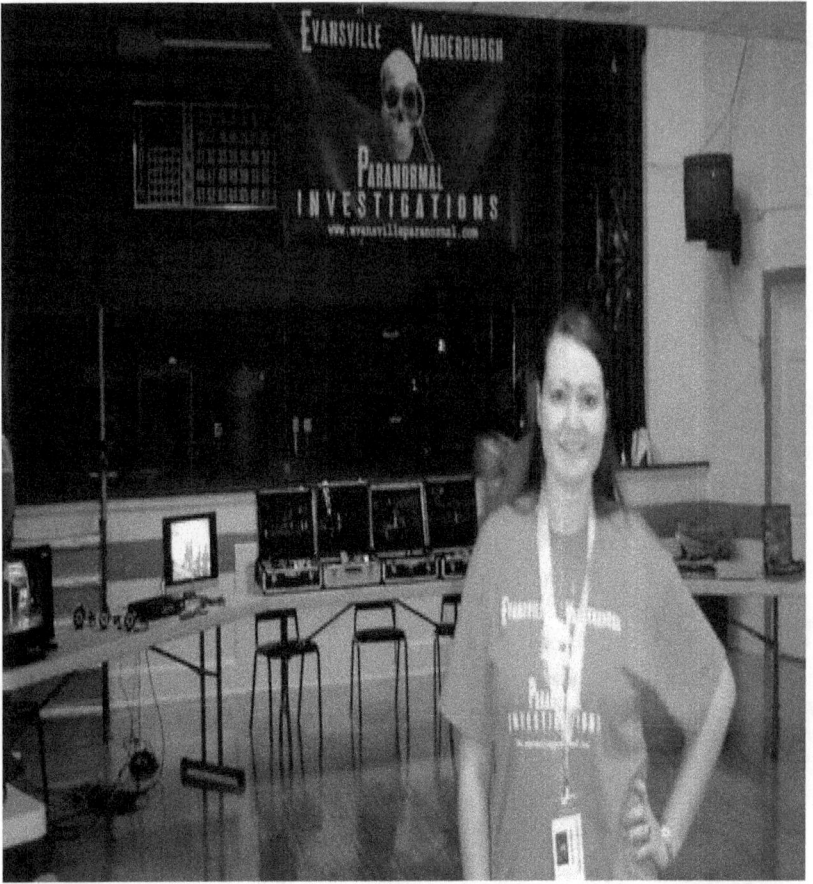

Chapter 16

An Introduction to the Past

We had souls to aid, and people's concerns and fears to ease. It was only a matter of deciding the most effective way to accomplish both in as little time as possible...not because we were in a hurry to move on to the next case, but because we had been warned, for a lack of a better term, that we needed to do this 'before it was too late', which gave us an uncomfortable sense of urgency. As we sat there taking in all that we had just been enlightened of, we began to formulate the steps we might take.

"I think it seems obvious to me, that the spirits of the children are hiding for a reason. Maybe they need to feel protected." Katie said.

"Agreed... and perhaps they feel abandoned by the very people who were supposed to protect them." Jenn added.

"I think it might be good to let them know that they aren't alone." Rick Hayes began to scheme. "That we not only know they are here, but that they are accepted and it's okay that we share the same space."

I thought for a brief moment. "I might have an idea worth thinking about. There was talk about doing a fund raiser for the Owl's Nest." I raised my eyebrows and looked around at everyone. "What about doing a ghost tour here... open to the public...and maybe a ghost hunt afterwards? We could let the spirits see that people not only know they are here, but that they want to experience their presence."

"That's a good idea. We can even tell their story to the people who come." Theo added to our thoughts. "We can make it very open and honest about the children being here, and let them know that they don't need to be afraid."

"This is all well and good, but don't you think we need to try to separate them from these malevolent entities, reunite them with their parents, or something? We were told to help them before it was too late, right?" Katie had a very valid point. "It might be a help to them to give them acknowledgment, and acceptance, but I don't think that's all we need to do. It just feels like we are missing something." Katie half mumbled to us, half to herself, but we all heard her, and we all knew she was right. Something felt off...missing... but it was a good place to start.

"I also believe that we need to somehow reunite the family members who have passed...the children need their parents." Theo recalled. "That was the focus of the message I received from my spirit guides. It is most definitely important."

"Okay. Let me see how quick we can set it up, and we will try to keep brainstorming on what else we can do." I said, still unsure of what else we *could* do, but I knew there must be more.

**

After parting ways, I made a call to the Heerdinks. I met them and the officers of the Owl's, to discuss the public event. We were just in time to get the announcement in the next 'HOOTS' newsletter before it went out later that week. It was short notice, but we made our plan to host the event in only three weeks. It was more than enough time for the team and I to prepare, almost too much time. I must admit that I was nervous since we had already been vaguely, and repeatedly, warned that our time was limited.

I confirmed the date with everyone, and it even though it was three weeks away, it conflicted with Rick Hayes' schedule. The plan had already been set, and instead of trying to alter it, it was decided to follow though. After a long discussion with Rick, and the Heerdinks, we thought we might need to all meet up at the Owl's Nest after the public event for another investigation to see if we had been successful on any level.

***

We went about our lives as if the time constraints didn't matter, but there was an overwhelming feeling that it mattered a great deal. It had been nearly two weeks since our meeting, and it felt like the event date would never arrive. We had the occasional phone call or text message between one of the team members and me, but an oppressive feeling constantly shadowed us. There was a sadness that I could feel in the tone of the voices and even in the content of the texts. It was as if the team and I were slipping into some sort of depression.

It was on a night almost a week before the event, when a cleansing rain came to our small town. The evening wore on with ever darkening skies, and steady showers that soaked the world around us. The random, low rolling thunder, in the distance, filled me with romantic thoughts, and I wished, with every grain of passion in my soul, that I had someone special to share it with...but I didn't. I loved a good storm, even though there were terrifying memories that I associated with them. Not having someone to hold, while I beheld nature's fury, filled my heart with gloom and sadness. Still, I couldn't help but love the tranquility and isolation that it brought to me.

My enthusiasm for atmospheric phenomenon was apparently not shared by everyone. Katie sat alone in her room watching the ending of her favorite movie, wishing that Sean hadn't had to work that night. When the film had ended, and she (feeling quite sappy) wiped the tears from her eyes, she turned out the lights. Well into the summer, she kept the air conditioning turned low. It made for good sleeping, and she found it nice to feel the coolness on her face while the rest of her was hidden, wrapped up and snuggling with her white, down comforter.

She lay there, draped in the warmth of her blanket, and listened to the rain tapping gently at her window pane. It was very soothing to her, but only until she began to hear the grumbling voice of the thunder. Though it wasn't close, it filled her with discomfort. The thunder and occasional lightning were separated by minutes, and Katie found herself beginning to doze in and out of consciousness. Deep in her sub-conscious, dreaming had begun, if only a few seconds at a time. The images and flashes of her alter-reality were vague at best, and like most dreams, made no sense to her. She found herself walking on a lake shore, feeling the grass under her bare feet, and looking, searching, for someone or something. Then the sound of raindrops becoming a deluge disrupted her sleep for only a brief a waking moment.

Katie found herself standing in the cool night breeze. It seemed as if she were in some type of an open tower, overlooking the darkened town. Looking down at her feet, she saw an open stairway leading down and felt uncontrollably compelled to descend. When she reached the bottom, only a dozen steep steps, she found herself in a cramped space. To her left was a wall, and to the right, the area opened up, only slightly. Stepping off of the stairs, she found herself facing a door...a door with a red glass knob. Her hand reached out, and just as her fingers touched the chilled glass, the sound of scuffling startled her from behind. She spun abruptly. From a small space beneath the steps, she heard the sound once again, hidden in the black shadows.

'Is someone there?' she spoke in her dream, and was terrified that a response may follow her question.

'Save the children, before it's too late.' came the persuasive voice of Ashley Sue. Her words brought a light to the hidden space under the stairs, and revealed the little burning girl, and four smaller children who were huddled, frightened in the corner. There was a light that came from everywhere, and nowhere, yet it refused to reveal the details of these hidden children.

'How, Ashley? How do I save them?' Katie cried out in distress and confusion.

'Home isn't home...not anymore.' Ashley's words trailed off along with her presence.

The children who had been hiding in the corner stood up, and the smallest of them, only a toddler, held out a small stuffed animal in his hand, as if it were an offering to Katie. Her hand stretched out to take to small toy elephant from the tot. Suddenly, all four of the children rushed to her with bluish faces, and dark circles surrounding solid ebony eyes. Their mouths silently screamed to her. Katie turned with a jump and grasping the red knob in her hand, found herself locked in with the ghastly children. She turned back around to face them, and slammed her back against the door. The children, all boys, began to surround her, reaching up with cold and clammy outstretched hands. Katie only wanted to escape, but it seemed impossible and she found herself giving in and giving up. Covering her face with her hands, she sank down with her back sliding against the door until her butt hit the floor. There was an eerie combination of a calming peace and dread. Her hands slowly slid down her face exposing her eyes to the see the faces of four lost and frightened boys, no longer the horrific ghouls that had her petrified. In a rush of screams and dust, and flying debris, the floor and walls gave way around and beneath her. Katie fell.

With a noisy gasp, and a reflexive jerk, Katie hit the bedroom floor and awoke. Sitting up, her right hand went, instinctively, to her tummy where her unborn child lay hidden inside her. She placed her opposite hand on her forehead where she felt the cold sweat that had beaded up. Deep breaths slowed, and her racing heart eased over time. She crawled back into bed, and though she feared the possibility of a reoccurring dream, eventually she found sleep again.

***

The day had finally arrived and Jenn, Katie and I met up at my apartment. We discussed Katie's dreams while we checked over our equipment's batteries and calibrations. We loaded up our banners and the numerous cases of equipment into the trunks of our cars, and anxiously waited for ten o'clock.

197

At nine-fifteen we showed up on the doorstep of the Owl's Nest. Our nerves were high, but the butterflies we felt were good. This was the first public event that we were hosting, and we hoped that not only would there be a good crowd, but that things would go smoothly. The last thing we needed was for someone to have a terrifying experience that caused them to run through the darkness and hurt themselves. Gathering my composure, I opened the door for the two ladies on my team. The bar room was crowded and the music played loudly. It felt as if every eye in the room suddenly stopped to stare at us as we entered. Maybe it was that we were strangers to most of them, or it may have been that we were all wearing our EVP shirts with the trademark skull and spyglass. Whatever the reason, we couldn't help but feel a bit uncomfortable, and slightly unwelcome.

The large entrance to the dance hall was closed off by a folding partition, from floor to ceiling. The girls and I stood frozen for a moment, wondering if we had somehow ended up in some twisted twilight zone episode, when the familiar face of Barb Heerdink appeared from the back hallway between the kitchen and the dance hall. There was an almost humorous and collective sigh of relief. From across the noisy and crowded room, she motioned us over to her, which we quickly obliged. We followed as she turned away and walked through a door that led us all into a much quieter, brighter, and emptier dance hall.

"Well, this is it guys. What do you think?" Barb said, as Del walked over to join us.

"Looks great." I said honestly. There were tables and chairs set up at the front of the room, just in front of the stage, facing the rear, and a dozen or more rows of chairs facing the front of the hall.

"Is it okay if we rearrange a few things?" Jenn asked politely.

"Of course." Del answered. "We just set this up, and thought it might work for you."

"Do you have any extra tables we could use?" asked Jenn.

"Sure, how many do you need?" Barb replied to Jenn's question, but looked at Del, as if letting him know it was his task to accommodate our needs.

"I think just a couple more." Jenn looked over to Katie and I. "We should set one up by the door where people come in, to take donations, and one over there," she pointed to the opposite side of the room, just past where the front tables had already been set up, "where Theo can set up to give readings during the 'ghost tours'. What do you think?"

"Yep, that should work." Katie smiled, knowing that things were coming together, and for some reason, she had a very good feeling about the night.

"Two tables? That's easy enough!" Del said, and then disappeared through a door in the rear of the room.

Barb pointed us to an exit door on the right side of the room, near the back wall. "You can bring all of your 'stuff' in through that door, just don't let it close, or you'll be locked out."

We proceeded to the parking lot, and after numerous trips we had unloaded everything and brought it in to the dance hall. Katie and Jenn began covering the tables with our hunter green table cloths, and while Jenn ran extension cords to plug in the laptops and monitor, Katie began to display our team t-shirts and photos. Jenn set up a slide show of photos on the monitor, and fired up the laptop to play the audio recordings of the phantom voices we had captured on other investigations. Del had already brought the first table and now returned with the second. Barb had directed me to a ladder, which I used (awkwardly I might add) to hang our rather large banner from the ceiling, and after getting permission, I hung a second banner on the chain-link fence in front of the club.

Upon reentering the dance hall, I was feeling very good about the professional look of the area. As true as that statement was, my slight OCD caused me to adjust everything that the girls had already done, something I was constantly teased about. Then as we started to open our equipment cases and display all of our gadgets, Theo walked in, with his arms loaded. While I decided the best way to showcase our meters, cameras, and recording devices, I watched Theo set up his table and display. It was difficult and I bit my tongue, but I did **not** suggest any arrangement tips, nor did I 'adjust' anything that had been placed (even though part of me, my OCD, knew there were things that just weren't spaced correctly).

"Hey, what do you think about this?" Theo said from the corner of the room.

"Looks great!" I shouted from the opposite side of the room.

"Perfect!" said Katie, standing with Jenn, in the middle of the space. Jenn smiled and gave Theo 'two thumbs up'.

The girls came walking over to me as I stood silently overlooking the entirety of the display. Jenn walked up very close and with her back to Theo, leaned in and whispered to me.

"It's killing you isn't it?" She smirked, knowing it was true, and causing Katie to grin.

I curled my bottom lip downward and shook my head 'no', but quietly said "Maybe a little."

I had no choice, but to accept that when hosting an event, and needing help from many others including the public, that it was literally impossible to control everything. I had to try to pack away my obsessive, compulsive personality, and not stress over details that were out of my control and probably were less important than I was able to believe. Suddenly in the midst of my contemplation, the lights dimmed slightly, and gave the room an ambiance of mystery.

"Is that better, or do you want me to turn them back up?" Barb said from the back of the room.

"No, that's great... I love it." I shouted back, and I honestly meant it.

"It's time... the place is closed, and people are starting to show up." Del popped his head in the door.

"Alright... who is going to man the donation and ghost hunt-ticket table?" I sucked my breath in and exhaled loudly. This was it. Would the patrons and public be pleased with our event? Would the spirits here make their presence known, or would they hide from the crowd for the entire night? I didn't have the answers, but at this moment, it didn't matter... I knew without a doubt that it was completely out of my hands. I swung my arms together and clapped my hands together, making a crisp and loud smacking sound. "Let's do this!"

The girls smiled at me nervously, Barb took her place behind the donation table, and Del opened the door. A few people wandered in, and after making their donations, and purchasing tickets for after-hours investigation, just hovered awkwardly in the rear of the dance hall. Alone, or in groups of two or three, others joined us, and I began to wonder if we were going to have enough participation to make the event seem worth-while to the officers and members of the private club.

A tall, young woman with long, straight, dark hair and almost elfish features entered the room. The lace fringed sleeves of her dress were the only parts that hung loose. The body of the paisley print clung tightly to her thin physique giving her a mythical appearance. Her dark eyes scanned the room, and stopped when they met mine. Not breaking the connection, she leaned in and whispered to Barb as she entered the hall, and then flowed across the room to where the team and I stood. She extended her slender hand to me.

"I am Sterling." She said confidently. "I work with Theo, assisting him as needed, and I am an empath."

"Pleased to meet you Sterling, I'm Rick." I said, pleasantly surprised at her unexpected appearance.

"Yes, I know. This is quite an incredible building. I have already encountered several spirits between the entrance and here. So much emotion, so much sadness... This should be a night to remember." She spoke openly and without hesitation. Once we had all been introduced, Sterling and Theo strolled over to Theo's table.

We had many friends, old and new, attend the 'open to the public' ghost tour. Katie's mom was in attendance, as was an old friend of mine who traveled from the opposite side of the state to come out. Even Jenn's friend from back in her high school days, Christian, had come to learn about the team, the haunting of the Owls, and to find out what Jenn had been up since he had seen her last. After talking with her, and being introduced to the rest of the team, Christian stepped over to Theo's table to get a reading. The accuracy to which Theo described the mother of Christian's son, and what they had been through, was so dead-on, that he asked Theo to please pause a moment while he grabbed up Jennifer to be a witness to its haunting truth. Both Jenn and Christian were in utter shock at the details Theo gave him.

I also had old friends, classmates, and even relatives attend the event, and a number of Facebook friends whom I had not yet met in person. One of those friends, Amanda Gish-Morris, would turn out to be invaluable in the future. Amanda and I spoke at length before the event began. Her enthusiasm and desire to assist was unparalleled. She quickly purchased and adorned one of our team shirts to show her support and to help her feel connected to the team. I knew immediately that Amanda would be someone we could rely on for help now, or in the future. Faithful and honest friends were a rare commodity in this world, and I had just met one.

Within a half an hour, we had mingled with many of the guests, sold numerous items, signed team photos, and eventually decided it was time to begin. There were nearly forty people who turned out to hear the chilling tales of the haunting of the Owl's. It was a large crowd, and I needed to formulate a plan that would accommodate them properly.

"Good evening everyone. If you would find a seat, I would like to get things started as soon as possible. We have much to do and discuss and not as much time as I would like. I'd like to start by saying, thank you all for coming. Tonight promises to be an informative and hair raising event that I hope everyone will be talking about for months and years to come!" I shouted to the back of the room with a smile that could not be contained. "Not only will you be getting a lesson in history, and seeing and hearing some amazing proof of the spirits that reside right here among us in this building, but you *may* all have an opportunity to interact, and meet them first hand." I paused briefly while heads turned and murmurs filled the air. Our guests were intrigued by what I had proposed and I could also see a tinge of fear in the eyes of a few of them at the thought of meeting a ghost face to face. Things were going as planned, and it was time to make some new adjustments to the tour. "Barb, could I ask a huge favor of you?" I spoke loudly so that not only Barb could hear, but everyone in the room would be in on our conversation.

"Certainly! I'm glad to help in any way I can." Barb said, and I could hear the excitement in her voice.

"Would you mind telling our guests about some of the ghostly encounters that have happened here over the years, and then, if you don't mind, tell a bit of the history of the building and the family who lived here a hundred years ago?" Eyes widened as I said the words. Strangers to the building were surprised that the paranormal team was not telling the tales of the hauntings, but instead, someone who had been an active part of the Owl's Nest and its history for many years. It gave the tales more credibility than it would have if a group of paranormal enthusiasts were trying to 'sell' a haunting to a crowd of eager participants.

Barb was flushed, and cleared her throat. "I'd be happy to, Rick." I could see the emotions pouring over her. She was thrilled and honored to have been asked to convey this important information, but she was also caught off guard which caused the slightest of embarrassment and stage fright. Barb quickly regained her composure, and turning towards the audience, began to recant the stories and histories of the Owl's Nest.

The four of us, and Sterling, sat behind the various tables in the front of the dance hall, filled with equipment, literature, and merchandise. While Barb began to recall the tales of frightened and confused Owl's members who had their brush with the spirits who existed within the building's confining walls, I motioned the others over to where I sat. They unobtrusively found their way to me and I began to whisper my new plan to them, in hopes that it would work.

"I am going to split up the evidence onto three flash drives and we should split up. Katie, do you mind going upstairs and giving the evidence review when the groups come up?" I whispered to them.

"Groups?" Katie asked quietly.

"With this many people, we need to split them up into a couple of groups." I explained.

"Okay, as long as I'm not up there alone for too long." Katie answered.

"Great...Sterling, would you mind going up with Katie, at least until the first group shows up? We try not to leave anyone

203

alone, if we can avoid it." It was an uncomfortable question to have to ask a stranger, but it was my first logical thought.

"Absolutely." She quietly answered.

"Theo, I want you to stay here with the group and Barb, and then split them up into two groups. You take one upstairs first, and I'll have Barb bring her group to the basement, okay?" It was a lot to throw together at the last minute, but I had to formulate a plan quickly.

"Sure." Theo whispered back.

"What about me?" Jenn asked.

"I want you to set up in the boiler room, and I'm going to be in the pool room. Once you have your laptop set up and ready to play the e.v.p.s, you can come into the pool room and help me tell the story behind the voices we recorded, and the story of the shadow children here."

"Sounds perfect to me." Jenn admitted, and it was a good plan. Now, we just needed to execute it as smoothly as we could manage.

I began to transfer the audio clips and photos onto the flash drives while Barb continued on with the stories of the original family that once lived at the home that became the Owl's nest, some of whom still occupied it spaces. With fine point sharpie in hand, I labeled each flash drive by where the evidence would be revealed, and passed them out accordingly. I unplugged my laptop, and the girls got theirs in order, and ready to transport to the various locations where the ghostly voices would be revealed.

Barb finished recanting the stories of the passing of the children and the grief-stricken family, though she hadn't heard the whole of the story yet. That much was intentional. We thought it was best, at this time, to not divulge too much of the devastating tale for fear that the spectral children might be listening in to our conversations, or the random conversations of our guests. Tonight's event was about raising some funds for the Owl's Nest #30, and raising awareness... the awareness of the guests and the awareness of the spirits who dwelt amongst us on this somewhat spooky night.

"If everyone would like to stand up with whomever you came with or whoever you want to tour with, Theo and Barb will be dividing you into two groups. One group will be going with Theo upstairs, and the second group will be touring with Barb and start out in the basement of the building." I said loudly, so that everyone could hear. When everyone stood up and began to mingle with their friends, and make new acquaintances, Katie, Sterling, Jenn and I crept out of the dance hall and headed to our respective spots to set up our laptops.

Chapter 17

YOU ARE NOT ALONE

From the pool room, I could hear the shuffling footsteps above and quickly worked to set up the laptop, and speaker system. Nervously, I clicked the play button for the e.v.p. I would be playing in this area. It came across the speakers loud and clear. A few seconds in, I stopped and reset the audio clip, and anxiously awaited the first group to join me. The hair on my neck rose when I heard quiet footsteps just outside of the pool room door. The overhead lights went out and my heart raced as I watched the door to the room slowly glide open without a sound. A shadowy outline of a figure stood in the doorway and began to move toward me.

"Holy crap! You freaked me out!" I whispered loudly, realizing the shadow person was none other than my team mate Jenn.

"Well, you told me to come join you once I was set up in the old boiler room... so that's what I did." Jenn sighed. "You are too damn jumpy... Just relax. Everything's going to be fine."

Upstairs, Barb led her group around the main floor, describing all of the chilling experiences that had been collected over the years, explaining about the many sightings of the man in the yellow shirt, and the hair-raising tales of her own frightful occurrences. Soon, they began descending the steps to the lower level of the old Bettiger home. With only flash lights lighting the way, the group entered the room.

"Barb, would you mind to turn on one of the lights, so everyone can see the room a bit better?" I asked.

Without a word, a dim light in the corner gave the room a hazy glow. I began my talk by thanking everyone for attending, and explained the importance of what we were trying to achieve. I told a tale of four lost children who felt compelled to remain hidden in the eternal shadows of the Owl's Nest. I told the curious gathering of onlookers about Jenifer, and her sensitivity to the spirit energies, especially the energies of children. Jenn then spoke up and detailed how she used specific triggers to connect with the spirits of children who we had encountered. Jenn opened the bag she had carried in and displayed the array of toys she carried. Kneeling down, as she had during our investigation, she placed the toys on the floor, explaining how she coaxed the children to interact with her.

"Play the clip Rick." She said, trying to not stare into the darkened corner to her left, where a pile of wood, and other construction leftovers lay, piled up...and also where Jenn noticed the slightest movement of shadows. The crowd gasped in amazement listening to the audio snippet.

"I want to talk to the children that are here." Jenn's voice echoed on the recording.

"You can't find us!" The child's voice eerily answered back.

Ashley caught Jenn's glance, and held the shadow boys still in the corner. They all concentrated earnestly on the people who had gathered just beyond the veil that separated our worlds. Ash helped the boys to focus their consciousness, and with each passing second the visions and sounds from the other side became more clear to them. Waves of comfort and peace came over them as they began to hear the voices of complete strangers telling them to not be afraid.

"You are welcome here." said one man.

"We are your friends." said another.

"We only want to talk to you, and try to help you if we can." said a woman, harboring genuine compassion in her voice. "I lost my daughter when she was seven, and I understand what it is to feel lost, but you don't have to feel that way anymore."

"Let us help you." I added. "If you can show us that you are here, or give us some instruction... let us know how we can help you...but for now, just know that we are telling your story, helping others to understand, and want nothing from you. We only want you to find peace and be happy, eternally happy." My voice was shaky, not from fear, but from shock. I had no idea that one of our attendees had lost a young child. The thoughts that ran through my mind ranged from hoping we hadn't said or done anything insensitive, to wondering how difficult it must be for her to hear the voices of these ghost children, and know that they are still earthbound spirits a hundred years after their passing. Like falling against a barbed wire fence, the reality of her confession ripped at my heart from many different angles, and each pain was disturbingly new. I kept my emotions in check as we continued on with the tour.

There were many questions and each was answered by myself, or Jenn, as best as we could, but our most important message that night was conveying the story of the lost shadow children of the Owl's Nest, and opening the public's mind to acceptance of things, even if we truly do not understand them. As it is with different religious beliefs and faiths, one does not have to agree with another's faith, to accept it and not be judgmental. Acceptance leads to understanding, and understanding leads to peace. It is there that we reach our goal, and the pinnacle of enlightenment.

I nodded to Jenn to let her know it was time to move on. She quietly passed behind the crowd, leaving her toys in their place. There was a buzz of whispers between friends, as our lecture and discussion came to an end in this area.

"Barb, if you would like to lead the group out, and tour them through the rest of the basement area, ending at the old boiler room, Jennifer and I will meet you all there." I spoke over the fascinated voices of the gathering.

"I'd be glad to... If you would all follow me out of this door, and to our left... our next stop will be the 'rat' room." Barb instructed everyone, and even in the dim light, I could see her smile as the guests imagined what horrors might possibly lay in such a disturbingly named room.

"Wow... it's really cold here in the doorway." One of the women said.

"Yes it is." Her friend agreed, looking around for an air conditioning vent, but there were none to be found.

I studied the exiting guests, and noticed their movement did not match the movement of shadows against the wall next to the exit. As each person passed through the doors, the shadows moved invariably closer to them, and many of the visitors, rubbed their arms to create a warming friction, or blew hot breath into their cupped hands and rubbed them together. I could image that if I had the abilities of Theo, or Rick Hayes, I might have seen the shadow children reaching up to touch their new friends on the arm, or attempting to hold their hands as the left the room. Perhaps they were not happy to see them leave this area for a place that the children found far less pleasant.

Barb led them through the lower level of the building describing ghosts of patrons sitting at the old bar, and the curiously humorous story of the 'rat' room, and though there were never any real claims of paranormal activity in that room, it raised the most shrieks and goose bumps for such a small room. The group toured past the stairway to nowhere, and to the doorway of the odd, octopus style furnace room. Some of our guests wandered through the uneven area, ducking under the round, tin, vent- pipe arms, and over unleveled floors to get a fun house feeling of fear. The room

210

held a certain look and feel to it. The old furnace, with its many arms had the look of a scene from a thriller movie, but nothing readied them for the last room on the basement tour... the boiler room.

Jennifer and I stood next to the old wheel chair, in near complete darkness. Only the screen of the laptop on a small tabletop lit our faces as Barb entered the room.

"Lights?" Barb asked, knowing the dangers that the pit in the center of the dark room evoked.

"Yes, please." I responded. "I only wanted to keep it dark in here until the rest of the tour was finished."

With the flip of a switch, the poor overhead lighting flickered eerily and then came on. The group of nearly twenty filtered in slowly, and encircled the pit in the center of the room. Jenn began telling the tale of Mrs. Bettiger, the children's grandmother, and the sad story of her confinement to the old wooden wheelchair that sat before them, dust covered and aged. In this room, everything seemed to have grown together over time. The rafters of the ceiling, the brick walls, concrete floor, and even the old wheelchair somehow appeared to be connected to each other through decades of dust, coal ash, and spider webs. This was the one room in the basement that felt untouched by modern times.

Instead of recanting the horrible story of Jennifer's own experience in this room, and the terrifying tale of 'Big Red' and his constable cousin stuffing bodies into the old boiler that once occupied the treacherous pit, she chose to leave an air of mystery to the e.v.p. that had been caught in the room, by explaining that the voice was creepy, but only mimicked our words, and one word in particular. She continued to say that the one word may have been a trigger of sorts, causing an emotional recollection and connection between our reality and the reality of the spirits who dwelt in this building. There were oohs and ahhs at the sight of the old wheel chair, and apprehensive gasps at the voice on our recording, as it played over and over, at the request of the visitors. Jennifer then turned the screen of the laptop towards the crowd, and displayed the photograph of the ghost-lady. Some of the guests immediately saw the ghost in the picture, while others were more skeptical until it was pointed out to them, and numerous other photos (taken in sequence) clearly showed only the brick wall behind her.

"What was that?" One of the young men who was near the back of the room shouted out.

"What?" I replied, excited to find out what caused him to raise his voice.

"Maybe it was nothing, but I swear I saw a shadow moving behind that wheelchair." He explained uncomfortably.

"Mrs. Bettiger, are you here with us tonight?" I asked nervously. "These wonderful people have come to hear your story, and the story of your family. We want to help your family find peace." The room was as silent as an abandoned church as I spoke, and for a moment or two afterwards, while everyone waited for a bone-chilling response. The whispers began to speculate, and some began to doubt, but all were immediately silenced when the overhead light flickered erratically and then   returned to its normal state of dimness. Several more minutes were spent in the room, discussing the entire story of the family and the haunting of the Owls-Nest, until we began to hear footsteps overhead, growing louder and more steady with each passing second.

"I think that's our cue. It sounds like the other group has finished upstairs, so, let's all follow Barb back to the stairs and we will take a few minutes on the main floor to take a break before we make the trek to the upper floor." Before I could finish speaking, our guests had begun to exit, passing by the wheelchair slowly, some stopping to take photos, while others pushed past, ready to get themselves to a far less creepy location.

"Thank you all for coming. Rick and I will see you in the dance Hall after the tour if you are staying for the investigation tonight." Jenn added to my instructions.

While Jenn and I reset our recordings, and prepared for the second half of the group to appear, Barb and the others made their way upstairs, and into the empty bar room. They all stopped for a moment and listened to the distant and growing sound of harsh footsteps. Soon, like a stampede of frightened gazelles, the second half of the guests busted into the bar area loud with conversation, and approached Barb's group.

212

"We thought you were already down here." Barb stated with a puzzled tone.

"Nope... we came down the steps just now. Why did you think we were already here?" Theo asked.

"Because we could hear people walking up here from the basement, that's why we came up when we did. Well... that and the tour downstairs was about over." She replied.

"Wasn't us." Theo smiled and looked over his shoulder to the group he had led down. "But there was some activity and experiences upstairs. I think everyone was ready to get out of there."

"I don't think they are going to find it any less active, or creepy, downstairs." Barb said with a wink.

The two groups became one momentarily, and traded brief stories of the unexplainable, letting those in the other group about their incredibly spooky experiences, and wishing them the same activity on their tour. Water bottles were passed out to any who needed to quench their thirsts, while some folks just had a seat, and rested their legs. After a ten minute intermission, the ghost tour continued. Barb and Theo separated the groups again, and Barb brought the new set of enthusiasts down to the where Jenn and I patiently awaited them. Theo took his new group down the hallway, and up the stairs where he and Katie would tell them even more stories, and play more recordings of the ghostly voices of the past.

As the new group ascended the stairs to the upper story of the home, Theo saw and felt the presence of one of the malicious male entities rush past him, down the steps. Theo paused only for a moment, turning to view the visitors who were filing up the steps. Amanda and her brother were a few steps back, and he watched as she stumbled, grabbing the rail, and regaining her composure.

"Be careful Amanda." Her brother prodded her from behind.

"I know... I almost fell backwards." She answered him, and trotted up the stairs to catch Theo. "I don't know if the steps are just uneven, or what, but I felt like I was being pushed backwards down the stairs. It was a creepy feeling." She whispered to Theo at the top of the stairs.

213

He acknowledged her concerns, and leaning over the railing spoke to everyone below. "Please be careful on the stairs. Amanda almost lost her footing, and it could be that the stairs are just uneven, or it could be the malevolent spirits that sometimes occupy this area. Whatever the case may be, we don't want anyone to get hurt. Thanks."

"Now, if you will all follow me into this room, we will begin telling the second story." Popping through the doorway at the top right of the stairs Katie made a pun about the second half of the tour.

The group filed into the room, followed by Theo, making sure there were no stragglers. Katie had her laptop set up at the far end of the room, with her back to the boarded up window. Theo ushered everyone through the area, and stood next to the door where the e.v.p. 'exciting' was captured. Stories recounting the investigations were told by both investigators, and the tales were passed back and forth between them quite comfortably and casually, as if it had all been rehearsed. The guests might have never believed that it wasn't until just an hour before that the decision was made to have Theo and Katie be the tour guides for the upstairs area.

The spirit voices were played, and the two demonstrated where they were caught and under what circumstances. When Theo and Katie had finished, they let everyone wander around the rooms, and analyze the areas that most intrigued them until it was time to gather everyone up in the dance hall once again and say our good-byes to those who were leaving, and prepare to begin our investigation with those who remained.

***

Del and Barb stood at the door, and thanked everyone for coming out as they left. They let in three people who had purchased 'Ghost Hunt Passes' in advance but weren't able to attend the tours. One of those people was a surprise visitor. When Del and Barb escorted the three newcomers into the room, Jennifer's eyes lit up, and with a big smile on her face, she crossed the room.

"Robby!" She screamed out. "Oh my god! I didn't know you were coming! How have you been?"

214

"I've been good." He answered, as I approached him, and shook his hand. "Rick said you guys might need some extra help here tonight, so...here I am to save the day... or night, or whatever." We all collectively laughed at Robby's intentionally goofy statement.

Robby Denton was one of the E.V.P. Investigations team members who had been a great addition, but unfortunately, had moved to Indianapolis, and being nearly four hours away, had to resign his position with the team. I was fortunate to have talked to him online and requested his help that evening. It was a pleasant surprise to Jenn, who was the only current team member who really knew Robby.

"Well, where do you want me to start, or what do you want me to do?" Robbie jumped right in to help.

"The DVR needs to be set up. I was thinking that if we could put it at the bottom of the stairs, we might get one camera that could cover the bar area, and the others spread out in the basement, we could cover a lot of square footage." I barked the order out, like I had back in the days when Robby was one of my team, and one of the family. We all smiled, and it felt like old times. We were experiencing a reunion of our own, and it was a great feeling to know, that even when team members had to leave, for whatever reason, that I could still count on some of them in our times of need.

"Right on." He answered me, grabbing up the cases that held the DVR system. "Who wants to help?"

"I will." Katie jokingly raised her hand, like a schoolgirl asking permission.

"Let's go!" Robby said, and I pointed out the box that held the monitor and the extra cables. Katie was quick to grab them up and the two disappeared.

Theo sat behind a table, draped in a multicolored table cloth and adorned with a deck of tarot cards a crystal ball, and various gemstones and herbs, the lot of which gave that particular corner of the room a mystical appearance. Its appearance conjured thoughts of a traveling gypsy wagon's vivid interior. Sterling accompanied him and spoke to many of those who waited for a reading from Theo, explaining her own unique gifts to them. Meanwhile, Jenn and I

215

powered up all of our hand held gadgetry, checking battery life, and explaining their functions and uses to a variety of paranormal enthusiasts. It wasn't long before I decided that the public investigation needed to begin soon.

"I'm going to see if Katie and Robbie need any help getting the DVR set up, so we can begin." I leaned over and whispered to Jenn. "Do you mind getting everyone's attention, after I sneak out, and separating them into two groups again?"

"Well, of course, I'd love to..." Her sarcastic whisper drew a grin to my face as I found my way stealthily out of the dance hall, and into the bar room.

"There you are." Robby exasperatedly called out from the hall way across the room.

"Yeah...here I am. If you needed me for something, you should have just came and got me. I was just talking to people in the dance hall." His statement puzzled me.

"But... I was just following you around the hallways." He looked back over his shoulder and then over to the other hallway entrance. "I saw you over there, and followed you all the way around to here. I tried to catch you, but you kept moving faster than me."

"Wasn't me. I just walked out here." We both knew what was going on. Robby was being toyed with, and possibly, intentionally delayed.

"Nice!" He snickered. "I think we have the DVR ready to go. You can go check out the camera placement, if you want."

"I trust you and Katie. Go ahead and start recording, and then come up to the dance hall, and we will split up into two groups and get this thing started." I gave him a cheesy, thumbs-up, to which he laughed and vanished down the stairs.

Reentering the room, I found it to be quiet and more orderly than I expected. There were two groups gathered neatly on opposite sides of the room. Barb and Del were speaking in a low tone to one group, while Jenn was encircled by the other.

"The group to my left," I gestured with my left hand, waving it in their general direction, "Will be accompanied by Barb, Del, Theo, and Sterling." I turned towards the other group, and motioning in a similar way said, "The group to my right will join Katie, Jenn, Robby and me."

The entire room turned to stare silently as if some universal mute button was pressed for a brief second, and then suddenly there was a murmuring buzz between the would be investigators. I couldn't tell what the tone of the discussion was, but I hoped it was excitement.

"Midway through the investigation, we will switch groups, so that everyone has a chance to investigate with everyone on the team." I added. The chatter quieted, and I could feel a sense of contentment come over the room, which also made me happy. "Most of the activity happens upstairs, and downstairs, so our two groups will go in opposite directions, and we will get less background interference and noises. Theo, do you want to take your group upstairs, and I will take mine to the basement?"

"Sounds good to me. It's about 12:30 now, what time do you want to trade off?" Theo responded.

"How about 2am? ...and then one of the group leaders will lead the rest to the opposite group." It was the fairest way for the guests who had donated money to the Owl's Nest to have the best experience possible.

Katie and Robby emerged through the doorway and using eye contact and hand motions I directed them to join my group. "Let's get this investigation started. I hope everyone has an experience they can take with them and a story to tell their friends and family when the sun rises tomorrow." And with that, I began to pass out flashlights, and distribute some of the equipment.

Both groups went their separate ways, and the hunt for the paranormal began. Lights were systematically extinguished, and the atmosphere grew more chilling by the minute. Theo, Sterling and Katie began upstairs with their group which included Amanda, her brother and several others, including Karen Daugherty, one of the Owl's members.

Some of the stories were told, but mostly, my team mates did their best to introduce the spirits to those who had come out to meet them. Our main intent was simply to help them be more comfortable and not feel the need to hide...at least not from us. The group had shared our equipment, taking turns to try and get some interaction with the spirits' energy. In the gentleman's business room, Amanda and her brother were trying to invoke some reaction by using the K-II meter.

"Hello... is there anyone here with us?" Amanda began. "If you could touch the little gray box with the light on it, you can show us that you are here and acknowledge our presence." They waited a few minutes in utter silence. Nothing happened.

"Hello. Can you do something to let me know you are here with us?" Amanda's brother asked, repeating her inquiry. Almost before the words had left his mouth, the meter lit up fully in response. Everyone focused their attention on the meter and awaited the next response.

"Are you one of the Bettiger family member's?" He asked, but no response was given.

"Did you do business in this room with Mr. Bettiger?" Amanda said cleverly, but also received no response.

"Did you do business in this room with Mr. Bettiger?" Amanda's brother then regurgitated, to which he received an immediate interaction with the lights on the meter. Amanda's brother laughed, poking fun at her inability to get any reaction.

"This actually makes perfect sense." Katie started. "This is the gentleman's business room. Women and children were not welcomed in here, so if this is the spirit of one of the businessmen, he might not communicate with a woman... no offense, Amanda."

There was other minor activity, but most of the overnight hours were spent talking casually to the ghosts of the Owl's nest, and doing our best to make them understand that they are not only recognized as existing, but that they are accepted. When the time came, to trade groups, Theo asked Sterling if she would escort the group to the lowest level of the building. She cordially obliged, but when she approached the edge of the stairs, she had the uncomfortable and consuming feeling that someone, or something wanted to push her down the steps.

218

"Everyone, please be careful descending the steps. They can be tricky, and I want everyone to have a good and safe evening." Sterling spoke, with a soothing and hypnotic voice that everyone heeded without question.

***

The activity in the basement had been relatively non-existent for the first half of the night, but things were not so quiet when the groups traded spaces. Even during the transition, the activity seemed to pick up. When the group from the upstairs made it to the main floor, Karen excused herself to use the restroom. As she reached over to flush the toilet in the ladies room, her entire ring of keys were somehow pulled from her pocket and thrown into the toilet, disappearing forcefully as the water in the toilet drained. She ran out of the restroom, and quickly found Del, to ask if there was anything that could be done to retrieve them. Although every effort was made, the keys remained lost forever.

After the groups had been traded out, we all found ourselves in the pool room, trying to connect with the lost Bettiger children. Speaking directly to them, and amongst ourselves, we attempted to interact with them as if they were just other people in the room. This seemed to work, as the boys, escorted by Ashley, made their way out of the corner of the room and began to intermingle with us.

"Do you feel that?" Barb asked those close to her, reaching down to her side and spreading her fingers.

"Yes. It's really cold all of the sudden." Amanda noticed.

"Uh huh... but it's just down here around my legs." Karen pointed out correctly.

The coolness swirled through and around our legs, chilling each of us, as the children passed by. There were energy fluctuations caught by our gadgets, and the presence of the children was undeniable. Our emotions were touched by their interaction, and their acceptance of us, but to at least one of us, it was more than that.

"I have to go... it's too much right now." Sterling said, almost crying.

219

The sadness that had been suppressing the children was being transferred to her, and it was nearly unbearable to such a strong empath. Sterling fled the room, and up the stairs, finding herself unintentionally in the dance hall, where one of the gangsters had been hiding out, attempting to avoid human interaction after fleeing down the stairs, nearly pushing Amanda down them with the force of his energy. The decades had changed him and his companions. Though they were still angry with the children, they longed to leave the space that they were trapped in, where they had been made to relive the deaths of the family they had caused, and even those they hadn't. The sadness she brought with her felt like the decades of the torture he had been subjected to, suddenly condensed into one moment of sheer hell.

He rushed from the dance hall as she entered, and flew to the basement, where he encountered my group, and came face to face with not only the children, but with their new protector Ashley. He felt her unequaled power and immediately knew of her ability to travel freely. The envy nearly consumed him and he screamed out his jealousy with such fervor, that the room quickly became an uncomfortable place for us, and his desire was caught on our digital audio recorder.

"Let's move on." I said, grabbing up the equipment and feeling the urgency to leave this room. The hour or so that remained of the evening were far quieter, and the magnitude of the activity had seemed to wane, as if the passing of the 3am hour sent the spirits into a peaceful slumber, or had at least distanced them from our physical realm.

The night ended with an easy feeling of comfort, and nearly everyone involved truly felt we had taken great strides in bringing rest to the lost souls of the Owl's Nest. As we packed our cases of equipment out to our cars, and the lights were all turned out/doors locked, there was a feeling of mixed emotions shared among us all. First, we felt that we had moved forward, in a very positive way, toward our goal, and second, we knew the most important achievements lay ahead of us. It was late... or I guess early, and my mind was already planning and strategizing for the next 'public event'.

Chapter 18

A TIME TO HEAL

It was a Wednesday evening in early August and the battery on my phone was growing dangerously low. I had called everyone on my team, everyone I knew from the Owl's, Rick Hayes, and many of the friends, old and new, who had attended our public investigation. The time had passed so quickly and I now found myself facing a rapidly approaching autumn. How much time did we have, before it was 'too late', I didn't know. The thought of making so much progress and there being an invisible deadline that could pass at any time worried my team and I. It was time for a Barnes & Noble/ Starbucks meeting.

I sat in the farthest corner table, sipping my vente, French vanilla cappuccino. Katie, Jenn and Theo wandered in, one by one, only minutes apart. My concern over the ominous and elusive deadline was overtaking my every waking moment. When would it be too late, and what happened when it became too late? All I could think of was all of the poor souls who had made the Owl's Nest their home in the afterlife, and if it suddenly became too late to help the children of the Owls, would it be too late for the other souls as well?

"It's set." I said in a low monotone voice, after drawing a deep breath. "The Owls have decided to let us host another public event... a week and a half from today."

"Wow... that's not much time to get the word out and prepare." Theo realized.

"Nope, it isn't. Do you think we can get anyone to come on such short notice?" Katie questioned the team.

"I've been on the phone all afternoon, since I found out, and I think we will have a decent turn out. Rick Hayes said he would come, and Barb said she could make a last minute addition to the Hoots newsletter, so between the two of them, I think we will draw enough people...but that's not what I'm concerned about, really." I explained.

Jenn and Katie looked at each other and their concern and confusion soon changed to a different concern and an understanding. Jenn spoke up first. "You aren't worried about having a good turn-out, because the real concern is helping the spirits, right?"

"The children..." Katie's voice was small and quiet, but held a heavy truth.

"If it's not already too late..." Theo added somberly.

"Yes, that's my fear...that's what has me anxious, and keeps me awake at night." I admitted, and it seemed evident that the rest of my companions shared in my endless worry.

"We have a lot to do in a short amount of time, huh?" Katie broke the silence after a few minutes of deep thought.

224

"Yep... do you think Robby is going to be able to help us out again? The extra hand was really helpful." Jenn asked.

"No, I already asked, but I did get an email from a guy who wants to possibly join the team named Jordan, so, I thought we would give him a shot. I talked to him on the phone and he seemed like a level headed, intelligent person." I sprung the idea on them to see how they would react without any prior notice.

"I think that's a good idea... I mean, at least it's good to have a back-up, or part time investigator." Theo said.

"Yeah, I agree." Katie added while Jenn nodded in agreement.

"He is meeting up with me this weekend, here for coffee, and you are all welcome to be here and we can make a decision...if we want to accept him into our team, or not." I purposed, and so it was.

That Saturday afternoon, we all met up again and were joined by Jordan, who probably felt like he was a part of the 'inquisition'. We pummeled him with questions about himself, his reasons for wanting to join us, and how he would handle different scenarios that we had encountered, or that we might encounter. He handled himself well, and spoke with intelligence and a sense of professionalism. The team, my friends, and I didn't have to meet in private to discuss Jordan's interview. It was an unspoken agreement that we all felt.

"Alright my friend, it looks like you will get a shot to join us at our public 'ghost tour' and investigation next Saturday night at the Owl's." I smiled. "Welcome to the team." I shook his hand, as did everyone else... well, except for Jenn. Jenn had to give the young man a hug, because, that's just what Jenn does. No one got away without a hug from Jenn. It was like some sort of unwritten law, and we all loved that about her.

The days drug by, like the moments between the unexpected meals of a man, starving and homeless. Waiting and wondering if the day we yearned for would ever come, and if so would it come soon enough. The thought of missing our warned 'dead line' by mere days, or even minutes gnawed at our hearts, minds and our very souls.

Saturday did finally arrive, and my greatest fear was that there would be no children, no small shadows of the once playful tots, and the mystery would remain forever. To me, that would be a haunting I could never separate myself from.

Jennifer had brought her teenage daughter, Grace, to help out with taking donations and attending the tables filled with equipment, t-shirts and other miscellaneous items of interest. The banners were hung, and the basement was decorated with our signs and our cases of paranormal investigating equipment. The only way we had been able to get our public event set was to agree to set up in the large bingo room, but we didn't mind. It wasn't as grand as the dance hall, but that wasn't important to us. All that mattered was time, which seemed ironic since I had always thought that once the veil to the other side, the afterlife, was crossed, time would make no difference whatsoever. This was not the case in our realm. The clock, high on the wall, mocked our anticipation, and seemed to slow with every tick, and taunted us louder and louder with each tock.

The room seemed to light up when Rick Hayes entered and gave us all a wave and a boisterous "Hey!" The mood lightened, and even the clock seemed to find its quiet place. As Rick approached the tables where we were preparing ourselves and our displays, we all dropped what we had been doing and gathered around him.

"Everything is going to be alright. I have an unmistakable feeling of peace... not a peace that is here, but a peace that is coming, soon." His words were like a warm blanket wrapping around us on a cold an unrestful night.

"I feel it too." Theo agreed. "You're right. It isn't here yet, but I think it will be...soon."

There was a mystical energy in the air that grew stronger with every participant who entered the downstairs room where we would be holding our 'seminar', before the ghost tours and public investigation. The room filled quickly, and even though the club remained open upstairs while we began, there was a quiet and easy feeling about the upcoming night. I introduced my team, Grace, and Rick Hayes to the crowd that had gathered, before turning the floor over to Barb to tell her tales of the history and haunting of the Owls. Onlookers, even those who had attended the last event, were captivated by the chilling stories of the past and the many

226

mysterious encounters since the Owl's Nest took over the space in the 1920's.

When Barb had finished her regale, and answered what questions were asked, I returned to take my place in the front of everyone. With only a short talk about my team, what we do, and our experiences at the Owls, I reintroduced our guest for the evening Rick Hayes who both entranced and delighted the crowd before him. His dialog with the audience included his own history and encounters, as well as his gifts of the supernatural, but more so, he spent the majority of his time teaching. His lessons taught everyone to be more open minded, less critical, and to open their eyes and their hearts to living their own magical lives...living their lives supernaturally, and all they had to do was simply believe.

Rick decided to make the situation less formal. While my team and I prepared for our ghost tour and a special surprise to kick off the night, Rick mingled through the crowd, answering questions and giving a most informal gallery reading, of sorts. It was an amazing time for everyone involved and the tales were recanted numerous times, (and still are to this day). Christian spoke often of Rick connecting with his grandfather and his uncle who had passed, and how overpowering the emotions were when they came through in his reading, and the feeling of close family flooding over him like warm waves. Barb received a few validating statements to let her know that her dad was still watching out for her.

"Barb, I keep seeing an old desk... you know the kind with the drawers that go down one side, the left hand side." Rick said to her, as he focused his thoughts.

Barb's eyes grew wide, as she recognized the description of her father's desk that she now owned, but, "Uh huh." was all she could muster.

"Don't take this wrong, but I sense a man, maybe your father, keeps saying the big bottom draw needs to be cleaned out. Does that make any sense?" Rick asked politely.

"Yes." Barb said as her eyes began to well up. "I have my dad's desk, and that bottom drawer has been crammed with 'junk' for a long time." She glanced over to a smiling Del. "I was just saying I needed to empty it out because my dad was very orderly, and it would have driven him nuts." Del nodded in agreement.

"I'm seeing one other thing, and don't laugh... but does a stick of butter mean anything to you?" Rick rubbed his chin, confused by this latest revelation.

"Ummmm... not that I can think of." Barb seemed just as confused.

"Sorry, that's all I am getting. Just keep that in the back of your mind and maybe it will come to you what it means." Rick smiled and soon moved on through the crowd to speak with others who patiently waited their turns.

I entered the room and quickly gathered everyone's attention. "It is time to begin our 'Ghost Tours'. It looks like we have about thirty people here, so if we could split up into three groups of about ten, we can get started." I announced, and everyone swiftly migrated to those they wanted to tour with.

Over half a dozen small groups were assembled and then those were combined until we had our groups. Because of the nature of the event, with Rick Hayes present, we decided to take one group at a time, and once the first group had finished in the basement, they were led to the main floor and the second group began to share our adventurous tales and the revelation of our evidence. The entire journey went very smoothly for all involved, and much like our first event there were a few skeptics, but mostly gasps of dismay at the voices of the departed that we had communicated with. There was one change on this tour, one small, yet significant, addition. The first stop on for each group was the pool room.

"I want to talk to the children that are here." Jenn's voice replayed over the speakers followed by moments of static-y tension. "You can't find us!" The voice of Ash called back in eerie response. Our visitors shivered at the haunting voice of the child.

"That is quite an impressive piece of evidence." One of the enthusiasts boasted.

"Yes, it is." I agreed. "But the last time it was played in this room, there was another voice caught, and my team and I believe it is a direct response." A hush came over the crowd as I played the second clip.

There were various people chattering away in the background of the recording, speaking about orbs of light, and other questionable paranormal evidence and then, over the top of every voice in the room, came a chilling insight.

"I WANT HER!" A cruel voice informed everyone. It was the belief of my team that this was one of the malevolent shadows, a ghastly gangster, if you will, speaking of wanting Ashley, for her powers and her ability to come and go at-will from this timeless prison.

The room broke out in a hushed murmur of voices, and several times I was asked to replay the chilling voices. The more squeamish of our friends began looking around, realizing that these specters may be joining us again, just as they had in the past, but there was no activity, no cold spots, and no one was pushed, or had their hair pulled. It would seem they were saving up their energy for something bigger, something more impressive, or perhaps...we were too late. I tried not to dwell on that possibility, especially since Theo and Rick had both seemed to think it was going to be 'alright'.

The tours moved on and through the building, and by the end everyone who attended was convinced that the Owl's Nest was truly haunted. I had decided to allow everyone to mingle and enjoy some fellowship, because we were able to start our event before the club actually closed, in fact, it was just before 11:30pm when our tours ended. When midnight approached, we escorted everyone from the building briefly, and then let the 'ticket holders' reenter. In total, there were twenty one attending the public investigation, nearly half of which were comprised of my team, Rick Hayes, the Heerdinks, and a couple of assistants.

Before anyone realized what we had done, the rows of chairs had been rearranged into a circle, with an old Gothic, throne-style chair at the head. The DVR was turned on and began recording as Theo took a seat in the head chair, with Sterling by his side, notebook in hand.

"If I could have everyone's attention for a moment, we are about to go dark, and we have a special event to kick off our investigation. Theo is a psychic-medium, but also a trance-medium and he will be conducting a séance in a few minutes. If anyone is uncomfortable taking part, I will have one of our investigators, Katie, lead you upstairs to begin investigating now. Otherwise, please find a seat in the circle." I motioned to where Katie waited by the stairway, and then to the circle of chairs that I stood in the midst of. There were no takers, and intrigue filled the room. Scuffling bodies of paranormal enthusiasts, teeming with curiosity, snatched up chairs and the circle was soon filled. The room darkened, and candles were lit on a small table in the center of the circle.

Theo's eyes closed, and the room fell deathly silent. Only the dull hum of the DVR filled the night. Once again the clock seemed to stop as everyone waited in anticipation of what might happen next.

"Will the children please join us in the circle?" Theo asked in a trance-like voice.

His words came out quiet and slurred, like a novice drinker who had consumed a few too many. Theo sat somewhat slumped over in the massive throne, and began to mumble as the spirit came to him. He could not sense the children in the room, but he could feel a presence behind him. The energy drew closer, leaning in, and began to speak to him.

"The children are hiding upstairs, as they often do." The voice said, and Theo repeated in a nearly indiscernible vocalization.

"It is I, Amelia." Again, Theo repeated while Sterling made every attempt to understand and scratch down her notes in the faint candlelight.

"You have brought me to my children, and for that I am grateful." The words were conveyed through Theo, and then penned to paper.

To Theo's left, about one quarter of the way around the circle, sat Rick Hayes. I stood almost directly behind Rick, and from my vantage point, I could make nothing out that was said, and impatiently waited for the séance to end. I had noticed that Rick seemed to not be able to keep his attention focused into the circle also. He repeatedly turned to look at me, and smile, and then look behind me towards the old bar across the bingo room. I could no longer hold my tongue, and stooped down behind him.

"So, what do you think, Rick?" I whispered as silently as I could.

"I'm not sure where the children are, but the three guys sitting back at the bar keep joking with each other, saying - I ain't goin' in the middle of all that." He smiled again. "These guys, I believe are part of the militia... the gun runners that Allison told us about."

"Interesting... So, how are we going to get them out of here? Those guys have to be the malevolent entities we've encountered." I asked, hoping Rick had some simple answer, and he did.

"We just try to help them cross over. It's all we can do." His words were directed at me, but as he spoke, he looked over his shoulder and mine, and I had a feeling that I wasn't the only one listening to him.

***

The séance had ended and Theo slowly awoke from his connection to the other side. The time had come to split up into two groups and try to find the ghosts that hid from us. It was much easier to divide this smaller group. Half of the visitors joined Jordan, Barb, Del, and I to begin investigating downstairs, while Theo, Jenn, Katie and Grace took the remaining guests to the second story.

The group I was leading was joined by Rick Hayes, and all was fairly calm and inactive as we investigated room by dismal room of the basement. The flashlights flickered, catching bits of dust in their beams as they scanned the dank passages and web filled, abandoned spaces in the oldest parts of the building. The dancing lights passed by the old boiler room, and Rick was immediately drawn back to the portentous, wooden wheelchair that sat hidden within its decrepit walls. He meandered slowly into the room, followed by several flashlight, and meter, bearing investigators. Eyes widened, and winced as Rick took a seat in the grimy layers of accumulated dust and debris of the chair. It popped, and groaned under the weight of a living being. Everyone, including Rick, was silent and anticipated some supernatural phenomenon. Nothing seemed to happen.

231

Our apprentice investigator, Jordan pulled me out of the boiler room away from everyone else. He was anxious to learn the proper way to investigate and to really do something that was more hands on. I reached into my front pocket and retrieved a digital recorder. I pointed to a door directly across from the boiler room. It was barely cracked open, and I motioned him to give it a gentle nudge. With a ghastly creaking sound, the door swung inward.

"Figure out how this digital recorder works in that dark room, with just a flash light, and when you get it to record, practice asking questions to an empty room. Electronic voice phenomenon is one of our greatest pieces of evidence, and it helps to be comfortable when you are asking questions and talking to someone you can't see. Give it a shot. At least if it feels embarrassing, there won't be anyone watching you." I handed him the digital recorder and smiled.

"No one I can see anyway, huh?" He smiled back, taking the recorder and cautiously entering the room, flitting his light around as if he were looking for bats or giant spiders that were poised to attack upon his entry. I turned and rejoined the group in the boiler room, leaving him to face his fears and insecurities. I stood just outside the open entry, and scanned the room. Everyone was focused on Rick, who was still seated in the antiquated wheelchair, and was deep in thought and meditation.

"I sense the presence of an elderly woman, the matriarch of the family. She is very angry, and still thinks she is confined to this chair." Rick spoke to the onlookers, then his tone and direction changed, and we knew he was no longer talking to us, but to a spirit that we were unable to see. "I understand that you have been bound to this chair for a *very* long time, but trust me when I tell you, that reality no longer exists for you. I am going to stand up, and I want you to stand up with me."

I listened to Rick, but I could hear the faint voice of Jordan from behind me as he began his audio recording session. I watched as Rick carefully, and slowly, stood. The serious look of concern and almost anguish on his face eased and grew into a childlike grin as he stepped away from the imprisoning chair. A chilling breeze blew past me, and for a moment I thought I smelled the faint scent of roses. It reminded me of past visits to the florist, the way the aroma and cool air would overtake my senses when opening up the cooler door to pick out an arrangement for a future ex-girlfriend, or ex-wife.

Jordan's voice had gone silent, and I wondered if he had already run out of questions to ask the emptiness, when there was a sudden commotion. Simultaneously my heart sank and I was amused. It sounded as if he had stumbled into something in the dark and knocked it over. I whipped around, thinking he could possibly have hurt himself. What I expected to see, and what I did see, were completely different. Jordan was backing out of the room, flashlight raised, and in its dim beam of light, I could see sheets of paper drifting down to the floor.

"Are you okay? What happened?" I asked being genuinely concerned. It was then that I could see the pale whiteness of his face.

"Bingo cards." He stuttered. "They just came flying out of that box up on the shelf there..." He pointed with his flashlight to the shelf and then to the floor where nearly a hundred bingo cards lay scattered in disarray.

"I would like to introduce you to the ghost of the Bettiger Matriarch, but it seems you have already met." I couldn't hold back my grin. "I think she was just elated that she isn't stuck in that old wheel chair any longer. Did you feel or smell anything?"

"Yeah..." Jordan thought. "I thought I smelled flowers."

I could tell by the way he said it he was unsure, or uncomfortable admitting it, but I quickly reassured him. "Congratulations on having your first supernatural experience with the team. I see the digital recorder is still on... is it still recording."

"Oh, yeah, I guess it is. Sorry." He apologized, not realizing it was a good thing.

"That's great. If you didn't capture any e.v.p.s, you have at least documented what happened by recording our conversation." I patted his shoulder. "Well done Jordan, well done."

***

On the second story of the home, Jenn and company were experiencing more typical paranormal activity. Unexplainable noises, random energy fields, cold spots that chilled one to the bone and then moved on were the order of the night. For a time, the group split again. Jenn and Katie taking half of them, and Theo and Grace worked closely with the others. In the gentleman's room, the same type of activity continued as before. Christian and Jenn were asking for responses to their questions using the various lights of the K-II meter.

"Is there anyone here with us?" Jenn asked politely after explaining how the response of yes or a positive response to a question could be given by lighting up the K-II. No activity occurred and no response was given.

"Does anybody want to talk to us?" Christian asked, half mocking Jenn. The lights glowed green, yellow, and red for a fraction of a second.

"Are you one of the Bettigers?" Jenn queried, but received no answer.

"Mr. Bettiger, are you here with us tonight?" Christian teased Jenn with his question, but once again, the meter flashed its answer. Jenn rolled her eyes, and there were several muffled chuckles in the room.

"Does it bother you that women are in this room, and asking you questions?" Christian asked cleverly, and there was a sudden burst of K-II lights that lasted a great deal longer than usual. It was an obvious response, and it was very fitting to the times that the Bettigers had lived in.

"Okay, this is a bunch of crap." Jenn said, half joking, half disgusted, and turned to leave the room. Just as she walked past the disturbing portrait of the Owl, she heard a voice coming from the empty corner where it was propped against the wall. Her head jerked in the direction of the mumbled words, to see if there was a ghastly apparition or some shadow person to be seen. There was not, but she and many others saw the painting of the owl pushed away from the wall and slide out into the middle of the floor. Jennifer took two quick and springy steps.

"Sor-ry!" She said in blatant sarcasm, which drew even more laughter from the half dozen on-lookers. The night wore on with more and more obvious, yet benign activity. While it may have been terrifying to some who beheld it, none of the phenomenon was intended to be harmful. The spirits of the Owl's Nest were finally becoming comfortable interacting with flesh and blood people, and not just one at a time, in a secluded setting, but out in the open, in front of several people at a time.

When the time came, and our groups traded places, Rick Hayes and I also found the majority of the activity occurring in the business, or gentlemen's room. Our group of guests circled around the K-II meter and began asking questions, to which we had no response. Rick observed from a distance, and after our frustration began to show, he made a simple suggestion.

"Let's think about this for a minute." He said, though he had already done plenty of thinking on the matter. "If you were a child, or even an adult, would you be comfortable walking into a circle of mostly, complete strangers...who just wanted to talk to you? I know I'd be more than a little intimidated. As a spirit, I might even be more hesitant. Why don't we open this up a bit. Try putting the meter down by the windows, and we can all stand, or sit at this end of the room. I think we should still be able to see if it picks up any energy responses."

"Yes, if we turn off all of the flashlights, it will be very obvious if the K-II lights up." I wish I had thought of the idea, but I was glad Rick had brought it up.

As soon as the meter was in place, lights were turned out, and we were all at the opposite end of the long rectangular room, we began receiving responses from one of the Bettiger boys, and our 'yes and no' questions and answers continued for nearly twenty minutes. It felt more like a conversation, with nearly everyone in the room taking their turn asking questions and simply talking to the spirit child, as if he were just another person in the room. An uncomfortable, yet not frightening feeling coming over me, and I wanted to turn around, but I dared not.

"Rick..." Rick Hayes began. "Do you feel something?"

"Yeah..." I said generically. Besides the uncomfortable presence, I could feel Rick grinning at me through the darkness.

"The boy's father, Charles, is right behind you... and his hands are on your shoulders." He explained, and I could feel the cool energy chilling my back, shoulders, and neck. There was a tingling as the hair on my head stood on end.

"He isn't angry, he is just protective of his son... and I think he is apprehensive about approaching him. It could be that they haven't had any contact on that side of the veil." Rick's words were somewhat comforting, but also saddening. I could not imagine being in the same world with my son and not seeing him. My heart truly went out to Charles, and I could sense that he knew it.

"Charles... could you and your son please wait here for us to return?" Rick asked, and then with a smile, said "Thanks."

We continued to investigate for a while, but eventually, we had to end the public event. The groups were reunited in the bar area, where water, coffee, or sodas were offered to our guests. We loitered in the room for nearly half an hour while everyone swapped stories of the supernatural events they had experienced. One of the events, experienced by the fewest people and talked about the most, was the explosive, flying bingo cards. I had wished that everyone could have seen it, but it didn't seem to matter to them. Many were just in the next room, and heard the noise, saw the aftermath, and listened to the recording. It was a tale that is probably still told by many of those fortunate souls who investigated one of the most haunted social clubs in existence.

Chapter 19

SUMMONING

Our guests had left, as did our newest team mate Jordan, and the evening seemed to be somewhat successful. The spirits were interacting on a much larger scale, but I still didn't feel like we were any closer to 'saving the children'. I found a seat in the back corner of the bar, and contemplated what more we could do, and how many times we would have to visit this location to remedy the dangerous situation that we had been warned about. Suddenly I had a brilliant idea... if it would work. I was about to get up and gather everyone together, when I realized they were already approaching my corner table.

"Hey... have a seat everybody. I have an idea." I said.

"Great! Let's hear it." Jenn said, excitedly.

"Okay... Katie, I'm going to need your help, if you can." Her eyes held a look of worry as I spoke. "I need you to try to contact Ash."

"Me! Why me?" She knew the answer but she was hoping that her tone might make me rethink my plan.

"From our first encounter with her, you have seemed to have the closest connection to Ashley. If you aren't comfortable, I understand, and we will just have to try to get her to listen to one of us instead." I reasoned.

"I'm not saying I'm at all comfortable with it... but I'll do it... I guess." She drug her sentence out as if it were a terrible burden to speak, but then she smiled. A calm came over her, and it was like an emotional light switch had been flipped. "Everything is going to be alright, isn't it?"

"Yes it is." Rick said calmly, and smiled back at her. "Okay, so what is your idea?"

"Our e.v.p. said 'I want her'. I believe this was one of the 'thugs' from Allison's story, and I think, maybe, he was referring to Ashley, and her ability to come and go as she pleases. So, my thought was... if you," I looked to Rick, "and Theo, could somehow round up all three of the malevolent male spirits, and Katie could 'talk' to Ash... perhaps she could lure, or entice them to crossing over. Okay, it sounds dumb, now that I've said it out loud, but it was just an idea."

"That's a great Idea." Theo said.

"Yes it is." Jenn agreed.

"But, do you think it might work?" I doubted myself.

"If it doesn't, we won't be any worse off than we are, but I think it might work." Rick reassured me.

"Step one of the plan is understood. Now, for step two... is anybody on a strict time schedule?" I asked, before I went any further, and was met mostly by laughter and a snide comment from Jennifer.

240

"Yeah... I have an important meeting at work... at 4am...ON SUNDAY." Jenn rolled her eyes and teased. "Come on E-V-Prick... we are here, in the middle of the night. What's step two?"

"Apparently, Charles Bettiger was upstairs with us tonight, and Rick connected with his mother in the wheelchair in the old boiler room. All we need is Amelia, and we will have the whole famn damily here." I joked.

"Huh?" Grace was puzzled by my twisted words.

"It's just something I say, instead of saying 'the whole damn family'. I dunno... maybe I've been up too long." I tried to explain my goofiness, to which the teenage girl smiled and slapped her forehead.

"Well, we would have everyone in the family, except for Allison." Theo pointed out.

"Ah... true. I was hoping, if we could bring them all together in one of the rooms, that maybe they could reconnect, and move on as a family...maybe." I felt the disappointment growing in the pit of my stomach. Maybe it wouldn't work. Maybe it was as far-fetched as it sounded, like some fairy tale ending.

"It's possible, and definitely worth trying." Theo remarked.

"And... how would we know it wouldn't work, if we didn't try, right?" Katie added.

"It's a worthwhile idea. It's important to not only try, but to believe. Doubt kills more dreams than failure. Don't doubt, believe in the plan, and believe in yourselves." Rick's pep talk gave me the boost of positivity I needed.

"Okay. Then, let's get this thing started. I *believe* neutral ground is going to our best bet for step one. First, let's all move into the dance hall. Katie, try to get Ash to manifest her spirit presence there, then let her know what we would like her to do. Rick and Theo, you two work it however you think is best to connect with the spirits of the 'business partners' of Mr. Bettiger, and somehow let them know Ash is there." I was suddenly confident in the plan. I simply believed.

"That won't be a problem." Theo grinned at Rick Hayes.

"No. I agree. I feel that if they think Ashley is there, and they can 'use her' to get out of this eternal prison, they will." Rick added.

Barb, Del, Grace, Jenn, and I sat at a table near the back of the dance hall. Theo and Rick disappeared out of the room, and were off to find the malicious shadow spirits. Katie, well...Katie sat, nervously, on the edge of the stage at the opposite end of the room from the rest of us.

"Ash? Are you here? It's me Katie. You remember me?" Her words were filled with mixed emotions, partly uncomfortable and embarrassed, unsure how to call the spirit to her, and partly afraid that she might actually *call the spirit to her.* Her thoughts digressed to a past time and place not that distant, when she had several encounters with the burning girl. Then as if her courage accompanied a memory from the past, she became a stern mother figure.

"Ashley Sue Helmach! Get in here now... I *need* to talk to you." Katie had a brief moment of timorous thoughts, but quickly regained her courage and composure.

From the rear of the room, we watched and listened to Katie as she reached out to the most powerful and frightening spirit we had ever encountered. I was proud and impressed at her determination. Katie became increasingly quiet, and still. Pale green exit signs dimly lit the vast space, and we struggled to see her from the far end of the room. Second by harrowing second, a light began to grow in front of her. Ashley began to manifest her presence, and soon, the small frame of a child, shrouded in a pale blue luminescence stood between where we sat, and where Katie was. The five of us at the table could feel our excitement, and the intense energy in the air, building. For Grace and the Heerdinks, this was their first glimpse of Ashley Sue, and though they had all heard our stories, over and over, and over again, nothing compared to that initial realization that these tales were not simply exaggerated fabrications. This girl existed.

We listened intently, but from that distance, all we could make out were the low murmurings of Katie, and occasionally, the sounds of Theo and Rick scouring the rest of the building. At length, Katie went silent, and bowed her head.

242

"I want to go up there and see her...face to face." Grace whispered curiously. Jenn and I exchanged looks of dismay.

"Naaaa... You really don't" I said in quiet persuasion.

"But, I really..." She started to argue, and then stopped short.

Ash half-turned and was staring in our direction, as if she had felt the desire of the young girl at our table. Glancing at Grace, I could see her eyes were fixed on Ashley, and her mouth fell open wide. The eyes of the ghost child began to blaze with a yellowy-orange fire. Without warning, the once childlike entity rushed towards Grace bursting into an inferno of flames and then disappearing just as she reached the table. Everyone, including myself, cringed, and ducked, closing our eyes tight for a brief second. We quickly opened them again to find that Ash was still, or once again, standing in front of Katie. Her stare was still on us, as she raised her hand to her mouth and let out a very childish giggle.

"Be careful what you wish for Gracie." Jennifer said to her young teenaged daughter.

"Right...mental note, made. Lesson learned." Grace said, her voice suddenly shaky and frail sounding.

The doors at both ends of the dance hall swung open nearly simultaneously. Rick Hayes and Theo entered, one at each end, and even in the extremely dim light, everyone noticed the movement shadows that followed closely behind them, and then rushed past them to surround young Ashley. 'Poor young Ash', I thought. Possibly, this was a mistake. Maybe there were flaws in my plan that I not only didn't understand, but couldn't understand.

Everyone watched intently. The shadows appeared to grow around her, encircling her, dimming her light. What had I done? I was just about to jump up and try to distract the shadowy figures, when something quite amazing happened. Overhead, the smallest pinpoint of light appeared, and shone down like the smallest of spotlights on the assemblage of spirits. As the pinpoint of light grew, so did my desire to move closer to it. I no longer felt the need to help Ashley (which, looking back, was a ridiculous thought), but the light called and beckoned me to come. Larger and brighter it became, until the spirits were barely visible. Katie's stare was fixed on the light, but she resisted the desire to join the spirits, and bathe in its brilliant beauty and warmth. In a flash, the circle of entities became engulfed in a raging fury of flames that were immediately extinguished, as was the heavenly light. Ash was gone, and so were the shadow men.

Although we should have had our doubts and concerns and we were slightly confused and uncertain of the facts, not a single one of us felt that anything bad had happened. It felt quite the opposite, actually. There was a sudden equanimity that washed over us, and all doubts were taken from us.

"Well, that was...something." Grace said with a long pause between words, still shaken by the sheer power of what she had seen.

"You get used to it after a while." Del joked, as if this were an everyday occurrence.

"Oh, yeah... this stuff happens all the time." Barb jested back to Del. Jenn's sarcasm was rubbing off on everyone.

"I wonder if we will ever see Ash again." I thought out loud.

"Whether we want to or not, we will." Katie said, as she wandered from the stage to where we sat.

***

"The room upstairs, opposite from the 'Gentleman's Room'..." Rick instructed, "...is where we need to go. I feel that is one of the few places left in this building, where the family used to spend time together, that hasn't changed dramatically in the past century."

"I agree. It feels right to me also." Theo commented, and so, without taking a proper rest to gather our thoughts, we trekked up to the second floor of the home.

The dark and dismal room now seemed inviting to us. We gathered ourselves in a semi-circle on the floor, and quietly waited. Exactly what we were waiting for, we weren't sure, but the moments passed and though I had no real idea of how to begin, I held no worries that we were doing the right thing. The silence was broken by the smooth sound of Rick's voice.

244

"Charles... bring your mother and join us, please." Rick's thoughts were far deeper than his words. In his mind he was connecting to the spirit world around us, as was Theo.

"Amelia... follow the energy of my voice. Find my thoughts." Theo drew himself deep into a state of mid-world-ness. The conscious, and the physical, part of him remained on our plane of existence, while his subconscious journeyed to the spiritual plane. His summoned his spirit guides to help him find and connect with Amelia, in a similar, yet different, way that Rick was connecting to Charles and his mother.

"There is no need to hide anymore, children. Come join us all." Jenn spoke into the blackness of the night.

"Donnie, Timmy, Brian, Little John..." Katie called out, looking around. "We are your friends, and we want to help you."

The rest of us remained mute, and simply thought about each of the seven family members who had been scattered like ashes in the wind. We imagined their reunion, and what a joyous time it would be. Our thoughts called out to them, or at least, that was our intention.

Rick Hayes and Theo watched as, one by one, the Bettiger family gathered in a room they once called home. Even those of us who do not have a sixth sense felt the growing presence of spiritual energy around us, and hoped for some sign that we were nearing our goal. The collective energy shifted and its power began to give Jennifer one of her migraines, the ones that we had always attributed to intense spiritual activity, or sometimes electro-magnetic frequencies that were off the charts. Rick spoke again.

"Seven is a powerful number, and family is a powerful bond. You have both." As he paused I realized that this must mean all seven of the Bettigers were now together. "Take each other's hands, reconnect, and look deep inside yourselves. Can you feel the warmth and the light?" Rick and Theo watched as the family embraced one another and formed a spiritual bond.

"Now, look outside of you. Focus on a point. See it as a point of light, and visualize as it becomes larger and closer to you." Theo continued where Rick had left off.

245

The two worked so well together, that it almost felt rehearsed, or as if this was something they had done countless times in the past. The power of belief and spirit was so strong that everyone in the room began to visualize this pinpoint of starlight, and we watched it become a glowing orb, ever increasing in circumference. A brilliant, white light flowed from it, and had the appearance of a luminescent waterfall, with its radiance splashing down in our midst. In the miraculous revelation of light, we saw them, for the first time. The Bettigers had been revealed to us, in a way that did not seem ghostly. In many ways, they appeared as a normal, everyday family. The vision we had been blessed with, however, was far from normal and 'everyday'. It was an unforgettable, and life altering glimpse at eternity, an eternity that was so full of omnipotent and omnipresent love and light, that no shadow could exist. We gazed, mesmerized as the utopian light engulfed the family, and the family consumed it, until there was no discernible separation between light and beings. They had become beings of light, and as miraculously as it had all began, we watched as the light shrank back to into the most beautifully incredible orb, and then even further, to become the most brilliant starlight we had ever experienced... and ever so slowly it faded from our sight.

Not a sound was made, and no one even moved for the longest time. We had been given a gift very, very few ever receive. The reality of our world was so harsh compared to the peaceful feeling of what I believe is a true universal consciousness, that there were parts of each of us that had no desire to return to our earthly lives...places deep within our souls that desperately longed to follow the family into that great unknown peace, but it was not our time. We each have a purpose here on this earth, and regardless of our accomplishments or lack thereof, when we have done our part, and played out our intended role, our time will come, and we will join with everyone who has gone before us, and all of those souls who will come after us, and the next great adventure will begin.

246

Chapter 20

A FAREWELL OF SORTS

It was a clear and cool Saturday morning in late October. The air was crisp. The smell of autumn was on the wind, and the leaves on the trees in southern Indiana were painting the landscape with reds, yellows and oranges. Linda and Barb were out for coffee, and discussing the new location for the Owl's Nest #30, when Linda's husband, Fred, called.

"You'll never guess who just showed up at our door." Fred started off the phone conversation.

"Well, no… I probably can't. So, why don't you just tell me?" Linda joked with her husband.

"I was getting ready to head next door to take one last look around before the crew fired up the equipment, when a knock came at the door." He led her on, trying to build her anticipation.

"So, have they started yet?" Linda didn't bite.

"You're no fun." Fred moped, but then his voice came to life. "Okay, I'll just tell you... I am standing here in our foyer, face to face, with Allison Bettiger."

"Well, why didn't you just tell me?...uugghh..." Linda groaned humorously. "We'll be right there. Tell the crew to hold off work for an hour, if they will." Linda hung up her phone, and putting it in her purse, shot a look across the table to Barb.

"What's going on?" Barb asked curiously.

"Ms. Bettiger is at my house, right now." Linda scurried to her feet and grabbed up her coffee, slinging her bag over her shoulder. "You comin'?"

"Of course!" Barb answered excitedly. "What's she doing at your house?"

"I don't know, unless she wanted to see the old house one last time. We had better hurry. I want to get there before the workers get started." Linda rushed the conversation, and Barb towards the car.

"I didn't even know that Ms. B. knew." Barb seemed puzzled.

"I don't think she did... at least I didn't tell her, so if she knows, I don't know how." Linda was just as confused, and somewhat concerned.

"Maybe it's just a coincidence." Barb tried to rationalize. "I know it's last minute, and everything should be in storage until the new building is ready for us to move into, but something is telling me we need to take another look around to be sure we aren't leaving anything behind."

"Fred said he would try to put the crew off for an hour, so maybe we will have a chance to do one last walk through...maybe with Ms. Bettiger." Linda spoke as she sped down First Avenue, leaving the Starbucks in her rear view mirror.

Her home and the timeworn building were less than two miles down the road from the coffee shop. It seemed that the stars were aligning as she drove and passed the nearly dozen green traffic lights. Within minutes, the two women pulled into Linda's driveway and parking the car hastily, they rushed into the house breathing heavy from the brisk walk and the adrenaline that was now coursing steadily through their veins. Neither of them knew what to expect, or what Ms. Allison Bettiger's reaction would be to the old family home and former Owl's Nest property being sold.

"Well hello ladies!" Allison Bettiger called out to them as they entered the front room where she and Fred were sitting immersed in conversation. The women exchanged hugs and greetings, and the nervousness of Linda and Barb vanished abruptly.

"So, what brings you to town?" Linda opened up with, not beating around the bush at all.

"I don't really know. I just needed to come." Allison pondered for a moment, as if in deep thought, trying to recollect why she had been compelled to make the long trip. "This may sound a bit 'coo-coo', but I had a dream last night, and a little girl told me that I needed to go home before it was too late. I can't say why, but it really made an impression on me, and I got up in the middle of the night, and called my nurse-friend. She is such a doll... she came over immediately, and we left out about four this morning... and so, here I am." She smiled at the three of them.

"If you'll excuse me, I need to run next door." Fred excused himself and trotted out the front door with purpose.

"Oh yes, by the way...what is going on next door? I noticed all of the construction equipment and dump trucks at the old home." Allison innocently queried.

249

"Oh, I am so sorry, to have not called you about this, but it just kind of snuck up on us." Linda admitted and looked to Barb for some help explaining the situation.

"I'm afraid the Owl's Nest just couldn't afford the upkeep on the old place, and the utility bills were outweighing the income... I don't know how to say this, but we've sold the property to the plastics plant that's just between us and the old Willard Library." Barb bashfully admitted.

"Oh dear!" Allison put her open hand to her mouth. "Whatever would a factory want with an old building like that?"

"Unfortunately, they aren't interested in the building. They are interested in the property for parking and future expansion." Linda finally spoke the inevitable, as heartbreaking as she knew it would be for Ms. Bettiger. "Fred has just gone over to see if they would delay starting the work for a little while so we could all walk through the building one last time, to make sure we hadn't left anything behind."

"I **would** like to visit the old place one more time. I have to check and see if something my mother told me is true, or if it was just a silly story." Allison smiled, but the ladies could see the tears growing in her care worn eyes.

The front door opened snappishly and Fred stuck his head in the room. "They said we can have two hours, so we may want to hurry."

He disappeared back outside again, and just as his words hit them, so did the brisk chill of the October breeze that entered the home with his news. Allison stood up and began to wrap her sweater around her shoulders, as the three headed out the front door. They made the short walk over to where a gate had been put up in the temporary construction fence that surrounded the property. Passing through the gate, over to the building and up the handicap accessible ramp, they found themselves at the front entrance of the old building. The small group noticed a sadness that seemed to exude from the tired old structure. The front door opened with an aged groan, as if the building itself were giving up its last breath.

Inside, an eerie silence filled the empty spaces that once housed the playful laughter of the Bettiger children, and the sounds of music, banters of friends, and the business hoopla of a social club. Every footstep felt burdened, and everywhere they looked, the memories that had hung on the walls or in the vast desolation of the enormous structure were now lost. An overwhelming sorrow grew around them as they escorted Ms. Bettiger from room to room, finding nothing left behind. Despite the unnatural solitude of the vacant building, Allison Bettiger collected memories from each room she visited, from the main floor, to the basement, and eventually to the upper floor, where the home was still mostly original.

Reaching the top of the stairs, the foursome stopped to take a breather, but the eldest of the group pushed past them and into the room to her left. She gazed around the room that the brothers she never known had not been allowed. This room was the 'gentleman's room' where the father (she also had never known) had conducted his business. When the others joined her in the room, they found her standing before the door with the red glass knob. Her frail hand quivered as she reached out and took hold of the knob. With what little strength she had, she applied pressure, attempting to turn the knob, but it was locked securely.

"I don't think that door has ever been unlocked as long as the Owls have been here." Barb informed her.

"I wonder..." Allison muttered to herself, as she turned slowly towards her friends. Then as if in a daze, she stumbled away from the door and with the labored steps of her tired old legs, brushed past them as if they didn't matter, or weren't even there. Fred, Linda and Barb, followed her out of the room past the stairwell, that no longer felt ominous, and through the room on the opposite side of the home. She walked intentionally through the room where her siblings once played...where many of them had also died. She stopped short of the grand front window that was boarded up and turning to her direct right, looked over her right shoulder with a childlike grin to her dear friends, and proceeded to enter the peculiar 'non-closet' room. The other three joined her quickly to see where she was headed and why.

251

"It's should be right over here somewhere, I'm certain." Allison said to them as they stood behind her and watched the elderly woman running her hands along the chair rail on the side opposite of the door they had all entered.

"What's over there?" Fred was curious and puzzled, wondering if their dear old friend was experiencing some mild form of dementia or Alzheimer's.

"The secret..." Her words trailed off and the ladies looked back and forth at each other wondering what she might possibly mean.

In the midst of the confusion there was an unexpected moment of clarity for all of those who were there, but especially for Barb. Allison grasped the chair rail with both hands near the corner of the wall, and gave it a stern tug upwards. "POP!" A piece of the wood trim rose in her hands and a panel on the lower wall opened up with a loud metallic popping noise.

"That's what we heard in the basement!" Barb blurted out, and suddenly felt flushed with a cold sweat on her brow.

"Be a dear and give me a hand please?" Ms. Bettiger looked over her shoulder with a grin, once again, while she pulled at the panel and swung it open, creaking on its piano hinge.

"What can I do for you?" Fred asked, stunned at the revelation.

"Just give me your hand for a minute." Allison Bettiger instructed and held her hand out, taking Fred's hand in hers. Clinging tightly to it, Allison knelt down on the floor in front of the small opening.

"Oh here," Barb called out to Allison. "Take this." She said. Pulling a small l.e.d. flashlight from her back pocket and turning it on, she handed it to the woman.

"Mother said my brothers used to hide in here where no one would be able to find them." Allison said, as she crawled into the small space, vanishing into the darkness that the flashlight refused to illuminate. The three friends were unsure

252

what to do, so they stood silently listening to the slow scuffling sounds coming from within this secret room. Momentarily, Allison appeared at the opening again and held her hand out. Fred reached out to take her hand and help the dusty old woman out of the time capsule of dirt and cob webs, but she refused to take his hand and instead, placed an old skeleton style iron key in his palm. Her bent, arthritic finger pointed and motioned for him to go unlock the door with the red glass knob. She disappeared back into the darkness of the hidden haven.

Barb knelt down, and took a seat on the dusty floor near the opening, while Linda and Fred reentered the room opposite from her. Barb could make out very little besides the silhouette of the old Bettiger woman who had also taken a seat on the dusty and dirty floor that hadn't been disturbed in a hundred years. There was a clicking and popping sound that came from within the dark space and slowly the light grew around Allison, revealing her surroundings.

Linda looked on as Fred placed the key in the old lock below the red knob, and turning it, the mechanism spun with quiet clicks, ticks and pops. He took the knob in hand, gave it a turn, and with a pull, the door moaned on its hinges and opened, letting the light of day fall on the area for the first time in numerous decades. Linda inhaled loudly.

There, before them, stood a beautifully ornate stairway that led to nowhere, and ended sharply at the wooden rafter ceiling.

"It's the stairs that went to the old tower!" Linda called out with excitement. "Oh, how gorgeous!"

The smallish room held a narrow space next to the stairs that led the couple to an opening under the oak stairwell. Leaning down to peer under the stairs, Fred and Linda found Allison sitting on the floor with her legs to the side. In her lap was a small, blue, stuffed elephant, and owl, both worn and slightly matted. Allison's Hand reached out towards the floor in front of her, turning the pages of a large, old, hard covered book... Little Red Riding Hood, and scattered within its pages were the crisp, blackened red petals of a number of roses.

Allison looked up with teary eyes. "Mother told me this existed, and I don't know if I didn't believe her, or if I didn't want to believe her...but here it is. The stories are true, they are all really true. I really did have a family, even if we didn't share the same time and space." Allison closed the book and pulled it snug against her chest, hugging it tightly, and allowing the tears to escape her eyes and adorn her spider-veined, rosy cheeks. She sat there in silence and solitude for a few minutes, and when she had gathered her thoughts and taken control of her feelings, she asked for help up. Fred and Linda helped her out of the secret hiding place under the stairs, where her siblings once hid from the villainous thugs their father had done business with. She emerged with spider webs in her hair, and her dress covered in the remnants of time that had gathered on the floor beneath her.

The friends held her by her elbows as they descended the stairs, as her hands were filled with the large book and the stuffed toy animals which she refused to release. Walking out of the front door, the bright autumn sky and cool air gave them a refreshing greeting, as if it were welcoming them back to the present day. They stood on the front landing just outside of the entryway and absorbed all that had just been revealed to them. There were smiles and a comfort that could not be explained, that was shared by all four of the friends. It was then that a familiar face appeared from around the corner, coming up the ramp.

"Well, how'd it go in there?" Del asked, noticing Allison's arms filled with her antique family treasures.

"Well..." Allison answered him with a squeaky, emotional crack in her aged voice. "Very well."

"Del," Barb began, "The door with the red knob is unlocked... Allison found the key. Could you take that lock off for Jenn?"

"Sure. Let me grab some tools..." He thought for a second. "She was kind of fascinated with that lock, wasn't she?" and then he disappeared to get his tools.

The three ladies returned to Linda and Fred's home next door, and began to prepare a lunch for them all. Fred remained at the front door and joined Del to help him remove the old lock from the once mysterious door. When they had finished, and Del had reassembled the lock, he and Fred joined the three women in the comfort of the beautiful home. The, now, five friends gathered at the dining room table and enjoyed the fellowship of good conversation, and great friendship while they savored the delectable meal that had been prepared.

When the meal was finished and the coffee was being poured, there was a loud, thunderous sound that intruded on the peaceful setting.

"I guess it's time." Fred spoke somberly.

"Time for what?" Allison asked sheepishly.

The others' faces had grown long, knowing the inevitable was upon them. Del stood up with Fred and gazed out of the window. The thunderous boom hit them again and brought a feeling of anguish to the deepest pits of their stomachs.

"Let's take our coffee outside. I think we should…" Linda's voice was meek, and though she didn't want to face the reality, she thought it was best. They gathered their jackets, and cups, and once again returned outside, walking slowly and regretfully to the cold, chain link, construction fence.

Looking on, their hearts broke as they watched the large buckets on the bull-dozers and scoops as they continued to rip apart the history and the memories that this amazing building held. As the equipment boomed against the structure, it crumbled bit by bit, filling the air around it with a cloud of brick dust and debris that floated through the air and slow settled on the surfaces of everything that surrounded it. Even Fred and Del couldn't keep their emotions bottled up, and the men's eyes watered, though they blamed it on the cool air and the dusty fog that rolled to them. The three ladies, on the other hand, cried openly, especially Allison.

255

Looking on, and focusing deep into the rubble, Allison caught the glimpse of a young girl, amidst the destruction, who smiled at her, as if to say 'Everything will be fine, it is finished'. Allison held her coffee cup in one hand and had the little blue elephant tucked neatly and cozily under her other arm.

She gave the stuffed toy a gentle squeeze and quietly said, "We weren't too late, were we? ...a rhetorical question that she knew the answer to. She smiled back at the young blonde girl who seemed to fade into the billowing dust-clouds that were created by the demolition crew.

The onlookers watched for nearly an hour as the angry, growling, yellow claws and scoops ate away at the stature of the times gone by. Their attention was distracted by a honking horn from Fred and Linda's driveway. Allison's nurse had returned from her shopping trip to the east side of Evansville and emerged from her car in dismay.

"What's going on?" She shouted above the roaring diesel motors and the sounds of falling rubble.

"The old home is being put to rest." Allison told her when she finally approached the cluster of friends.

The nurse shook her head saying, "Now, that's a real shame."

But, Allison held up her elephant and smiled at her, as the salty deluge embraced her cheeks once again. "It was time... not a moment too soon, and not a moment too late. This was meant to be."

The friends waved good-bye as Allison and her nurse drove away, and then returned to the harsh reality that this was the end of an era and most definitely, a very sorrowful end indeed.

Chapter 21

HOLIDAY GATHERINGS

The weeks passed after the Order of the Owls had moved into their newly renovated location. A Christmas party had been planned for the Saturday before the holiday, which would also be the first weekend the new location was open. Barb, Del, Linda, and an assortment of other volunteers had spent all morning decorating the new dance hall and putting up the Christmas tree, and other festive holiday decorations in expectation of the big party.

"Barb, who are the guys in the bar room sitting in the corner?" One of the helpers asked.

"I didn't think there was anyone in there." She said as she rushed in to see who the unknown guests were, but no one was there. Her holiday helper had followed her into the room.

"I swear there were just three guys sitting right there." He pointed to the corner. "Two of them were wearing black jackets, and the other one was in a yellow shirt. Maybe they realized we weren't open yet and left."

"Maybe..." Barb smiled. She had a feeling that these patrons were still around, and though she didn't know their names, she had a good idea of who they were.

Holiday themed music played quietly in the background, fat, flurrying snow fell silently outside and the combination put all of the helpers in a very jolly mood. It was on that Saturday afternoon, while using a step stool to hang clusters of mistletoe over the various doorways, that Barb received a surprising phone call.

"Hello?" she said inquisitively, not recognizing the phone number on the screen of her cell phone.

"Hi, is this Barb?" The cheery voice on the other end said.

"Yes it is, who may I ask is calling?" She said in a professional tone, still puzzled at who this anonymous stranger was, calling her by her first name.

"Well, hey there Barb, this is Rick Hayes. How have you been?" and suddenly the voice became not only recognizable, but familiar.

"Oh, hi Rick. To what do I owe the pleasure?" She asked with a spark in her voice.

"I hope you don't mind, I got your number from the 'other Rick'. He said it would be okay." He wanted to be sure he hadn't over stepped any boundaries.

"Of course! You're fine." The tone in Barb's voice happily fluctuated as she spoke.

"Okay, good... you all have been on my mind a lot since I was down there to visit your club, and all day today, I couldn't get Ms. Allison off of my mind. She seemed very happy, and peaceful... not that she wasn't before." Rick paused for a moment in thought. "I feel like she has reconnected with someone she hasn't seen in a very long time, like a very close friend, or even a family member. Does any of this make sense to you?" He stopped for a breath, and to await an answer.

"No, I'm afraid it doesn't. Unless you are thinking of when she was down for a visit, when the old Owl's Nest building was torn down, but that was ...oh gosh... a couple of months ago." She scoured her memory, but that was definitely that last time she had heard from, or about, Ms. Allison Bettiger.

"Well, alright... I don't think it is anything to worry about. It actually feels like a very happy time for her. I just thought maybe you had talked to her, or knew something I didn't" Rick said politely.

"Well that's a first!" Barb said with joyous sarcasm. "The psychic thinks I may know something before he does." She chuckled at the thought.

"Just because I am a psychic-medium doesn't mean I know everything." Rick laughed along with Barb. "Alright, I'll let you get back to decorating for your party, and just keep that in the back of your mind, and next time you hear from her, see if anything made her exceptionally happy today."

"Oh, I will... heeeey..." Barb drug out her word. "How did you know I was decorating for a party?"

"Psychic, remember?" Rick and Barb bubbled with holiday laughter. "Keep BE-lieving, and have a great holiday! Talk to you soon." Rick said.

"I will, and you have a great holiday too, Rick! Oh, while I have you on the phone, I wanted to tell you that the week after you came to the club, I got a call from my doctor's office. I had some tests done, and it seems my cholesterol was really high. They asked me to cut out a few things... like butter." She smiled as she told the story.

261

"Wow... I'm glad they caught it, and let you know. That may explain the stick of butter I saw when we were talking. Those kind of validations are what keeps *me* believing. Okay, tell everyone I said hi, and I wish them all a joyous holiday! Talk to you soon." Rick ended the conversation.

"I will. You have a wonderful holiday too! B-bye." Barb hung up the phone and found that she had a small audience around the foot of her step stool.

"What was that all about?" Linda loudly joked to her friend.

"THAT... was Rick Hayes. He called *me* to ask if I had heard from Ms. Bettiger recently, and he wanted me to tell everyone hi, and happy holidays." Barb went through the condensed version of their conversation, telling it to all of the volunteers who had surrounded her while she was chatting on her phone.

"I haven't talked to her since the day she was here. She called me that night to let me know that she had arrived home safely. Oh, and she did send me a Thanksgiving holiday card, but other than that, I really haven't heard from her." Linda said to Barb, but everyone was listening to hear what was going on. "Maybe I'll call her this evening before the party starts, just to see how she is doing, and to let her know everyone is thinking about her."

"Thanks a nice gesture." Del interjected. "Tell her Barb and I said hello, and merry Christmas."

"I sure will." It warmed Linda's heart, knowing that she would be talking to her old friend so close to the holidays.

The snow flurries had grown steadily thicker and the snowfall was now a beautiful shower of white, cottony fairies that danced and twirled in the twilight of the late afternoon. It was nearly four o'clock when the decorating was finished, and the friends all gathered around a couple of tables telling stories and reliving precious memories from the past.

"There's my ride." Linda stood up and gestured to the front of the new club. Through the windows, everyone could

262

see the warm car that Fred had pulled up in, waiting by the curb to pick her up.

"See you in a while, right?" Barb asked for confirmation.

"We are just going to dinner, and then we'll both be back for the party by seven or eight." Linda reassured her. Causal good-bye waves were given as she headed out into the snowy wonderland.

"I didn't think we were supposed get anything but a few flurries." Fred joked as she stepped into the car. He had been surprised by the early arrival of wintery weather in southern Indiana.

"Supposed to, or not, it's here. I just hope we don't get too much. People might stay home, or worse, come out and have to drive home on slick roads." Linda was concerned, but didn't let it dampen her mood.

"So where do you want to go for dinner?" He asked, half expecting her to say, 'Home.'

"I don't care, as long as it isn't too loud. I want to try to call Allison Bettiger before we head back to the Owls." She mumbled, half to herself.

"Oh, about that... Kind of an odd coincidence, but you had a call at home while you were decorating." Fred's voice had fallen to monotone, and not as cheery as it had been when he joked about the unexpected snowfall.

***

It was Friday evening, and Allison peered through the front window as the snow began to fall. Though it had been many decades since she had anyone to share the holidays with, she loved this time of year. There was a smile in the heart of the elderly woman, who had seen so much change in her lifetime, but one thing remained the same, her love for the mother that she gravely missed. Allison wandered from the front window to the small pine Christmas tree that had been placed on a short table in the corner of her living room. She had always insisted on having a real tree, and in her later years, she demanded a live tree that she could donate to the local Boy Scout troop, to be planted after the holidays were over.

This year, she had a three and a half foot blue spruce. It was covered in silver tinsel and white and blue lights that twinkled slowly. A hand made angel from Allison's childhood adorned the tree-top, and its branches were tipped with ornaments that spanned nearly a hundred years. She gazed at it lovingly, for all that it stood for, and all of the memories it held on its boughs. Beneath the tree there were no wrapped presents, but three gifts had been placed there by the old woman's shaky hands... a tattered, old, blue elephant, an owl, whose 'feathers' were now a beautifully matted mess, and an old hard cover book with worn and frayed edges, that hid rose petal memories within its pages. The soft and thin skin of Allison's hand gently touched the needles of the tree, an occasional light, and caressed a few of the ornaments. She knelt down cautiously before the tree and, picking up a plastic pitcher from the floor next to the table, watered the young evergreen. She stayed there for a moment and ran her hands across the 'presents' under the tree that she had been given earlier that year.

Standing up, she went to turn off the lights and find her way to her invitingly warm bed, and the goose down comforter that patiently waited for her. With the switches off, the only light in the room was the faint twinkling of the Christmas tree lights. Allison's nurse, who had brought the tree, put the lights on a timer so that they came on every evening just before dusk, and turned themselves off every night at midnight. She glanced at the tree one last time on her way to her bed, and detoured her path. It was truly a beautiful thing to her. Happy tears filled her smiling eyes, as she reached under the tree and retrieved the old elephant. Tucking it under her arm, she headed off to bed.

Allison sat on the edge of her bed, where she could still see the lights twinkling in the front room, and held the little elephant in her lap. "Dear lord..." She spoke out loud in the solitude of her bedroom. "...Thank you for this beautiful world and for my friends that you have given me..." She paused, deep in thought and humble gratitude, "...and thank you lord for this long and blessed life. Amen" She pulled back the comforter and top sheet, and slid herself into their warmth. Hugging the elephant tight, she drew a deep breath and closed her eyes. "Good night, my little friend." She whispered to the stuffed toy that now meant more to her that everything she had accumulated in her lifetime.

Allison slipped off to a peaceful slumber, and in the early morning hours a dream came to her. She stood in a mist of bright, white fog and three figures approached her, two adults and a child. The child stepped forward and out of the haze that shrouded her identity. Allison quickly recognized her as Ashley, the little girl from her dream, and the girl that appeared to her in the dusty cloud at the old family home.

"Ally, these are my parent's. Come with us." The girl's voice was hollow and haunting, as she stretched out her hand to Allison. Allison reached out to her, and now saw that the hand she reached out with was no longer riddled with arthritis. In fact, it appeared to be a child's hand. She looked down, and remembered the dress she wore as being one she had been so happy to receive on her thirteenth birthday. The two girls strolled hand in hand into the mists, and were joined by Ashley's parents.

"Where are we going?" Allison asked curiously.

"Home." was the only answer she received, and though it didn't seem to come from Ashley, or her parent's, the voice sounded familiar.

The four strolled through the foggy mist in a seemingly aimless and carefree fashion. After a bit, the cloudy fog lightened and the four travelers emerged into a bright and beautifully sun-shining day. Allison stopped in her tracks. The familiarity of the beautiful home before her struck her as odd. She pieced together her memories with a sudden knowledge that simply 'was', and found herself filled with amazement for the sight that stood before her.

"It's the old family home... but it isn't old anymore." Allison spoke in a breathless whisper. It was true. The old home was now beautiful, white, and pristine. The windows sparkled in the sunlight, and a bell rang in the tower announcing their arrival. The front doors swung open wide and Allison's Grandmother, mother (now young again, only in her thirties), Father, and four younger brothers rushed out to greet them.

Arms wrapped around each other, and joyful tears filled their eyes. Allison met her grandmother, father, and brothers for the first time, but felt as if they had known each other for a lifetime and longer. As they embraced, Allison looked over her shoulder to her friend Ashley and her parents, who held smiles across their faces that could not be dimmed, and as they waved to the newly reunited family, they vanished back into the mists that had brought them. Allison was not sad to see them go, for she knew in her heart they would see each other again. She turned back to her family, and her arms felt a weight in them. She looked down, to see the owl, elephant and book, resting in her folded arms, each looking crisp and new as it had on the day they were made. Allison smiled and knew this was far better than any Christmas gift she had ever hoped to receive.

"Oh, Ally-girl, welcome home!" Her mother cried out to her.

"It is good to be home... it is good to be a family. This **must** be Heaven!" Allison responded and the celebration continued for an endless amount of time. Her thoughts were filled with wonder and the possibilities of where this new life would take her were limitless.

***

Ashley Sue and her parents had slipped back into the fog, and their joy was met with contentment as they were joined by a council of spirit guides, and Angels, thanking them for guiding Allison home. It was now time for their family to return home again. They felt truly blessed and their souls held a completeness that is only attained by the selfless act of helping another in need, as they had once been helped.

***

Allison Bettiger never awoke again on this earth, and though her friends mourned her passing, there was a comforting feeling that none could deny. As Rick Hayes had so aptly put it, 'She seemed very happy, and peaceful... not that she wasn't before. I feel like she has reconnected with someone she hasn't seen in a very long time, like a very close friend, or even a family member'.

The EVP Investigations team held a holiday party of our own, and even with the passing of Ms. Allison Bettiger, it was a happy time for us. We had helped the public, and the patrons of the Owl's Nest, to understand that a haunting isn't always *just* a scary situation. Often times, it is merely a situation that requires understanding and guidance for a lost soul, and many times the needs transcend the planes of existence. Katie was beaming and the thrill of being a first time mommy showed on round tummy, and the radiant glow of her face. Sean was a proud 'future' papa, and we could all hear the paternal excitement in his voice when he and Katie chatted about how different Christmas would be next year, and the years to come.

"I just want to let everyone know how proud I am of you." I boasted to my team mates and friends. "Once again, you have gone far above and beyond the call of duty. I only wish there were some medal of honor I could award each of you with, but since there isn't, let me just make a toast." I raised my glass of spiced rum eggnog towards the center of the group, and was met by every glass in the room, including Katie's glass of sparkling flavored water.

"Here's to the most amazing paranormal team I could have ever imagined... here's to a team that is made up of friends... and to friends that are more like a family. I am honored to call each of you my friend." With the clinking of glasses and cheers of 'here, here,' and 'we love you too, E-V-Prick!', we all toasted one another's uniqueness *and* our similarities. I choked back the tears as I drank my toast, and blamed my watery eyes on the drink being too stout.

"So, what's next?" Jenn shouted over the racket of conversations and slightly too loud holiday music.

267

"A break!" I shouted back, and was shot looks of dismay. "Take it easy guys... just a short break... and that's only if nothing imperative comes up, but I think we all need a little family time, and time away from the all-night frights and emotional roller coasters that we've been on."

"I'll second that." Katie cringed as she spoke up. "I'm going to have to take a break for a while, whether I want to or not." She rubbed her belly in reference to her 'son' who would be arriving in a few short months.

The conversation ran on and on, all afternoon and evening. Everyone ate and drank to their heart's content, and before the night was over, we found ourselves all gathered around a big, flat screen T.V. watching 'It's a Wonderful Life', and it truly was.

EPILOGUE

The time off from paranormal investigating was needed and well appreciated. The winter months were typically slower for us anyway, so it was not as if we were greatly missed, but as soon as the spring thaw came, so did our next request. This time it came in the form of a phone call from a   friend whom we had grown close to through our world-wide paranormal family.

"Hello?" I answered the unknown phone number.

"Hi, is this Rick?" The woman on the other end said.

"Yes it is. Can I help you?" I kept my professional tone until I could figure out who I was talking to.

"It's Hilary. Remember me from the conventions?" she said lightly.

"Hilary! How have you been?" I did remember her, a sweet young woman who was raising money to save a wonderfully historic landmark near her home town...in northern Ohio.

"Been pretty good... okay, look... I know we both know hundreds of people, famous and not so famous, in the paranormal field... but I really want you and your team to help me out here if you can." She wasn't exactly beating around the bush, but she hadn't gotten to the point yet either.

"What can we do for you?" I expected her to ask for help with a fund-raiser, or something like that.

"It's Maddie...she has gotten worse and I can't handle her anymore... I can't even bring myself to go to the 'Infirmary' alone now. There is no real rush... she's been waiting a hundred years, but if you think you could pencil us in, we could really use your team's expertise." Her voice was troubled.

"Send me what you have... everything... history, photos, time lines, whatever you have managed to dig up, and if you need help with that let me know and one or two of us will come and work with you. Once we have that in hand, we can form a plan." I knew this was a serious situation, just from the sound of her voice as she spoke about it.

"Thank you so much! I won't keep you, and I'll be in touch via email, in the next few weeks, okay?" Hilary, once again, asked for confirmation that we would be willing to help.

"Of course! Just email, or call, or whatever you need to do. We're here for you." I meant every word I said, but part of me was honestly worried.

***

I met up with Jenn, Katie and Theo on a fairly regular basis throughout our winter break. Like most, this particular meeting was at the Starbucks inside of our local Barnes & Noble Booksellers store. Our chatter rambled for quite some time about family and friends and the reappearance of the ground, after a long and 'white' winter, but mostly about Katie's new little boy, and how difficult and stressful parenting could be. Jenn and I tried to give her comforting advise, but Theo just sat back blushing and grinned.

"I have no idea about being a parent, and I don't plan on ever having an idea about it." He chuckled knowing his choice of lifestyles had taken that possibility out of the equation. "But, I think you will make a wonderful mom."

"Well, no sense in prolonging the inevitable." I said, and stopped the conversation cold. "We have another investigation request... in Northern Ohio."

All eyes turned to me, and mouths dropped open. Even though there were mostly complaints about taking a break, I knew it would be a shock to the system to jump back in to investigating 'with both feet'. It was obvious to the team that this case must be important, and someone must be in dire need, for me to suggest trekking to northern Ohio.

"When do we go?" was the first question that was asked...by Katie, who smiled.

"I haven't set it up yet, but there is apparently no rush, so we can probably do some research and planning before we have to set a date. Theo, Jenn... are you two on board?" I asked, already knowing the answers.

"Uh.... nah... I'm just going to sit this one out." Jenn replied calmly.

"Really?" I asked, both confused and concerned.

"DUH! Set it up! You know I'm in!" Jenn's sarcasm had, for the first time in a while, surfaced and caught me off guard. We all laughed at how I had fallen for her comment, hook, line and sinker.

"Just let me know ahead of time so I can make schedule the time off, but you know I'll be there." Theo said, still laughing a bit between words.

"It's settled then. I'll contact Hilary and let her know, and then we will have another meeting to plan a schedule, probably in a couple of weeks." I sat back in my chair and sipped at my French vanilla cappuccino.

"No rest for the wicked." Katie said jokingly.

"Or us..." I mumbled under my breath. "...here we go again."

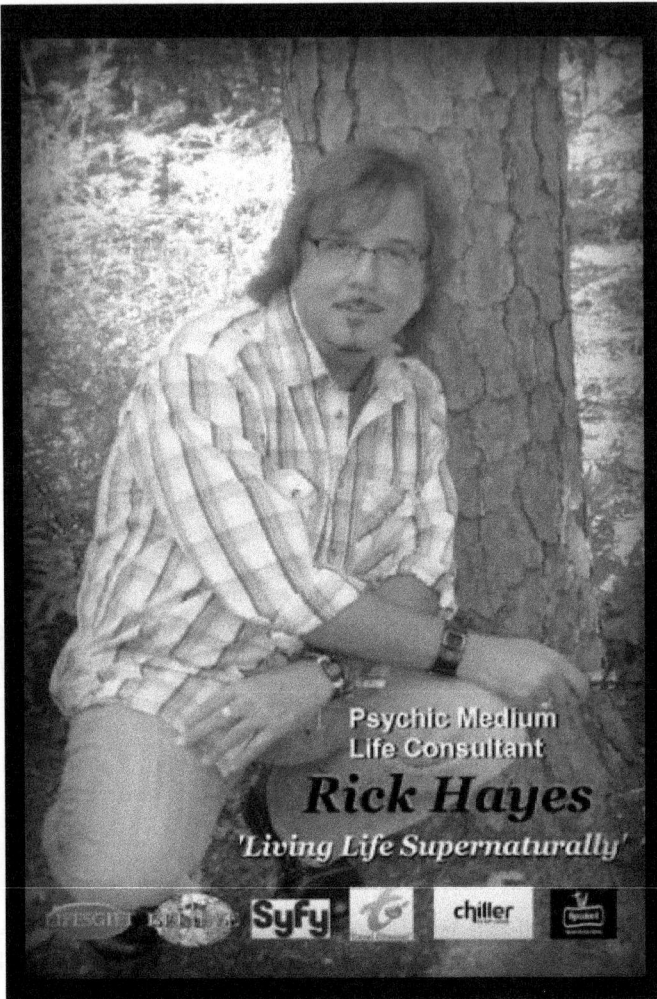

Psychic Medium
Life Consultant

Rick Hayes

'Living Life Supernaturally'

Psychic Medium/Life Consultant
Rick Hayes
'Living Life Supernaturally'

Rick Hayes
"Amazing and very real - The best at what he does"
Christopher Saint Booth – Producer/Director Spooked Productions

2013 Psychic Medium of the Year – Paranormal Awards Association

A Top 50 Psychic in America
"Top 100 Psychics and Astrologers in America"
2014 book by Paulette Cooper and Paul Noble

Rick Hayes is the founder of LifesGift, Inc. – an association that supports his consultation and speaking engagement services. As a psychic medium and life consultant with unique abilities, Rick consults on a daily basis with those that have questions on life and the life-after.

As a speaker and lecturer, Rick has shared his unique insight with inspiration and enthusiasm to thousands since 2003. Rick's speaking invitations range from a small organization group to major events and conventions attended by thousands. Rick's wide range of topics is designed to accommodate each speaking invitation.

As a published author, Rick's books include 'Stepping Stones –Thoughts Along Life's Path' (ISBN# 0-9765434-1-9) and 'You're not Crazy, You Have A Ghost' (ISBN# 0-9765434-0-0). Rick's articles appear on numerous print and online publications.

Rick is a media favorite appearing on television, film, radio, and print media including appearances on The Travel Channel, SYFY Network, Chiller Channel, Fox Television, and Sirius Satellite Radio. Rick is also the host of the weekly syndicated internet radio show, 'Reflections with Rick Hayes'.

THE Psychic Medium from SYFY's 'The Possessed'

Rick is featured in the docu-film 'The Possessed' (NBC Universal/Spooked Productions) and 'Soul Catcher' (NBC Universal/Spooked Productions) on the SYFY Television Network. Rick also appears on the Travel Channel's 'Most Terrifying Places In America' and 'Children of The Grave 2' (NBC/Chiller Network).

Rick Hayes
Living Life - Supernaturally

JENNIFER

KIRSCH

Jennifer is a 40 something mom of three and with the recent marriage of her oldest son, is now the proud mother-in-law to one.

Jenn's interest in the paranormal began when she was only a small child. Her grandmother's spirit would visit and comfort Jenn, while her father was away serving in the Vietnam War. Though as a child she didn't recognize it, Jennifer had a strong sensitivity to spirit activity.

Growing up in a Christian household, her interest in the paranormal was squelched as a child, but was rekindled as an adult when she found herself living in a house that had a wide variety of frequent paranormal activity.

While living in an actual haunted house, and EVP Investigations was still in its infancy, she contacted Rick Kueber to come investigate the house and was asked to join the group. Jennifer has been the Team's Lead Investigator ever since. Her interest in the paranormal has spread to her youngest child, who wants to follow in her footsteps.

KATIE
COLLINS

Katie Collins was born and raised locally in southern Indiana. Her interest in the paranormal began around the age of 8, when she had her first personal paranormal experience involving the spirit of her Grandmother. Katie joined the EVP team and quickly grew to be an integral part of the group. Known to be the "McGuyver" of the EVP team, she always has a backup flashlight, batteries or spare roll of duct tape in her equipment case (pink of course).

As a level headed and forward thinking member of EVP, she's always looking for an explanation behind paranormal happenings. Katie has also been known to be quiet at times and is an excellent observer, though she can also cut-up and infuse sarcasm in her rhetoric as well as any team member.

The mother of a young toddler, she has a maternal and sympathetic approach to investigating, and is readily aware when a situation needs to be handled cautiously and sensitively.

Like all of EVP's members, Katie is a great asset to the team on many levels, such as paranormal, social, research, and planning, and she can be individualized by one obvious constant... Katie loves PINK.

THEO
KOSTARIDIS

     At 41 years old, and a sixth generation psychic with a long family ancestry of intuitives, Theo was born in Athens, Greece. He moved to the United States at the age of 4 and lived in Florida until after college, when he finally accepted his destiny of intuitive arts, accumulating 20 years of professional experience in psychic readings. In 2001 Theo moved to Evansville, Indiana and now resides in Henderson, KY. He has worked various psychic fairs in numerous states as well as New Age and Spiritual Shops. Over the years, Theo started by honing his natural abilities, and then became very proficient in the use of tarot cards, psychometry, tea leaf and Greek coffee readings, and a variety of other tools. Theo has become the talk of the psychic world in Indiana and hosts seminars and workshops at Barnes & Noble and other locales. Theo has also worked missing persons cases with local police departments with phenomenal results.

     Working with Evansville Vanderburgh Paranormal on several investigations as well as hosting seminars with E.V.P. as his invited guest speakers, Theo has become an integral part of the EVP family. Being a Trance Medium*, Theo specializes in communicating with those who have crossed over and channeling messages from your spirit guides and angels.

*A Trance-Medium is a person who is in contact with spirits and communicates between the living & the dead. A spirit uses the medium's mind & body to communicate. The medium does not have clear recall of the messages conveyed while in an altered state; such people may sometimes work with an assistant. The assistant records the medium words as they are delivered.

Terms and Equipment:

EMF: acronym for either electro-magnetic field, or frequency. EMFs are generated by many sources, both natural and manmade. The human body emits a natural e.m.f., while a cell phone or microwave oven would emit a man-made e.m.f. EMFs are measured with several different devices, and can have a wide range of strengths and 'speeds'. Much like a sound wave, an electro-magnetic frequency is measured by the strength and frequency of its waves. An e.m.f. detector registering a .5 would represent a wave that occurred .5 times over the set length of time and space, whereas it would take an exponentially stronger e.m.f. to register a 1.5 on the same scale.

Various EMF Detectors/meters used in paranormal investigating:

K-II Meter	MEL-Meter	Cell Sensor

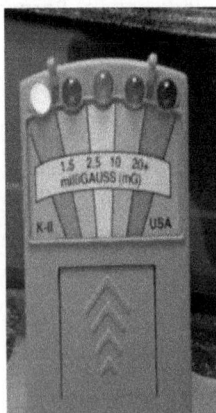 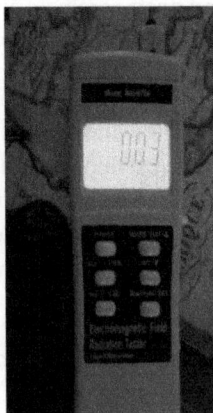 

EVP: acronym for 'electronic voice phenomenon'. Many times people experience hearing voices in a haunted location. An 'e.v.p.' is a voice or sound that is not heard by the human ear, but instead it picked up by electronic means, such as an audio or video recording device.

Often times a paranormal researcher will use a digital recorder to perform an 'EVP Session'. This is a series of standard and site specific questions that will later be reviewed and scrutinized using high tech computer programs to detect any voice phenomenon that may occur randomly, or in response to the questions being asked.

Any type of recording device can be used for these e.v.p. sessions, but a digital recorder records the audio into files that can be easily transferred to a computer for analyzing:

Infra-Red Camera: often called I.R. cameras and 'night-vision', these cameras can film in complete darkness by capturing infrared light that cannot be seen by the human eye, the video or photos captured by these cameras often has a green cast, or will only be in black and white. While these images are not always the best for capturing shadow phenomenon, they are very helpful due to many investigations being done at night in complete darkness. Many times the un-natural movement of an object has been recorded using this type of camera. A series of infra-red lights can be seen surrounding the camera lens and though they are only seen when looking directly at the camera with the naked eye, the I.R. light allows the images to be recorded into a format that can be seen.

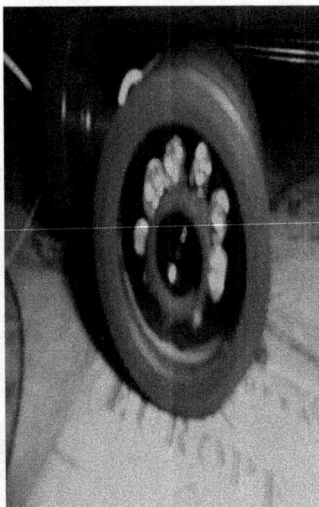

Digital Laser Thermometer: this hand held tool uses a laser beam projected onto any object and reads its surface temperature. It can often be used to detect 'cold spots' and temperature fluctuations which may indicate paranormal activity. It can also be used to find the source of these temperature fluctuations, and at times can prove the opposite: that there is a logical reason behind an apparent cold or hot spot.

Laser Grid : a laser grid is a series of laser beams that can be used to identify distant shadow movement that may not be obvious to the naked eye when lighting is minimal, or non-existent.

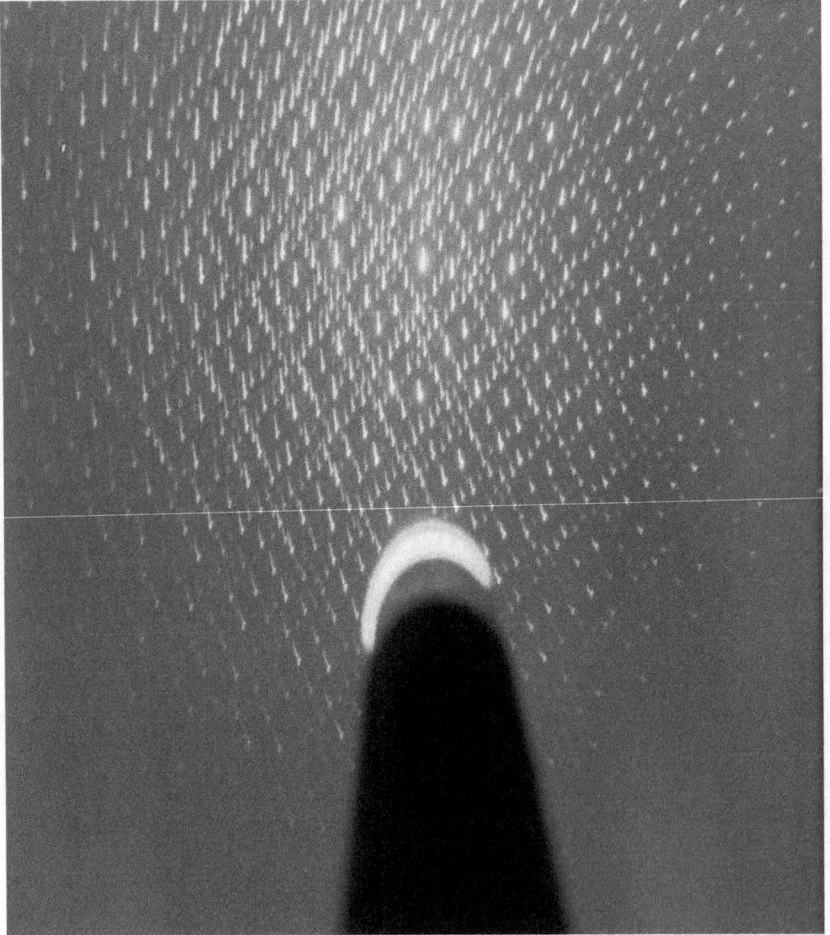

About the Author:

RICK

KUEBER

Rick Kueber was raised Catholic, and has attended many different churches and denominations. He has always had a knack and immense love of science, graduating high school with more than a double major in science. This combination has given him an edge as a paranormal investigator and team leader.

Rick has spent more than two decades in the construction industry working his way from an apprentice, journeyman, foreman, superintendent, and finally, a representative of hundreds of union workers. This leadership ability has been key in every aspect of his life.

Rick has appeared as a guest and speaker at many paranormal events and on numerous radio programs. He has also written smaller published articles.

While he writes about the experiences of his team, Rick says he finds his greatest inspiration and motivation comes from his love and bond with his son Daniel.

Frost & Flame Trilogy by Rick Kueber

Stellium Books

Book One

Forever Ash:

The Witch Child of Helmach Creek

Revised Edition

Book Two

Shadows of Eternity:

The Children of the Owls

Book Three

Never-ending Madness:

A Girl Lost to the World

Autumn 2015

www.ingramcontent.com/pod-product-compliance
Lightning Source LLC
Chambersburg PA
CBHW071408090426
42737CB00011B/1396